WHISTLEBLOWERS

Whistle blowers

HONESTY IN AMERICA FROM WASHINGTON TO TRUMP

ALLISON STANGER

Yale

UNIVERSITY PRESS

New Haven and London

Published with assistance from the foundation established in memory of James Wesley Cooper of the Class of 1865, Yale College.

Yale University Press books may be purchased in quantity for educational, business, or promotional use. For information, please e-mail sales.press@yale.edu (U.S. office) or sales@yaleup.co.uk (U.K. office).

page v: From James Baldwin, "As Much Truth as One Can Bear," *New York Times*, January 14, 1962. Reprinted with permission from the James Baldwin Estate.

Set in Janson Text and Janson Antiqua types by IDS Infotech Ltd.
Printed in the United States of America.

Library of Congress Control Number: 2019933343
ISBN 978-0-300-18688-8 (hardcover : alk. paper)

A catalogue record for this book is available from the British Library.

This paper meets the requirements of ANSI/NISO Z39.48-1992 (Permanence of Paper).

10 9 8 7 6 5 4 3 2 1

The whole art of government consists in the art of being honest.

—THOMAS JEFFERSON, 1774

Not everything that is faced can be changed; but nothing can be changed until it is faced.

—JAMES BALDWIN, 1962

Contents

WHISTLEBLOWERS

Introduction

The Paradox

We are unknown to ourselves, we knowers, and with good reason. We have never looked at ourselves.

—FRIEDRICH NIETZSCHE, 1887

WHISTLEBLOWER RIGHTS AND PROTECTION in the United States are as old as the republic itself. In 1777, during the Revolutionary War, ten American naval officers revealed that their commodore, Esek Hopkins, had tortured captured British sailors. They submitted a petition to the Continental Congress alleging that Hopkins had "treated prisoners in the most inhuman and barbarous manner." Congress voted to remove Hopkins from his position, and Hopkins retaliated by accusing two of the whistleblowing sailors of libel and having them arrested.[1]

The imprisoned whistleblowers, Richard Marven and Samuel Shaw, petitioned Congress to secure their release from prison. Congress ruled in their favor and in response to the situation issued the world's first whistleblower protection law on July 30, 1778. Its language captures the intimate relationship that the founders perceived between the upholding of whistleblower rights and the maintenance of the republic: "That it is the duty of all persons in the service of the United States, as well as all other inhabitants thereof, to give the earliest information to Congress or any other proper authority of any misconduct, frauds or misdemeanors committed by any officers or persons in the service of these states, which may come to their knowledge."[2]

Congress did not stop at upholding whistleblowing. Although the country was at war and strapped for resources, Congress paid the legal fees of Marven and Shaw. Congress also passed a law to ensure that future whistleblowers would have legal counsel to fight libel charges. In a final demonstration of its convictions, Congress authorized that all records related to Hopkins's removal be released to the public. Thus, even before the Constitution became America's basic law, the importance of whistleblowing as a means of exposing important truths was part of the new nation's DNA. Ideals and practice, however, would too often diverge.

What Is Whistleblowing?

Whistleblowing has been present since the United States' founding, but the concept means different things to different people. To have a meaningful national conversation on whistleblowing, we have to start with a common definition, stripped of partisan leanings. That is the only way to see what has changed and what hasn't in the treatment of American whistleblowers.

For starters, just thinking oneself a whistleblower isn't enough. A whistleblower cannot be defined as "an advocate for the change I'd like to see." That definition confuses whistleblowing with political activism, and it invites partisan interpretations. The usually precise *Oxford English Dictionary*, showing an awareness of this confusion, skirts it with a circular definition: a whistleblower is one who "blows the whistle" on a person or activity, especially from within an organization. The *Cambridge Dictionary* definition is narrower: a whistleblower is "a person who tells someone in authority about something they believe to be illegal that is happening, especially in a government department or a company."

The Whistleblower Protection Act of 1989, which was strengthened in 2012 through the Whistleblower Protection Enhancement Act, comports with the *Cambridge* definition.

Federal employees who disclose "illegal or improper government activities" are protected from supervisors' or coworkers' retaliation.[3] According to the U.S. Merit Systems Protection Board (MSPB), whistleblowing is "disclosing information that you reasonably believe is evidence of a violation of any law, rule, or regulation, or gross mismanagement, a gross waste of funds, an abuse of authority, or a substantial and specific danger to public health or safety."[4]

The MSPB's "reasonable belief" standard depends on an evidence-based, nonideological approach to determining the truth. For our purposes, a whistleblower is an insider (meaning an employee, customer, auditor, or other stakeholder) who has evidence of illegal or improper conduct and exposes it, either to the authorities or to the press. In government, improper conduct is illegality or a violation of constitutional norms. In the corporate world, it is illegality or the violation of company norms. Put another way, whistleblowers draw attention to self-interested actions that undermine public trust. They often reveal misconduct involving the use of public power for private gain, otherwise known as corruption.

Whistleblowers thus betray their organization or its leaders in service of the truth. Their motives for doing so are irrelevant. Most are heroic. Some are saving their own skin. In the heat of the moment, motives can be impossible to identify with accuracy. Motivation is thus somewhat important but not definitive, especially in the corporate realm, where current law gives whistleblowers a share of the money recovered from a successful suit. That is why the main focus should be on whether behavior exposed is illegal or shameful.

Comparing this definition with partisan alternatives brings into fuller relief the vital role truth telling plays in sustaining civil discourse and American constitutional democracy. Whistleblowing is not merely a weapon for advancing partisan or personal interests in a fake-news world. Its purpose is not to denigrate others or vindicate our own political biases. The extreme Left and Right may view any revelation of secret information as whistleblowing, but that definition blurs important lines. All whistleblowers are leakers, but not all leakers are whistleblowers. Leakers expose secrets, but secrets are not always a cover for misconduct, even if their revelation can often embarrass individuals and destroy careers. Whistleblowers expose lies and wrongdoing.

Equally, dissent is not the same as whistleblowing. All whistleblowers are certainly dissenters in that they refuse to accept current circumstances, but all dissenters are not whistleblowers. Whistleblowers reveal truths that the powerful do not want to be made public, whereas dissenters simply disagree.

Whistleblowing is a cousin of civil disobedience, but they are not one and the same. For Hannah Arendt, "Civil disobedience arises when a significant number of citizens have become convinced either that the normal channels of change no longer function . . . or that, on the contrary, the government is about to change and has embarked upon and persists in modes of action whose legality and constitutionality are open to grave doubt."[5] Civil disobedients break laws that they want to see changed. In this sense, like whistleblowers, all civil disobedients are dissenters, but all dissenters are not civil disobedients. Yet whistleblowers differ from civil disobedients in that they appeal to the law or the Constitution—to the American rule-of-law tradition—for justice, whereas civil disobedients challenge the legitimacy of existing laws. Both variants of dissent require political judgment.

Arendt saw civil disobedience as uniquely American. It was a manifestation of what Tocqueville deemed America's greatest strength, the vitality of its associations, more commonly known as civil society. "Civil disobedients," wrote Arendt, "are nothing but the latest form of voluntary association . . . quite in tune with the oldest traditions of the country." Civil disobedience is "primarily American in origin and substance . . . no other country, and no other language has even a word for it," and "the American republic is the only government having at least a chance to cope with it—not, perhaps, in accordance with the statutes, but in accordance with the spirit of its laws." "To think of disobedient minorities as rebels and traitors," Arendt continues, "is against the letter and spirit of a Constitution whose framers were especially sensitive to the dangers of unbridled majority rule."[6]

The same can be said of whistleblowers, who often illuminate the gap between American ideals and a fact-based world. While whistleblowing is now a global concept, the United States has a unique and long tradition of respecting whistleblowers, especially in regard to whistleblower protection legislation, that is the envy of other countries.[7] In this sense, whistleblowing, like civil disobedience, is distinctly American and an indirect call to renew the rule of law through new legislation defining corruption and the abuse of power.

Since they challenge business as usual, whistleblowers are by definition troublemakers who remove blinders that many people would prefer to leave in place. For that reason, they can be difficult people. They do not turn away from wrongdoing but choose to confront it. They can be annoying to those averse to conflict, but they are also people of conscience who are willing to be seen as disloyal to the institutions that employ them in order to remain true to their own values. Acts of conscience are always motivated by loyalty to a conviction, but they usually demand defiance of other loyalties.

A review of the archives of the *New York Times*, the *Washington Post*, the *Los Angeles Times*, the *Chicago Tribune*, and the *Wall Street Journal* reveals that the term *whistleblower* was first deployed in the early 1970s. Ernest Fitzgerald, about whom more below, played a critical role in fostering media interest in whistleblowing by flagging waste at the Pentagon in 1968. With the exception of the *Wall Street Journal*, which focused more on corporate misconduct, the vast majority of news stories in the 1970s and 1980s involved whistleblowers from government agencies, especially the Central Intelligence Agency, the Department of Defense, and the Environmental Protection Agency. In the 1990s, the coverage was about equally split between public- and private-sector whistleblowing. As a general trend, the total number of articles about whistleblowers in these five newspapers has risen steadily since the 1970s.

The same growth in coverage can be found in data from Google Ngram Viewer, which tracks the frequency of a word's use in published books over time, an innovative way of evaluating the zeitgeist. Although the project ran into legal problems and is now abandoned, 4 percent of all published books had been digitized for the database as of 2010, giving us a reasonable sample.[8] Typing *whistleblower* into the Google Books search tool shows virtually no use of the term before the 1970s, followed by an explosion of use after 1975, most likely sparked by the Watergate and Pentagon Papers scandals. Interest in the subject has continued unabated. For example, from 2012 to 2017, whistleblower tips to the Securities and Exchange Commission rose by 49 percent, thanks to the whistleblower statute that was part of the 2010 Dodd-Frank Act.[9]

Whistleblower protection legislation parallels media coverage. The more coverage, the more Congress has paid attention to the issue and passed legislation, some of which has been effective, although some of it amounts to nothing more than window dressing. The First Amendment provides the ultimate whistleblower protection, but because the Supreme Court balances free speech against competing interests, whistleblowers always run the risk that the balance will not tip in their favor. Congressional statutes are more effective because they tell you what classes of persons are protected, what they can and can't do, and what their rights are.[10]

Although corporate whistleblowing is obviously an important topic, the several hundred pages I wrote about it have wound up on the cutting-room floor, leaving the public sector as my primary focus in the pages that follow, although I will draw comparisons when instructive. Restricting our investigation to public servants serves the interests of concision and clarity while bringing some important truths to light.

Committing Truth

Whistleblowing serves the interests of truth, and all whistleblowers commit truth. Because they highlight the gap between American ideals and lived reality, they unveil behavior that the rich and powerful would like to keep secret. The #MeToo campaign, for example, exposed sexual misconduct that could be ignored so long as women did not speak out for fear of retaliation or not being taken seriously. Sheryl Sandberg's advice on new processes for sexual harassment could be generalized to whistleblowing more broadly:

> Every workplace should start with clear principles, then institute policies to support them. First, develop workplace training that sets the standard for respectful behavior at

work, so people understand right from the start what's expected of them. Second, treat all claims—and the people who voice them—with seriousness, urgency, and respect. Third, create an investigation process that protects employees from stigma or retaliation. Fourth, follow a process that is fairly and consistently applied in every case, both for victims and those accused. Fifth, take swift and decisive action when wrongdoing has occurred. And sixth, make it clear that all employees have a role to play in keeping workplaces safe—and that enablers and failed gatekeepers are complicit when they stay silent or look the other way.[11]

The backlash against #MeToo, of which Sandberg warns, is an example of whistleblower retaliation.

Viewed from a slightly different perspective, whistleblowers also uphold individual rights that would otherwise be trampled by majority preferences. Rights always matter most to those who must struggle for them. Slavery and the subjection of women, for example, were once both legal and popular, despite being built on the lie that Blacks and women were not full humans worthy of rights and legal equality. Enfranchised white males were able to turn a blind eye to gross injustice because they did not suffer its consequences, and it is always the privileged who decide whether rights have been violated.

The right to privacy is part of the foundation of all rights. If Americans lose the right to privacy, they lose the right to freedom of thought. They also lose the very mechanism that allows the people to control their government rather than be controlled by it. Whistleblowing, which both depends on and protects the right to privacy, is a powerful antidote to the tyranny of the majority that the founders feared. Whistleblowers expose practices at odds with the world as it should be. Both liberty and equality demand their protection.

Whistleblowing is thus an important part of what makes American democracy distinctive. The pursuit of a more perfect union is impossible unless we are free to identify instances where we have fallen short. American constitutional democracy depends on a common understanding of the proper place of whistleblowing in America. That is what this book seeks to deliver.

The National Security Exception

Whistleblower protection statutes have been on the books since the Revolutionary War, but if your work has any connection to national security, the shield they provide is unreliable. The Civil Service Reform Act of 1978 established new statutory protections for whistleblowers and created the Office of Special Counsel for investigating claims, but its protections explicitly excluded national security employees. This exclusion continued in the 1989 Whistleblower Protection Act. In 2012 there was another attempt to include national security employees through the Whistleblower Protection Enhancement Act, but that effort was also defeated. The result is that in the eyes of the law, whistleblowing in the national security arena, although it is at least as vital there as in other forms of government service, remains a contradiction in terms.[12] After the 2012 legislation, President Obama tried to rectify the continued exclusion of national security workers via Presidential Policy Directive 19, which offered some protection for both classified information and employees reporting waste, fraud, and abuse. The resulting friction between statute and executive order provided little reassurance to government contractors who believed they had uncovered wrongdoing. Edward Snowden was a case in point.

National security whistleblowers will always be the most controversial, because protecting the United States does require some degree of secrecy. There is a feeling that revealing classified information is always a betrayal of the national interest. In the pre-Internet world, when spies stole secrets and passed them to the enemy, they sought to do so in secret, because the advantage gained would be undermined by any publicity. In the Internet age, secrets are more difficult to keep, and those in power face new challenges to their legitimacy. The Obama administration, as we shall see, considered any leak of classified material to the press to be a form of espionage, even if the information was shared with everyone rather than with a specific enemy. This policy both expanded the definition of a spy and constrained the possibilities for whistleblowing in unprecedented and troubling ways.

Because national security whistleblowing is a variant of dissent, framing it as a contradiction in terms has significant political implications. Without dissent, there would be no United States. Senator J. William Fulbright saw dissent as an act of faith, service, and respect for one's country. "To criticize one's country is to do it a service and pay it a compliment," he wrote. "It is a service because it may spur the country to do better than it is doing; it is a compliment because it evidences a belief that the country can do better than it is doing. . . . Criticism, in short, is more than a right; it is an act of patriotism, a higher form of patriotism, I believe, than the familiar rituals of national adulation."[13] President Dwight D. Eisenhower applauded honest dissent: "Here in America we are descended in blood and spirit from revolutionaries and rebels—men and women who dared to dissent from accepted doctrine. As their heirs, may we never confuse honest dissent with disloyal subversion."[14] Thomas Jefferson held "that a little rebellion now and then is a good thing. . . . It is a medicine necessary for the sound health of government."[15] When their higher allegiance is to the Constitution, whistleblowing dissenters in the national security realm can provide a vital public service.

The Paradox

Research conducted in other countries confirms that whistleblowers play an important role in keeping elites honest. In an effort to understand the root causes of economic crime, the consulting firm PricewaterhouseCoopers (PwC) conducted an extensive survey of global economic crime, the largest survey of its kind, in 2007. PwC's investigations and forensics team conducted fifty-four hundred interviews in forty countries. The survey found that whistleblowers make a significant contribution to rooting out corruption.[16]

The paradox of whistleblowing in America resides in the gap between ideals and practice. Whistleblowers in the United States are all too often first commended for speaking truth to power, and then persecuted for it when media attention has moved on. The stories of individual whistleblowers, which offer plenty of examples of this paradox, are supported by aggregate statistics. The MSPB, established in 1979 to protect federal employees from management abuse, assessed the status of whistleblowing in the federal government in 1980, 1983, 1992, and 2010.[17] These studies were initiated to investigate whether the federal inspectors general, established by the Inspector General Act of 1978 to combat fraud and other abuses in government agencies (a reform that grew out of the civil disobedience of the Vietnam era that Hannah Arendt saw as appropriate and American), were doing an adequate job of preventing reprisals against whistleblowers. With the support of the inspectors general, the focus of the studies was expanded to government as a whole.[18]

The MSPB studies provide a series of snapshots of the changing status of whistleblowing.[19] Two general trends can be observed. First, employees are today more likely to report misconduct when they see it in the workplace (30 percent did so in 1980 versus 50 percent in 1992 and roughly the same in 2010).[20] They are also less likely to have observed waste or illegal activity in the last twelve months (45 percent in 1980, 17.7 percent in 1992, and 11.1 percent in 2010). Second, employees experienced greater retaliation over time: 20 percent in 1980 reported threats or acts of reprisal versus 36.2 percent in 2010. Not surprisingly, the desire to remain anonymous also increased: from 24 percent in 1980 to 57.5 percent in 2010. Federal employees today are more likely to report corruption, yet more vulnerable to retaliation.

These trends show that more people are taking the great risks that whistleblowing entails, but doing so in a system that does not protect them. The most likely outcome for whistleblowers is self-destruction. According to whistleblower attorney Stephen Kohn, "The MSPB system is an absolute failure, even with the Whistleblower Protection Enhancement Act."[21] A recent MSPB survey found that federal whistleblowers were roughly nine times more likely to be fired in 2010 than they were in 1992.[22] Whistleblowers who lose their jobs are usually branded troublemakers and find it hard to secure new employment.

The obstacles for whistleblowers are daunting. An Office of Research Integrity report on whistleblowing in science, for example, showed that more than two-thirds of whistleblowers experience negative consequences from speaking out. One in four loses his or her job. Despite this, in a 1995 study, close to 80 percent said they would do it again.[23] According to the 2013 *National Business Ethics Survey*, 86 percent of those who had been the victims of retaliation claimed that they would be willing to report again, versus 95 percent of those who did not suffer retaliation.[24]

Only a small percentage of federal whistleblowers succeed in having their assertions believed—5 to 20 percent, according to professors Marcia Miceli, Janet Near, and Terry Dworkin.[25] The Occupational Safety and Health Administration (OSHA) gets involved in cases that have stalled or in which there is alleged retaliation against the whistleblower. Between 2007 and 2017, OSHA dismissed 54 percent of the nearly thirty thousand whistleblower claims on which it rendered judgment. Another 15 percent of cases were settled; only 2 percent were upheld as meritorious.[26]

The same pattern held after the passage of the 2002 Sarbanes-Oxley Act (SOX), which established whistleblower protections for employees of publicly traded companies. As of May 2006, 499 out of 667 complaints were dismissed, and 95 of the remaining 178 were withdrawn. Of the 286 cases that went before an administrative law judge, only 6 resulted in a ruling favorable to the employee.[27]

None of these studies is definitive, but they highlight the challenges whistleblowers continue to face despite unprecedented legal protection. Because whistleblowing law is complex (for example, the Occupational Safety and Health Administration alone is responsible for enforcing at least fifteen different pieces of legislation related to whistleblowing), it is very difficult for whistleblowers to emerge indisputably victorious.[28] An astonishing labyrinth of whistleblower protection legislation is on the books in the United States, but navigating it is virtually impossible without legal guidance.[29] Despite the legislation, whistleblowing remains a risky endeavor and is seldom undertaken frivolously.

The paradox of whistleblowing in America—embracing the ideal of whistleblowing while failing to protect those who do it—was on full display in the debate over Edward Snowden. On one hand, the fiercest arguments were over whether Snowden deserved to be called a whistleblower. On the other hand, because Americans after 9/11 have grown accustomed to thinking of perfect security as a precondition of liberty, they are divided over the realms in which whistleblowing should be supported. If it undermines security or prosperity, many Americans have little use for it. And powerful insiders would be happy to do without it—so long as that preference is not openly revealed to the public. Americans thus celebrate whistleblowing in theory but give it only half-hearted support in practice.

It is easier to acquiesce in the persecution of those who challenge majority opinion or powerful institutions when they are seen
as undermining American prosperity or security. Secrecy is considered indispensable in keeping America safe. Money is also made
through secrecy and information partitions, the gap between those
who are in the know and those out of the loop. That is why government and big business alike will continue to pursue leaks and
punish leakers. The paradox of whistleblowing in America will prevail until Americans insist that it change.

The Journey and the Stakes

While whistleblowers often bring about changes that serve their
fellow citizens, their personal sacrifice is immense. Legitimate
whistleblowers are risk takers for the truth, and what they risk,
above all, is their own well-being. They pay dearly after they jump
ship to expose corruption or abuse. When they regret their decision, it is generally because they vastly underestimated the potential damage, especially for their families. When whistleblowing
succeeds, there is always a loss of innocence, not only among the
public but for the whistleblowers themselves.

The story of whistleblowing in America challenges all of us to
think differently. We have lost an appreciation for whistleblowers,
but as greater power comes to be concentrated in ever fewer hands,
they are ever more necessary for holding government and business
elites accountable. Whistleblowers disrupt business as usual and expose—sometimes bring down—those who put self-interest above
the good of the country. They create pressure for reform.

The taboo on national security whistleblowing makes it easier
for Americans simultaneously to revere whistleblowers and to acquiesce in their persecution. Emergency measures can be justified
as temporary evils when the nation is at war and existentially
threatened, but the reaction to the 9/11 attacks made the emergency unending and enabled an implicit belief that security should
always trump all other considerations. This thinking has had a cor-
rosive effect on democratic values. Ultimately, if we fail to grapple
with the paradox of whistleblowing in America, we risk losing what
has made this nation exceptional.

PART I

From the Revolution to 9/11

CHAPTER ONE

Truths

ESEK HOPKINS, FIRST COMMODORE of the first United States Navy and a Rhode Island slave runner, was the catalyst for America's first whistleblower law. To fight and win the Revolutionary War, the newly minted United States needed loyalty from its citizens that trumped parochial state allegiances. But for Hopkins, this larger commitment involved sacrificing financial opportunities. He had difficulty taking that leap of faith and tried to hedge his bets.

The state of Rhode Island is well known for its celebration of tolerance. Less well known is that one of the things it tolerated was slavery. Rhode Island passed the first colonial antislavery statute in 1652, abolishing African slavery and stating that "black mankinde," just like white mankinde, could not be indentured for more than ten years. But the law was never enforced for Blacks.[1] As a result, the Museum of African American History and Culture reports that Rhode Island merchants had "sponsored at least 934 slaving voyages to the coast of Africa and carried an estimated 106,544 slaves" by the 1750s, and Newport was North America's top slave-trading port.[2] Rhode Island in 1750 had the highest percentage of enslaved humans in New England.[3] After the Revolution, Rhode Island merchants controlled 60 to 90 percent of the American trade in African slaves.[4] Scholars estimate that for every one hundred human beings seized in Africa, only sixty-four survived the march from the interior to the coast, fifty-seven actually boarded the ship, and just forty-eight lived to become slaves in the New World.[5]

A Maverick Commodore

Commodore Esek Hopkins acquired much of his transatlantic sailing experience on slave ships, including captaining and provisioning the 1764–65 voyage of the *Sally* for Nicholas Brown and Company, a Providence merchant shipping firm. Brown and Company was owned by four brothers, Nicholas, John, Joseph, and Moses. With Hopkins in command, the *Sally* set sail for West Africa on September 11, 1764, laden with over 17,274 gallons of New England rum—Newport alone had nearly two dozen rum distilleries.[6] The Browns had instructed him to sail to the windward coast of Africa, "dispose of your Cargo for slaves," and then to sail to Barbados or any other suitable port in the West Indies and sell the captives; the proceeds from the sale of Africans would be used to fill the emptied hold with molasses and sugar for Rhode Island's booming rum industry. Hopkins was to return to Providence with 4 young slaves for the Brown family's own use. In payment, he would receive the "privilege" of 10 slaves to sell for himself, as well as the standard captain's compensation of 4 slaves for every 104 he delivered alive.[7]

Hopkins reached Africa in November and spent the next seven months selling liquor to purchase his return cargo, mainly at the mouth of the Grande River in what is today Guinea-Bissau. At first he accounted for his transactions in pounds and shillings, but soon switched to the standard of the coast, which was bars (for a bar of iron). A yard of cloth went for 1 bar, a barrel of rum for 10 bars, and slaves for anything from 70 to 130 bars. Unlike iron, cloth, and rum, human beings were fragile merchandise; as Hopkins maneuvered to fill his ship with Africans, twenty of his captives died, including at least one woman who hanged herself.[8]

All told, Hopkins purchased 196 Africans, including the 20 who died. He sold 21 human beings to other traders before departing Africa, bringing his homeward-bound total cargo to 155 men, women, and children. Hopkins set sail for the West Indies on August 21, 1765. A woman, two boys, and a girl died during his first week at sea. On the seventh day, the surviving captives staged a failed uprising. According to an account Hopkins later gave to the Brown brothers, the Africans had grown "so Desperited" after their failed insurrection that some drowned themselves. By the time Hopkins reached Antigua, the death toll had reached 68. Twenty more died before they could be sold. The 77 Africans who had survived the ordeal failed to command high prices on the auction blocks in Antigua, and the whole enterprise lost money.[9] Having failed to deliver the 100 live humans for sale, Hopkins is unlikely to have been compensated.

When they heard that the voyage they had bankrolled was a bust, the indebted Browns complained about 'the Heavy Loss of our Int[erests]" but were pleased that Hopkins had survived.[10] Rather than lament the loss of African life, the Browns were sorry that Hopkins had to be involved in "so Disagreeable a Trade."[11] Noting the disappointing results, one of the slave traders, Alex Millock, expressed his sympathy to the Browns for the dismal return on investment (he wanted return customers, after all). "I am truly sorry for the Bad Voyage," he wrote. "Had the Negroes been Young and Healthy, I should have been able to sell them pretty well. I make no doubt if you was to try this Markett again with Good Slaves I Should be able to give you Satisfaction."[12]

It was not that Rhode Islanders—at least some of them—didn't know slavery was wrong. A decade after the *Sally*'s voyage in 1774, the Rhode Island General Assembly prohibited the further importation of slaves to Rhode Island. In 1787, the state made it illegal for Rhode Islanders to participate in the slave trade *anywhere*, the first such ban of its kind in the United States. Enforcing the law, however, stood in direct conflict with powerful citizens' economic interests. Over the next decade, more than fifty ships per year ignored the 1787 statute and continued to sail from Newport to Africa. Even after Congress passed federal anti–slave trafficking laws in 1794 and again in 1800, Rhode Islanders persisted in these practices. In 1796, John Brown, a cofounder of Brown University, became the first American to be prosecuted in federal court for violating the new federal trafficking laws, but a Newport jury acquitted him. The wealth to be had was more persuasive than either Rhode Island or federal law.[13]

Rhode Island's persistent championing of states' rights, a fig leaf covering its naked economic interest, led the legislature to refuse to send delegates to the Constitutional Convention. Its leaders saw the proposed federal project as taking away its livelihood, and in 1788 the state rejected the Constitution by popular referendum. It would be the last of the thirteen original colonies to ratify the Constitution and did not join the United States until 1790.

Rhode Island's refusal to ratify the Constitution, even with the appended Bill of Rights, and its enthusiastic pursuit of human trafficking in defiance of Congress help explain the many references to wayward Rhode Island in the founding documents. In Federalist 7, for example, Alexander Hamilton refers to "enormities perpetuated by the Rhode Island legislature." In Federalist 63, James Madison cites the state's "iniquitous measures." In July 1787, at the Constitutional Convention, Nathaniel Gorham of Massachusetts proclaimed Rhode Island "a full illustration of the insensibility to character produced by a participation of numbers in dishonorable measures, and of the length to which a public body may carry wickedness and cabal."[14] Jonathan Dayton of New Jersey, in making the case for federal review of territorial claims, "mentioned the conduct of Rhode Island, as showing the necessity of giving latitude to the power of the United States on this subject."[15] Finally, in a letter to Gouverneur Morris in 1789, George Washington wrote that he would feel more confident that Rhode Island would eventually ratify the Constitution "had not the majority of that People bid adieu, long since to every principle of honor—common sense, and honesty."[16]

The Founders and Corruption

When they included King George's long train of abuses in their document, the writers of the Declaration of Independence were not focused initially on indicting monarchy in favor of democracy. Rather, they saw the British Crown as a fount of corruption that had betrayed its own values, necessitating the break, lest London's moral deterioration prove contagious. The classical republicanism that enchanted America's founders had coexisted comfortably with monarchy in eighteenth-century England.

Yet the Declaration also contained the seeds of something brand new. Those who believed in the self-evident truths that all men are created equal and endowed by their creator with certain inalienable rights presupposed that it was the purpose of government to protect those rights and defend the equality of all human beings. The subordinate position of the colonies, which became more and more irritatingly apparent over time, was incompatible with such a conception of government.

In her brilliant exegesis of the Declaration, Harvard University professor Danielle Allen emphasizes the centrality of equality in the Declaration's vision. Focusing on the punctuation in the original text (currently in the National Archives), she notes that many reprints have inserted a period after "Life, Liberty, and the Pursuit of Happiness" that does not exist in the original:

> We hold these truths to be self-evident, that all men are created equal, that they are endowed by their Creator with certain unalienable Rights, that among these are Life, Liberty and the Pursuit of Happiness.—That to secure these rights, Governments are instituted among Men, deriving their just powers from the consent of the governed,—that whenever any Form of Government becomes destructive of these ends, it is the Right of the People to alter or to abolish it, and to institute new Government, laying its foundation on such principles and organizing its powers in such form, as to them shall seem most likely to effect their Safety and Happiness.

Yet there is no period at that point in the original text. This punctuation underscores the link between inalienable rights and the indispensable role of government in upholding them:

> We hold these truths to be self-evident, that all men are created equal, that they are endowed by their Creator with certain unalienable Rights, that among these are Life, Liberty and the Pursuit of Happiness—That to secure these rights, Governments are instituted among Men, deriving their just powers from the consent of the governed—that

whenever any Form of Government becomes destructive
of these ends, it is the Right of the People to alter or to
abolish it, and to institute new Government, laying its
foundation on such principles and organizing its powers in
such form, as to them shall seem most likely to effect their
Safety and Happiness.

Since the Declaration went through multiple drafts, the punctuation choices that appear in the final version are significant. The
signers of the Declaration believed that only the right form of government could make life, liberty, and the pursuit of happiness realis-
tic possibilities for all citizens. Without the period, Allen writes, the
passage laying out the self-evident truths "leads us from the individual to the community—from our separate and equal rights to what
we can achieve only together. The Declaration really is *ours*, not
mine." For the signers, government is what we do together, not indi-
vidually. It can be an instrument of freedom only when it is rooted
in equality, and "political equality is equal political empowerment."[17]

Equal political empowerment, in turn, required virtuous public
servants. The classical republican tradition that informed the English outlook was instinctively suspicious of involvements in the
marketplace, which could create conflicts of interest. Classical republicanism was the ideology of the Enlightenment, and invoking
its ideals—integrity, virtue, disinterestedness—was a major means
by which Britons and Americans alike objected to selfishness, lux-
ury, or corruption in the monarchical world they shared. When it
came to governing the community, virtuous citizens were free from
the petty interests of commerce. Virtuous public servants did not
allow their political decisions to be influenced by personal economic interests.

In her masterful book *Corruption in America*, Fordham legal
scholar Zephyr Teachout argues that corruption for the founders
was not limited to explicitly buying votes, what today's Supreme
Court, in its campaign finance rulings, has called "quid pro quo
corruption." Instead, corruption encompassed all manifestations of
self-interested behavior at the expense of the common good. "By
corruption, the early generation meant excessive private interests
influencing the exercise of public power," Teachout writes. "An *act*

was corrupt when private power was used to influence public power for private ends. A *system* was corrupt when the public power was excessively used to serve private ends instead of the public good. A *person* was corrupt when they used public power for private ends."[18]

The American revolutionaries saw containing corruption as the very foundation of representative democracy. The common good could not be secured when citizens elevated private interest over public service. Nor could the common good be served when the Crown's interests always trumped those of the colonies: they viewed their treatment as second-class subjects as a manifestation of corruption. In their nascent republic, the revolutionaries sought to thwart corruption through measures designed to encourage public virtue and discourage the exploitation of public office for private gain.

It was often difficult for colonists to appreciate how extreme their thinking was. As the historian Gordon Wood writes, "Republicanism was as radical for the eighteenth century as Marxism was for the nineteenth."[19] Yet the American revolutionaries did not initially see themselves as doing anything radical at all. They thought they were upholding, not challenging, British values. In 1767, Samuel Adams told his fellow Englishmen across the Atlantic, "We boast of our freedom and have your example for it. We talk the language we have always heard you speak."[20] Just as Rhode Islanders professed opposition to slavery while perpetuating it, Parliament talked about rights and principles while denying their relevance to the colonies.

Since corruption was a cancer for any republic, public servants ought to follow what Jefferson called "the Roman principle." This principle, a value ostensibly shared by all of the Revolution's leading figures, saw the common good as best upheld through disinterested service. It informed Benjamin Franklin's proposal to the Philadelphia Convention that all members of the federal government's executive branch serve without salary. It led George Washington to refuse a salary as commander in chief of the Continental Army, and later to try to do the same as America's first president.[21] The Roman principle inspired Robert Morris, the wealthiest merchant in Pennsylvania and one of the wealthiest men in North America, to divest himself of his lucrative shares in banks and of his involvement in the merchant trade once he became a congressman in order to prevent a conflict between his personal interests and the public good. Instead, he shifted all of his entrepreneurial energies into speculation in land, something considered more respectable than trade and wholly compatible with public service in a country where land was abundant. Morris wound up in debtor's prison, but with his civic virtue intact.[22]

Respect for the Roman principle led many American readers of Edward Gibbon's *History of the Decline and Fall of the Roman Empire*, the first volume of which was published in 1776, to see a direct connection between the corruption of the Roman and British Empires.[23] America's founders and some English citizens saw themselves fighting to put right a system that had lost its way. Benjamin Franklin, who spent five years in England, found it a nation that considered "itself so universally corrupt and rotten from Head to Foot, that it has little confidence in any Publick Men or Publick Measures."[24] The American Revolution was a sustained effort to exorcize the corruption demon and build a new republic that might withstand the temptations that had ruined America's former overseers.

The 1762 transatlantic uproar over the treatment of John Wilkes provides an excellent example of the British hypocrisy the colonists found so appalling. John Wilkes, the publisher of an English newspaper called the *North Briton*, had criticized the king and his officials in his paper. The king's officials, in response, issued a general warrant commanding authorities to root out the authors, printers, and publishers of the offensive material. In conducting their "strict and diligent search," as prescribed in the warrant, the authorities searched at least five homes, breaking down doors and locks and dumping books and papers on the floor. They arrested forty-nine people, nearly all of whom were later found innocent. The press in both England and the New World roundly criticized this excess, and British courts ultimately withdrew the general warrant, declaring it "totally subversive of the liberty of the subject."[25]

Yet what was condemned at home remained a common practice in the colonies. The king issued "writs of assistance" to his agents there—primarily though not exclusively customs officials—giving them permission to search the homes and belongings of anyone suspected of subverting the king's authority. Though writs of assistance might sound like modern-day search warrants, they were very different. A judge did not issue them, they did not require any evidence of wrongdoing, and they remained valid for the lifetime of the king who had issued them. Although they did not authorize arrest and permitted searches only during daylight, they were effectively licenses to intimidate and harass.[26] Because they were designed to silence dissent, and since there were always spoils that might be seized in any search, they facilitated the use of public power for private gain. What was impermissible in England was perfectly acceptable in the colonies. Americans rightly saw this disparity as an instance of the Crown's embrace of tyranny to protect imperial interest.

Americans were fully aware that they were being treated differently. With the death of King George II in October 1760, all writs of assistance were set to expire in April 1761. Charles Paxton, the chief customs official in Boston, petitioned for new writs to be issued. A group of sixty-three Boston merchants, represented by Boston lawyer James Otis, filed suit to challenge the legitimacy of the writs, effectively challenging the authority of the king and Parliament. Otis and the Boston merchants lost: the Crown granted new writs and would continue to do so until the colonies won their independence.[27]

After his defeat in court, Otis continued the argument in a 1765 pamphlet in which he maintained that general writs violated the (unwritten) British Constitution. His arguments had a powerful impact on John Adams, then twenty-six, who had been present at the trial. Years later, in 1818, Adams wrote in a letter to Hezekiah Niles, "Mr. Otis's oration against the writs of assistance breathed into this nation the breath of life."[28] Otis's arguments were also in James Madison's mind when he designed the Fourth Amendment. The Supreme Court in 1886 called Otis's suit against Paxton "perhaps the most prominent event which inaugurated the resistance of the colonies to the oppressions of the mother country." In the 1980 case *Payton v. New York*, the Supreme Court noted, "It is familiar history that indiscriminate searches and seizures conducted under the authority of 'general warrants' were the immediate evils that motivated the framing and adoption of the Fourth Amendment."[29] Specific warrants to search a citizen when there was evidence of probable wrongdoing were necessary, but general warrants that enabled indiscriminate searching—"suspicionless surveillance"—violated the Fourth Amendment.[30] Tyranny is corrupt by definition, both in a limited monarchy and in a professed republic, since it always serves the interests of the powerful rather than the people.

While the British Crown asserted that the government in London was the supreme arbiter of law in the colonies, the colonists had no seats in Parliament. To our twenty-first-century minds, this seems obviously unrepresentative. How could the Crown claim to support representative government when it did not extend this principle to its North American brethren? The simple answer is that the understanding of representation was still developing. At the time, not all Britons had actual representation in the form of an MP they could identify as their own. Quid pro quo corruption, or vote buying, was rife, especially in the absence of a secret ballot.[31] Many regions back in the home country had only what was called virtual representation, meaning that Parliament collectively spoke for all British subjects, regardless of where a particular MP actually resided. This is how Prime Minister George Grenville could argue that the colonies had virtual representation like other subjects in Great Britain, and therefore they could not claim tyrannical mistreatment.

Taxing the colonists who had no actual representation in Parliament, however, inflamed the sentiments of many who were ostensibly loyal to King George III—but not for the reasons twenty-first-century Americans might think. There was widespread fear in America that there was an active conspiracy against liberty that would have negative consequences for Britons and Americans alike. The colonies were thus being exploited, the patriots reasoned, because the corrupt Crown was behaving unconstitutionally at home. If liberty were lost in Great Britain, the home country would take the colonies down with it.[32]

To the framers of the Constitution, corruption (in their expansive definition) and tyranny were inseparable. The Emoluments Clause of the Constitution, adopted with almost universal agreement, was designed to inoculate the new republic against political corruption. The concern was that the president could use emoluments—such as offices, pensions, grants of income, or gifts—to compromise congressional independence, imitating the misdeeds of the British Crown in buying off Parliament and thereby undermining the separation of powers and self-government. There was an American consensus, present at the nation's founding, that corruption was a threat to both liberty and equality.[33]

America's First Whistleblower Protection Law

In December 1775, Esek Hopkins was named commander in chief of the new Continental Navy. This appointment was engineered, in part, by Rhode Island's social elite, in which his own family was prominent. Hopkins's brother Stephen, later a signer of the Declaration of Independence and the first chancellor of Brown University, was the chair of the Continental Congress's Naval Committee. Hopkins also had the backing of another prominent committee member, John Adams of Massachusetts.[34]

The new navy addressed the need for a more unified force than the privateers General Washington had hired to back up his Continental Army, who ultimately answered to the profit motive rather than to General Washington. The new force, starting with four vessels authorized by an October 1775 appropriation, would answer solely to the Continental Congress. From the start, its officer ranks were dominated by Rhode Islanders. Commodore Hopkins's flagship was the *Alfred*. Dudley Saltonstall (son-in-law of Rhode Island Supreme Court justice Joshua Babcock) commanded the *Alfred*; John Paul Jones (who grew up in Scotland) was his first lieutenant. Esek Hopkins's nephew, John Burroughs Hopkins, was given command of the *Cabot*; Abraham Whipple, commodore of the Rhode Island Navy (and Esek's brother-in-law) became captain of the *Columbus*; and Philadelphia's Nicholas Biddle (the only captain without a Rhode Island connection) headed the *Andrew Doria*. By January 1776, four more boats had been added: the sloops *Hornet* and *Providence* and the schooners *Fly* and *Wasp*.[35] Christopher Gadsden of South Carolina, who also served on the Naval Committee, bestowed upon Hopkins, as his personal standard, what later became known as the Gadsden Flag: a yellow flag bearing a serpent coiled above the slogan "Don't Tread on Me."[36]

There were disputes from the start over how the navy was to be deployed. The southerners were having trouble with British raiders and wanted to see an initial engagement in the Chesapeake Bay. Hopkins received his first orders from Congress on January 5, 1776, to clear the southern coasts and then sail north to do the same in Narragansett Bay. But he had other plans. Disregarding Congress entirely, he took the fleet south to the island of New Providence in the Bahamas, without engaging the British at all until he reached Nassau.[37] Finding the British garrison undermanned, he seized more than one hundred cannons.[38] Then he headed home. On April 4, he also captured two British vessels off the eastern end of Long Island, as well as two merchant vessels bound from New York to London the following day; the latter two were taken as prizes. His renegade mission appeared wildly profitable.

At midnight on April 6, however, Hopkins's luck changed. Sailing near Block Island, his fleet encountered the HMS *Glasgow*. Despite the navy's overwhelming superiority, the *Glasgow* managed to elude capture and escape to Newport, leaving eleven Americans dead and seventeen wounded.[39] The entire Continental Navy had failed to defeat a twenty-gun British frigate.

Commodore Hopkins met with General Washington on April 8 in New London, Connecticut, the first meeting of the two commanders. It did not go well. Washington wanted to coordinate navy operations with the army. Hopkins had other priorities and instead took his fleet back home to Providence. Washington would fight the British alone in New York, just as he had in Boston.[40]

Hopkins was roundly criticized for the *Glasgow* fiasco and for the insubordination that led to it. Rather than take responsibility for his own choices, Hopkins blamed his own brother-in-law, Abraham Whipple, captain of the *Columbus*, and John Hazard, captain of the *Providence*. Both were court-martialed for the *Glasgow* debacle. Whipple, cleared of the charge of poor judgment but not of cowardice, was reprimanded; Hazard was dismissed for not following orders, embezzlement, and failure to do his duty.[41] The *Andrew Doria*'s captain Biddle called the whole encounter "a shameful loss. . . . A more imprudent ill-conducted affair never happened."[42]

Congress, however, was not pleased with Hopkins. On May 8, 1776, the legislature appointed a special committee headed by John

Adams to investigate his behavior.[43] "I saw nothing in the conduct of Hopkins, which indicated corruption or want of integrity," wrote Adams in his autobiography. "Experience and skill might have been deficient in certain particulars; but where could we find greater experience or skill? I knew of none to be found."[44] Thomas Jefferson, however, saw the matter differently. In his personal brief in preparation for the inquiry, he noted that Hopkins's suspicious conduct had continued after his return, as the Continental Navy "has merely acted in defence of trade of Eastern colonies. . . . The objection is [not] that he did not exercise an honest discretion in departing from his instructions but that he never did intend to obey them."[45]

In addition to ignoring the needs of his compatriots, Hopkins was accused of favoring Rhode Island in distributing the spoils. Congress had ordered him to turn over all of the captured cannons to Governor Trumbull of Connecticut, but Hopkins again defied orders and sent some of them to his old friend Governor Cooke of Rhode Island.[46] On May 30, Congress intervened, ordering that six cannons be returned from Newport and fourteen from New London. Despite Adams's unfailing support for Hopkins, Jefferson's perspective carried the day. Congress found Hopkins "guilty of not paying proper attention to his orders" and voted to censure him on August 16, 1776. Adams wrote, "This resolution of censure was not in my opinion demanded by justice."[47] Three days later, however, Hopkins was ordered to resume command and on August 22 given orders for a new expedition.[48] "I had the satisfaction," Adams noted, "to think that I had not labored wholly in vain in his defence."[49]

The fall of 1776 found Hopkins in Providence, having difficulty manning his ships because of fierce competition from privateers. A sailor could make better money in the private sector than serving in the Continental Navy. In an effort to prove his loyalty to the United States, Hopkins asked the Rhode Island General Assembly to declare an embargo on privateering until his Continental Navy ships could be manned, but since many members of the assembly had investments in privateering, the motion was defeated. The Continental Navy under Hopkins's command remained a chimera. On December 7, 1776, a British ship sailed into Newport uncontested and took possession of Rhode Island, shutting the American ships inside the bay.[50]

After being reprimanded by Congress and losing control of Newport, Hopkins continued to look out for himself. He reimbursed his own accounts before considering the needs of others. John Hancock wrote to him on January 21, 1777, urging him to pay his seamen the share of captured spoils that they were due.[51] Hopkins responded by holding the *Alfred*'s first lieutenant John Paul Jones responsible for the nonpayment and asked Hancock to court-martial him.[52] Jones, however, was hardly to blame for not paying his debts. While residing on the docked *Warren*, Hopkins seems to have been withholding reimbursements of the *Alfred*'s bills, despite Jones's persistent requests.[53]

Outrage at Hopkins's self-serving maneuvers reached its apex in February 1777, when he defied Congress yet again by issuing counter-orders to Joseph Olney, who had replaced John Hopkins as captain of the *Cabot*. Congress had wanted Olney to report immediately for a multi-ship mission under the direction of John Paul Jones.[54] Hopkins instead ordered Olney to complete a six-week cruise already in progress. His defiance of congressional authority fatally undermined the loyalty of his crew. On February 19, 1777, ten officers of the *Warren* delivered a petition to Congress demanding his removal from command. Hopkins, they wrote, was guilty of defying congressional orders on multiple occasions, the *Glasgow* fiasco, and had deficiencies of character that rendered him unfit for command of the Continental Navy.[55]

The collective testimony that accompanied the petition paints a portrait of a self-serving man with a profound sense of entitlement. One petitioner, James Sellers, said that Hopkins repeatedly cursed the Marine Committee (successor to the Naval Committee) as "a pack of damned fools." According to Sellers, he also said, "If I should follow their directions, the entire country would be ruined. I am not going to follow their directions, by God." In addition, Sellers maintained that Hopkins "treated prisoners in a very unbecoming and barbarous manner." Three other petitioners—Richard Marven, George Stillman, and Barnabas Lothrop—described Hopkins as "a man destitute of principles, both of religion and Morality," who frequently profaned "the name of almighty God." Samuel Shaw testified that he heard Commodore Hopkins call the Continental Congress "a pack of damned rascals." John Reed maintained that Hopkins "treated prisoners in the most inhuman and barba-rous manner" and believed that "no man yet ever existed who could not be bought." John Grannis described Hopkins's mistreat-ment of prisoners in detail and referred to his conduct in general as "wild and unsteady."[56] In response to the avalanche of condem-nation, Congress suspended Hopkins on March 26, 1777, pending formal inquiry into the charges.[57]

Once he became aware of the "plot" against him, Hopkins re-sorted to his reliable tactic of accusing his critics. One of the signers of the complaint, Richard Marven, was tried by court-martial aboard the *Providence* on April 3, 1777 (before the news of Hopkins's sus-pension had reached him). Marven was found guilty of insubordina-tion, which rendered him "unworthy of holding a Commission in the American Navy."[58]

But there was blood in the water, and public criticism of Hop-kins mounted. In a letter to John Adams on May 19, 1777, minute-man Joseph Ward lamented America's "sleepy navy" under Hopkins.[59] John Paul Jones, now promoted to the rank of admiral, wrote to the American commissioners in France (who were pro-curing guns and ships for the war effort against England) on De-cember 5, 1777, complaining that the jealousy of "the then Commodore Hopkins" had deprived him of the ships he needed to fulfill an order from Congress.[60] Hopkins's crew blew the whistle on his character. Hopkins's peers focused on his insubordination, which they saw as having compromised the war effort.

In bringing charges against Commodore Hopkins, the ten offi-cers who signed the complaint were upholding principles that had been delineated in Congress's original "Orders and Directions for the Commander in Chief of the Fleet of the United Colonies," which stipulated that prisoners of war be "well and humanely treated." The orders also urged commanders to promote and pro-tect whistleblowers: "You will . . . very carefully attend to all the just complaints which may be made by any of the People under your Command and see that they are speedily and effectually Redressed . . . for on a careful attention to these important Subjects the good of the service essentially depends."[61]

Several months later, on January 2, 1778, Congress dismissed Hopkins from "the service of the United States."[62] Enraged at having been undercut by those he saw as his inferiors, Hopkins retaliated by filing a criminal libel suit against the ten petitioners. Richard Marven and Samuel Shaw had the misfortune of being residents of Rhode Island, where the Hopkins family was powerful, so of the ten, only they were jailed. They again turned to the Continental Congress for justice, and again they were vindicated: Congress ruled that Marven and Shaw should be released. But the legislators went even further: on July 30, 1778, they passed the world's first whistleblower protection law. America's public servants were obligated to report wrongdoing in government whenever they encountered it.

Congress did not stop at extolling whistleblowing as an expression of American values. It went on to protect whistleblowers from retaliation. Despite being at war and strapped for resources, Congress paid Marven and Shaw's legal fees, a sum of $1,418.[63] Since this payment was in continental dollars, a currency in use only from 1775 to 1779, it is difficult to calculate its equivalent today. Nevertheless, it was no insignificant amount, given that the first issue of continental currency in 1775 was just $2 million.[64] Congress clearly considered it crucial to support whistleblowers, as it also passed a law ensuring that future whistleblowers would have legal counsel to fight libel charges, just as Marven and Shaw did. Finally, it authorized all records related to Hopkins's removal to be released to the public, which is why this story can be told today.

It only added insult to injury that Hopkins lost his libel suit, despite its taking place in Rhode Island. Being well known there does not appear to have helped him.

Congress did not pass the first whistleblower protection law or pay Marven and Shaw's legal fees solely to stand against torturing prisoners of war. The group of ten and others blew the whistle on abuse of power and disrespect for the newly independent United States of America. For that union to be viable, Rhode Island corruption could not prevail against the authority of the Continental Congress. A union of free and equal states and a collective commitment to the rights of individuals within that new entity were necessary if the new republic was to put down sturdy roots. These were revolutionary times, and both norms and law were being remade. What was at stake was no less than the authority of Congress and the supremacy of the people over special interests.

The Founders and National Security

Proponents and opponents of the new Constitution (Federalists and Anti-Federalists) both condemned British imperial excess, but they parted ways on the question of how the new United States of America was to be governed. For the Anti-Federalists, to recentralize power in a federal system was to succumb to the temptations of their predecessors and trade security for liberty. The Federalists, in contrast, thought they were proposing a free government that could withstand the threats from the hostile European powers then menacing America's borders. The 1787 Constitution and 1791 Bill of Rights encapsulate both Federalist and Anti-Federalist concerns in an effort to keep America both secure and free.

The First Amendment grew directly out of the 1778 whistle-blower protection law, which had recognized freedom of speech and the press as instruments and reflections of liberty. It states, "Congress shall make no law respecting an establishment of religion, or prohibiting the free exercise thereof; or abridging the freedom of speech, or of the press; or the right of the people peaceably to assemble, and to petition the Government for a redress of grievances." If American public servants have a duty to inform Congress of misconduct, fraud, or abuse, they must have the ability to bring such abuses to light: they must have the rights of free speech and a free press. Suspicion of centralized power thus coexisted with faith in federal institutions. The founders assumed that a virtuous people would defend both the new republic's security and its citizens' rights.

In practice, however, when national security was threatened, the Constitution and Bill of Rights did not always succeed in upholding free-speech principles. The Alien and Sedition Acts of 1798, passed under Federalist president John Adams with the aim of silencing opposition to an anticipated war with France, trampled on constitutionally guaranteed rights in the name of national security. The Alien Act allowed the president to deport aliens judged dangerous to the peace and safety of the United States. The Sedition Act punished false, scandalous, or malicious writings against the government, if published with intent to defame or to stir up sedition. Their combined force led to the indictment of the owners and editors of the four most important Jeffersonian (Anti-Federal-ist/Democratic-Republican) papers. Opposition politicians were imprisoned as well, and even congressmen were prosecuted for criticizing Adams, Washington, and the Federalist administration.[65]

James Madison believed that too much had been sacrificed in the pursuit of stability. In the 1798 Virginia Resolutions, which were written by Madison and passed by the Virginia legislature, he identified the Alien and Sedition Acts as unconstitutional assertions of federal power. The Kentucky Resolutions, secretly drafted by Vice President Jefferson and passed by the Kentucky legislature, also challenged the constitutionality of the acts. Both resolutions insisted that Congress had no power whatsoever to infringe on freedom of speech. They were a prominent issue in the 1800 presidential campaign.[66]

Much was at stake in this battle. Jefferson's first inaugural address upheld the principle that "error of opinion may be tolerated where reason is left free to combat it." Not every difference of opinion, Jefferson pointed out, is a difference in principle. "We are all Republicans. We are all Federalists" because Americans hold dear both republican and federalist principles. For Jefferson, a republican federalist government firmly committed to freedom was the strongest government possible: "I know, indeed, that some honest men have feared that a republican government cannot be strong; that this government is not strong enough. But would the honest patriot, in the full tide of successful experiment, abandon a government which has so far kept us free and firm on the theoretic and visionary fear that this government, the world's best hope, may, by possibility, want energy to preserve itself? I trust not. I believe this, on the contrary, the strongest government on earth."[67] Put another way, we are all Republicans and all Federalists because both perspectives inhabit the Constitution and Bill of Rights.

Twentieth-century Supreme Court decisions such as *New York Times v. Sullivan* (1964) and *Watts v. United States* (1969) would uphold Madison's and Jefferson's view that the Alien and Sedition Acts violated the Constitution. But since American judicial review began only in 1803, the acts were never explicitly ruled unconstitutional. Instead, they were repealed, amended out of existence, or allowed to expire shortly after Jefferson assumed the presidency in

1801. The appropriate relationship between the demands of national security and the imperative of whistleblowing thus remained an open question, despite the powerful precedent set by Marven and Shaw.

Those two were America's first whistleblowers. The reprimand and removal of Esek Hopkins clearly demonstrates that whistleblowing was not off limits for the founders, even in the national security realm, even in wartime. The ideals that brought down Hopkins while protecting Marven and Shaw stood at the heart of the new republic. The patriots had faith that a better world could be constructed when authority was subjected to scrutiny. They viewed power as a corrupting force that required constant vigilance in order for liberty to be kept alive. To be an American was a matter of belief, not of blood or soil; the foundation of national unity was a set of shared values. As Gordon Wood explains, it was "the Revolution, and only the Revolution, that made them one people. Therefore, Americans' interpretation of their Revolution could never cease; it was integral to the very existence of the nation."[68]

The 1778 downfall of Esek Hopkins and the steps Congress took to promote and protect whistleblowing were necessary conditions for forging a United States greater than the sum of its parts. Ultimately, Hopkins was more committed to Rhode Island's past, which had given him wealth and social prestige, than to the Revolution's unifying ideals. He was a powerful man accustomed to pursuing his own interests in his own way, and he continued to do so even as Congress repeatedly demanded that he serve a higher cause.

It was a measure of the distance the thirteen colonies still had to travel before they could think of themselves as one people that Hopkins's reputation in Rhode Island remained intact.[69] He served as a member of the Rhode Island state assembly from 1777 to 1786. He was elected a trustee of both Rhode Island College and Brown University. Upon his death in 1802, his obituary did not mention his dishonorable discharge from the U.S. Navy. His tombstone describes him as "Commander in Chief of the Continental Navy during the American Revolution from December 22, 1775 to January 2, 1778."[70] A middle school in Providence continues to bear his name.[71]

Edward Field's hagiographic biography, published in 1898, suggests that Hopkins was a patriot brought down by fellow Rhode Islanders who profited from privateering, but the weight of evidence does not support this view. His story as whitewashed for local consumption leaves his real significance unrecognized: if Jefferson's natural aristocracy of merit and equality were to prevail, American democracy could not tolerate the attitudes and actions of traditional aristocracy. In the United States, no citizen could be above the law because of race or birth. Inherited privilege and entitlement are inconsistent with self-government. Whistleblowers keep us focused on that simple truth.

CHAPTER TWO

Corruption

THE CIVIL WAR BROUGHT many reports from the front lines of fraud by government contractors. Union soldiers might discover that their shells were filled with sawdust rather than gunpowder; the Union cavalry was double- and tripled-charged for horses; cheap, shoddily made boots and uniforms were provided to Union forces at exorbitant prices.[1]

Naval procurement was not immune. When Cornelius Vanderbilt was asked in late 1862 to assist in outfitting an expedition for Union general Nathaniel P. Banks, he selected T. J. Southard to broker the transaction. Southard proceeded to charge the government $900 a day for leasing the boats for the first month, and $800 a day thereafter. The actual value was $500 a day. To add insult to injury, he added a 5 percent commission to the transaction, despite having promised Vanderbilt he would not charge a commission during wartime.

The overcharge for the boats seems to have been overlooked, but when the chartered vessels were launched into battle to occupy New Orleans, the disastrous consequences of wartime profiteering were exposed. One of the ships, the SS *Niagara*, had to return to port after less than twenty-four hours because the sea had removed the fresh coat of paint on the hull and exposed its rotting timbers.

Sold to the navy as a new ship at full cost, it had actually been out-fitted in 1845 for service on Lake Ontario and had long been considered unfit for passengers.[2] Vanderbilt had been warned that this was the case, yet he insisted that the procurement go forward.

Senator James Grimes of Iowa told Congress, "In perfectly smooth seas, the planks were ripped out of her and exhibited to the gaze of indignant soldiers on board, showing that her timbers were rotten. The committee have in their Committee Room a larger sample of one of the beams of the vessel to show it has not the slightest capacity to hold a nail." Vanderbilt escaped without congressional censure, but Commodore Van Brunt and Charles H. Haswell, who were in charge of supervising the outfitting, were found guilty of negligence. Southard was forced to issue a full refund to the government.[3]

The Union soldiers' uniforms were also vehicles for rampant fraud. The word *shoddy* was first used to describe recycled wool: fabric manufacturers would buy old clothes and rags, grind them up and saturate them with oil, milk, and chemicals, and then mix in small quantities of new wool to produce cheap fabric. *Shoddy* became a synonym for "unusably cheap" when Union military uniforms, supposedly made of durable wool, would wear out or disintegrate within a few days. Shoes were also instruments for profiteering. Supposedly made of leather, they were discovered after acquisition to be made of much thinner horsehide, or worse, made of paper. Some were found to have wood inside the soles, placed there because its stiffness would camouflage substandard upper materials until the traveling salesman who provided them was far away.[4]

These scandals were emblematic of the era's contracting fraud, which was regarded as dangerous not only to the soldiers' physical welfare but to the entire enterprise of self-government. "The wholesale swindling that has been practiced upon the Union soldiers, is a disgrace to the nation, and if the evil is not corrected, will disgust the people and break down the administration," warned the *Sacramento Daily Union* in 1861. Contractors "are public robbers, and should be punished as such. Either the contract system should be abolished, as one which is only a cover for frauds upon the service, or contractors in every instance should be mustered into the service of the United States when they signed the contracts, and subjected to the articles of war. One of these articles should be that any contractor or officer of the army convicted before a Court Martial of having practised a fraud upon soldiers should be shot."[5]

Among the public robbers was Brooks Brothers, the oldest men's clothier in the United States. Two weeks after the war began, the company was awarded an initial contract for twelve thousand uniforms, and by the end of 1861 had delivered some thirty-six thousand. The uniforms were shoddy and often missing buttonholes or even buttons. It cost the New York state legislature $45,000 (approximately $11 million in today's dollars) to replace them.[6]

President Lincoln and Civil War Corruption

Given the Union army's sudden demand for goods, it was a seller's market. Unscrupulous defense contractors sold the federal government ill horses and mules, defective ammunition, and inedible rations.[7] President Lincoln was enraged by such treasonous business. "Worse than traitors in arms," he wrote, "are the men who pretend loyalty to the flag. [They] feast and fatten on the misfortunes of the nation while patriotic blood is crimsoning the plains of the south and their countrymen are moldering in the dust."[8]

In response to widespread fraud, in 1861 the House of Representatives created the Select Committee on Government Contracts. New York representative Charles Van Wyck originally chaired the seven-member committee until he was replaced by Elihu Washburne, a close ally of the president. The committee released three reports with over three thousand pages of findings, delineating frauds in the outfitting of horses, ammunition, uniforms, and food as well as frauds by government procurement officers in awarding contracts to friends and associates instead of to the lowest bidders. The frauds committed by agents working under John Frémont, the Western Department head, were so numerous that Washburne wrote to the president to alert him of impending catastrophe. One official, Major Justus McKinstry, the Western Department quartermaster, was eventually court-martialed on sixty-three separate counts of bribery and fraud.[9] Frémont was also involved in the "Hall Carbine Affair," in which carbine guns were sold to Arthur

Eastman to be "modernized" at $3.50 apiece, and then sold back untouched to Frémont for $22 each.[10]

In January 1863, as both the war and the corruption continued, Senator Henry Wilson of Massachusetts introduced Senate Bill 467 to "prevent and punish frauds upon the Government of the United States." Investigation committees in both houses of Congress, Wilson said, "have reported the grossest frauds upon the Government." While the government was doing what it could to stop these frauds and punish those who committed them, the War Department saw no law authorizing it to address the problem. Senator Wilson argued for passing his bill to "put fraudulent contractors in a position where they may be punished."[11]

Rising to Wilson's challenge, Congress passed the False Claims Act, or Lincoln Law, on March 2, 1863.[12] Under the Lincoln Law, whistleblowers could bring "qui tam" actions on behalf of the government against those accused of submitting false claims to the government. Qui tam comes from the Latin phrase *Qui tam pro domino rege quam prosi ipso in hac parte sequitir*, or "One who sues on behalf of the king as well as for himself." If a court agreed with the whistleblower, he or she could receive half of any damages won by the government.

The legislation seems to have been an effective deterrent.[13] The qui tam provision went unused for fourteen years until 1877, when B. F. Dowell sued on behalf of himself and the United States government to recover $35,228 plus costs of around $2,800 from William Griswold, who was accused of falsely claiming $16,114 as payment for supplies furnished during the Oregon Indian War of 1854.[14]

In the decades after its inception, the act fell into disrepute due to "parasitic" lawsuits in which civil relators tried to piggyback on suits already brought by the federal government, filing civil qui tam suits based directly on federal criminal indictments returned against companies and contractors.[15] The government grew concerned that the qui tam provision detracted from the attorney general's proper control over litigation, potentially harming national security interests and the effectiveness of law enforcement.[16] While the Supreme Court upheld the qui tam provision against these policy concerns, Congress acted to limit the provision.[17]

The 1943 amendments to the False Claims Act further reduced the incentives for whistleblowing. They cut the relator's maximum award. They also prohibited the filing of qui tam lawsuits based on information that the government already possessed. In other words, a whistleblower claim was viable only if it revealed something the government did not already know. An anonymous tip to the government that mirrored any civil claim disqualified the citizen whistleblower from compensation. This ended the piggybacking suits but also undermined the incentives for reporting waste, fraud, and abuse to the government. As a result of the 1943 amendments, the False Claims Act again fell into disuse until its fortification via amendment in 1986 in response to public outrage about corrupt defense contracts under the Reagan administration.[18]

Greed and Corruption in the First Gilded Age

Technological change in the growing nation transformed the stage for whistleblowers. American revolutionaries had pamphlets and the printing press but no means of disseminating information quickly across the entire American territory. The development of the post office in the 1820s and 1830s had made it possible for newspapers to both create and reach a national audience. The telegraph, first used in 1842, accelerated this process. Abraham Lincoln had used the telegram to enormous advantage during the Civil War. Since the North controlled fifteen thousand miles of telegraph wires and the Confederacy only one thousand, communication between Washington and the Union army was far more efficient than counterparts in the South could manage. But rapid communication also meant that political controversy and conflict could no longer easily be locally contained, and these technologies assumed a central role in national politics.[19]

In the latter part of the nineteenth century, the possibilities for progress seemed unlimited, and politicians thought big. Building the infrastructure of the United States presented vast opportunities for self-enrichment. William Magear "Boss" Tweed played the game of public servant on the make better than most. Corrupt practices went hand in hand with infrastructure development that advanced public interests.

The political corruption machine known as Tammany Hall did not end with Boss Tweed, but he certainly epitomized its tactics, ethics, and power mongering. Tweed held sway over New York City and New York State politics through the city's Democratic Party organization, nicknamed Tammany Hall. Tammany Hall grew out of a fraternal organization—the Tammany Society of New York City—founded in 1786. The Tammany Society's activities were at first social but became politicized over time, ultimately becoming the main proponents of Jeffersonian policies in New York City.[20] Jimmy O'Brien, who served as sheriff of New York County from 1867 to 1872 while Tweed was a member of the New York State Senate, played the same game as Tweed until an opportune moment, when he brought the entire enterprise crashing down to save his own reputation.

Tweed rose to prominence slowly and methodically. In 1850 at the age of twenty-six, he was elected foreman of the fire brigade and became the Democratic candidate for assistant alderman in the Seventh Ward. He lost that race, but a year later, in 1851, he won the more powerful post of alderman in the Seventh Ward through clever electoral manipulation. He had his acquaintance Joel Blackmer run as a Whig against the favored Whig candidate, John B. Webb, splitting the Whig vote and giving Tweed, the Democrat, the election. Tweed saw corruption and patronage as necessities in democratic politics. As he would later tell a jailhouse interviewer six months prior to his death, "The fact is New York politics were always dishonest—long before my time. There never was a time when you couldn't buy the Board of Aldermen. A politician in coming forward takes things as they are. This population is too hopelessly split up into races and factions to govern it under universal suffrage, except by the bribery of patronage, or corruption."[21]

In 1852, Tweed won election to the U.S. Congress, where he sponsored no legislation and made just one speech but maintained his connections with New York's Seventh Ward and with Tammany Hall. After serving only one term, he returned to New York and devoted his full-time attention to slowly and carefully nurturing an elaborate web of patronage relationships. At one point or another, he was a member of the New York City Board of Advisers, commissioner of public works, New York state senator, the third-largest landowner in New York City, director of the Erie Railroad, director of the Tenth National Bank, director of the New York Printing Company, proprietor of the Metropolitan Hotel and, by 1863, boss of Tammany Hall.[22]

Two years before taking the helm of Tammany Hall, however, Tweed first went bankrupt after his chair business failed.[23] His bankruptcy filing lists his worldly assets at the time: "Three Hats, Two Caps, Two Thick Overcoats, One Thin Overcoat, Three Pair Pants, Six Vests, Two Dress Coats, One Business Coat, Three Pair Boots, Two Pair Shoes, Ten Pair Socks, Thirty Collars, Twelve Linen Shirts, Twelve Cotton Shirts, Ten Handkerchiefs." He recovered from this bankruptcy by opening a private law office at 95 Duane Street, where he used city contacts to "fix" problems for paying customers.[24] Five years later, he owned homes in Manhattan and Greenwich, Connecticut.[25]

Two of Tweed's contacts were the young New York City moguls Jay Gould and James Fisk, who were battling Cornelius Vanderbilt and Daniel Drew in 1868 for ownership of the Erie Railroad. As a state senator that year, Tweed at first supported Vanderbilt, but Gould and Fisk won him over with a bribe of Erie stock and a seat on the executive committee. With Tweed's support, Gould and Fisk gained control of the Erie Railroad. The Erie Railroad then funded Tweed's judicial and legislative favors.[26]

Though not gifted at honest business, Tweed turned out to be a virtuoso of city politics, enriching himself by taking 15 percent from every city contract and cooking the books to disguise the flows into his own bank account. The main vehicle for Tweed's skimming was public investment in the infrastructure of New York City, which he first financed by borrowing from abroad, rather than by raising taxes on New Yorkers.

Using Erie Railroad money to turn himself into a patronage playmaker, Tweed effectively took control of the city government, which brought with it tremendous opportunities for additional graft. One trick was to buy up undeveloped property in the Upper East Side and Harlem, use public resources to develop it (for example, installing pipes to bring in water from the Croton Aqueduct), and then sell the upgraded real estate at a huge profit, which he would then reinvest in more real estate. By the late 1860s, he was one of New York City's biggest landowners and was lauded for developing modern New York. Under Boss Tweed's influence, the city developed the Upper East and West Sides of Manhattan, launched the Brooklyn Bridge, and set aside land for the Metropolitan Museum of Art. Tweed got rich and New York City got developed. Millions of dollars of taxpayer money went walking.

Tweed took to wearing a large diamond in his shirtfront. He bought a brownstone on 36th Street, then a very fashionable area, and a mansion on Fifth Avenue and 43rd Street. He stabled his horses, carriages, and sleighs nearby on 40th Street. By 1871 he was on the board of directors of not only the Erie Railroad and the Brooklyn Bridge Company but also the Third Avenue Railway Company (of which Gould seized control in 1884) and the Harlem Gas Light Company. He was president of the Guardian Savings Banks, and with his cronies, including Gould, established the Tenth National Bank.

Tweed's carefully constructed political machine showed his grasp of human psychology. Instead of keeping the benefits from his graft all to himself, he spread the wealth widely, expanding the network of people indebted to him. The Tweed "ring" was really a corrupt pyramid, and the base was sufficiently broad to ensure both satisfaction and political support. His machine ultimately depended on the tolerance of citizens, who seemingly overlooked his corruption, nepotism, and attempts to manipulate the press. That cynicism, in turn, fueled bolder exploits, until the greed and envy of Tweed's partner-rivals brought the entire enterprise crashing to the ground.[27]

Tweed's heavy hand shaped the election of 1868, when voting fraud dominated in New York City. The Democrats lost the presidential election to Civil War hero Ulysses Grant, but still managed to win all the important state and city positions. That discrepancy led Congress to appoint a special committee to investigate; it found the 1868 elections to have been grossly manipulated. The Tammany leaders had wanted an early count of upstate votes so as to be able to manipulate the downstate votes enough to secure a Democratic majority and carry the state. In their zeal to consolidate their power, they had committed frauds too large to be disguised. For example, the 156,054 votes cast in New York City that year exceeded the total number of eligible voters by at least 8 percent. The committee estimated that some 50,000 of those votes had been added by Tammany Hall.[28]

The Tweed ring's ability to conjure up voters out of thin air was not confined to New York City. As scholars have pointed out, it is hard to assemble convincing evidence of electoral fraud, in large part because the manipulators took such pains to camouflage their activity. But the available data indicate that such fraud was widespread in the Gilded Age.[29] The very structure of the electoral process encouraged it. For most of the era, there was no secret ballot. Voters used party tickets, which were printed by the competing parties and contained only the names of their candidates, not any sort of slate from which to select a favorite. Party tickets varied wildly in size and color, and they were distributed at the polls by partisan ticket peddlers, making a voter's choice a highly public act. Such a system facilitated vote buying as well as considerable social pressure on how citizens voted.[30] Both kinds of electoral manipulation are hard to document.

Where the Tweed ring is concerned, however, we have at least one smoking gun. A confidential letter to Tweed from George J. Magee of Watkins, New York, dated September 16, 1868, contained the names of Irishmen from Pennsylvania who desired naturalization papers. Magee wrote, "We cannot procure them in this section or in Pennsylvania. Cannot it be done in New York? To be of any service to the cause they should be obtained at once and for use on the second Tuesday of October. We need every vote at that election. These papers should be dated back from December to July last. Most of these have been in the country five years and none of them less than three but they would not get even their first papers owing to the war and a fear of drafts. Hoping that something can be done to secure these certain democratic votes."[31] When questioned by a special committee of the New York City Board of Aldermen in 1877, Tweed more or less confessed to his machine's ballot manipulation when he admitted, "The ballots made no result; the counters made the result."[32]

The fall of Boss Tweed shows that whistleblowing is not always heroic: it can emerge from impure motives. He was done in not by a noble act of conscience but by rivals who envied his success and aspired to emulate him. One of these rivals was Manhattan County sheriff James O'Brien. After it was over, Jimmy O'Brien spent the rest of his life as the hero who brought down Boss Tweed. Yet he merely passed along evidence that he had instructed others to collect; those others died in obscurity.

As sheriff, O'Brien had patrolled the ballot boxes for Tweed during the 1868 election. In theory, the sheriff was a natural point person for anyone seeking to expose or prosecute corruption. This particular sheriff, however, was mainly concerned with getting his proper share of the spoils. The records show that between September 1869 and May 1871, Tweed paid O'Brien four checks totaling $23,000. Tweed had also lent him $12,000 on a thirty-day promissory note due on June 1, 1871. On June 3, O'Brien refused to pay and pocketed what he had borrowed as profit. We also know that he repeatedly pressed Tweed to reimburse him for exorbitant sheriff's expenses, by one account as much as $350,000.[33] Later in June, after having benefited from Tweed's patronage for years and having pocketed Tweed's $12,000 loan, O'Brien delivered explosive evidence on Tweed's dealings to the *New York Times*, thereby turning himself into a hero in the anticorruption fight. In so doing, he avoided prosecution while sending his adversary to jail.[34] Jimmy O'Brien exposed wrongdoing only when he could no longer count on his fair share of the spoils.

Every account I have read of the Tweed machine has focused on O'Brien as the instrument of Tweed's demise, but the real whistleblowers in this story are William Copeland and Matthew O'Rourke. In January 1870, before he broke with Tweed, O'Brien had helped Copeland land a job in the auditing department of the city comptroller's office, serving as assistant to county auditor James Watson, the main man in charge of cooking the Tweed ring's books. After several months on the job, troubled by some irregularities he had noticed in the city's books, Copeland turned to O'Brien for advice. O'Brien told him to start copying, by hand, anything he found disturbing or anomalous, and to bring the copied records back to him.[35]

Copeland spent the next three months laboriously copying out suspicious entries by hand, meticulously documenting everything. By late 1870 he had compiled a voluminous collection of incriminating information, in large part consisting of incredibly inflated expenditures for items such as furniture. He turned all the copied records over to O'Brien. In March 1871, he was fired, in his own words, for "political reasons."[36] Most likely, comptroller Richard "Slippery Dick" Connolly had come to believe that Copeland was leaking incriminating material. O'Brien silently waited for his opportunity.

Matthew O'Rourke, who had previously served as a newspaper reporter on military affairs, was hired on to replace Copeland in comptroller Connolly's office in early 1871. He too quickly noticed (and copied) immense irregularities in the books, and in May he quit in disgust, taking his incriminating records with him. He brought the evidence to the *New York Times* in early July 1871. O'Brien appears to have caught wind of the imminent exposure of the Tweed ring before the *Times* published anything on the subject, and rather than initiate an internal investigation, which as sheriff he surely could have done, he gave Copeland's materials to the paper as well. This evidence corroborated what O'Rourke had submitted, and together the two sets of records made up the case against Tweed. The *Times* hired O'Rourke, since he was closest to the evidence, to work with reporter John Ford and editor Louis Jennings on the story.[37]

When the story broke on July 22, New York's mayor A. Oakey Hall, known as "Elegant Oakey" and an instrument of Tweed's patronage power (Tweed himself never served as mayor), retaliated by trying to evict the *Times* from its own office building, but the paper stayed put.[38] Using the documents supplied by Copeland and O'Rourke, the *Times* laid out the full story of Tweed's corrupt practices for its readers. On October 3, 1871, a judicial warrant was issued against Mayor Hall for "various offenses and malfeasance." In the ensuing trial, the witnesses against him included William Copeland and James O'Brien as well as Governor Samuel Tilden and *Times* publisher George Jones, none of whom testified that they suspected Hall of personally committing unlawful acts. The jury ultimately dismissed the charges.[39] Despite his having been tarnished by association with Boss Tweed, when Hall died in October 1898, the *Times* gave him a glowing obituary, describing him as an "eccentric" but "remarkable man."[40]

At the end of 1871, the *Times* ran an editorial informing readers that Tweed had been "banished from public life . . . after a long but ineffectual attempt to become a permanent burden on the public he robbed." The editors pointed out that in September 1870, the *Times* had been the only paper willing to criticize the Tweed ring. "Every paper was against us," they reminded readers. "It is easy enough to fight the Ring now—it was very different work in 1870." The editors also predicted that Oakey Hall would be next, although that did not happen.[41] With the Tweed organization's corruption no longer in doubt, the New York State Senate began to follow the Tweed money in earnest in 1872.[42]

Boss Tweed's first trial, in January 1873, ended in a mistrial when the jury could not agree on a verdict. His retrial in November resulted in his conviction on 204 of 220 counts and a prison sentence of twelve years. A higher court reduced the sentence to one year.

The transcripts of the trials as well as the media coverage make fascinating reading. Copeland testified that he first thought something was amiss—something that could only be fraud—when bills seemed impossibly large for the items in question.[43] In one of the more sensational transactions, $5 million had passed through the account of furniture maker and bag man James Ingersoll, ostensibly to decorate and furnish the new courthouse. In early 1871, Ingersoll offered the cartoonist Thomas Nast, known for his devastating cartoons lampooning Tweed's exploits, $500,000 ($10 million in 2008 dollars) to go to Europe until the elections of November 1871 were over.[44]

Throughout Tweed's trial, there was no suggestion that Copeland or O'Brien had violated confidentiality or loyalty norms by making the evidence of fraud public.[45] Copeland was a public servant who had discovered wrongdoing, and the working assumption was that he had no choice but to turn his findings over to the authorities. No one probed Copeland's motives. He took note of wrongdoing and took the requisite steps to confront it. Nor did anyone question James O'Brien's decision to leak his materials to the press rather than pursue the matter internally. O'Brien, celebrated as a hero, milked his fame for all it was worth.

After Tweed was released from prison, New York State tried to recover $6 million in embezzled funds by filing a civil suit against Tweed. He was unable to pay the $3 million bail and was sent to Ludlow Street Jail. He was allowed home visits, and on one of these, he fled the country and managed to make it all the way to Spain via Cuba, but Spanish authorities seized him and sent him back to his captors. His options exhausted, he agreed to testify about the inner workings of his corruption network to the New York Board of Aldermen.[46]

Copeland's and O'Brien's whistleblowing shook Tammany Hall to its foundations, but Tweed was the only member of the ring to be punished, even though Copeland had testified that he had never seen Tweed's signature on any warrant. Everyone else who was implicated escaped jail time. Connolly fled to Europe, Ingersoll was pardoned, and Hall was acquitted.[47]

Looking back on his career from his jail cell, Tweed is said to have remarked, "I was always ambitious to be influential and to control ... [now] my vanity sees nothing to delight in. I recall nothing eminent."[48] When he died, the *New York Tribune* opined that "his life, as a whole, was a wretched failure, in every possible way and from whatever point of view it may be regarded."[49] People like Governor Samuel Tilden, whom the *New York Times* repeatedly lambasted for lacking the courage to speak out against Tweed until it was safe to do so, piled on to condemn him.[50] The public's tolerance for corruption had reached a breaking point, and O'Brien had anticipated that shift. Tweed's last words reportedly were, "I hope they will be satisfied now they have got me."[51]

Crony Capitalism and the Transcontinental Railroad

If developing New York City took a stack of cash, building a transcontinental railroad took a bushel. The federal government needed a railroad spanning the entire country, but private investors found the venture too risky. Both Collis P. Huntington, an organizer of the Central Pacific Railroad, and Thomas Durant of the Union Pacific Railroad came to Washington in 1864 in order to encourage (bribe) Congress to alter the laws governing railroad construction westward.[52] Through the Pacific Railroad Acts, Congress authorized the issuance of bonds and grants of land to railroad companies bent on expanding into the frontier. Congressional backing mitigated the risk for investors. Huntington and Durant got what they wanted, and so did Washington.

Having gained federal government backing, the Central Pacific Railroad and Union Pacific Railroad were empowered to harness the power of financial markets to their cause. President Lincoln chartered them to build the railway, and Congress gave them land donations, loans, mineral rights, and other advantages. To raise money, the companies sold stocks and issued bonds, which sold easily because they had the direct backing of the U.S. government.

Scandal started brewing when Union Pacific created another corporation, the Credit Mobilier of America construction company, to carry out the actual construction. Union Pacific contracted with Credit Mobilier to build the Union Pacific railway at rates significantly above cost. Since Union Pacific's bonds were also backed by the U.S. government, raising the capital necessary to expand the Union Pacific line westward was not difficult.[53] The board of directors of Credit Mobilier consisted entirely of members of the Union Pacific board. As a result, the subcontractor Credit Mobilier could charge Union Pacific whatever it saw fit, while Union Pacific, the recipient of government funds, would report Credit Mobilier's charges to the government as actual expenses—which, on its own books, they were. This method of indirect billing was the principal means of fraud. In essence, the symbiotic relationship between the government, Union Pacific, and Credit Mobilier allowed for creative bookkeeping that could mask any evidence of fraud or profiteering on the part of the directors.

In early 1865, with Union Pacific floundering under Durant's leadership, President Lincoln turned to Massachusetts congressman Oakes Ames to get things back on track. "Ames, you take hold of this," Lincoln told him. "The road must be built, and you are the man to do it. Take hold of it yourself. By building the Union Pacific, you will be the remembered man of your generation." Thus anointed by the president, Ames bought into Credit Mobilier and sought to represent it in Washington.[54]

After Lincoln's assassination, the plot thickened. In 1867, Union Pacific issued a new construction contract to Credit Mobilier, now ostensibly overseen by Congressman Ames, and reported a 90 percent profit at year end. Since he had joined Credit Mobilier, Ames had been offering his congressional colleagues shares of the company's stock at a discount in hopes of winning their continued support for the project; now everyone wanted in. Credit Mobilier stock had a high market value precisely because the railroad venture had the obvious backing of the U.S. government. A congressman could buy discounted shares and then immediately sell them at a high profit. This machine could keep rolling as long as Congress kept appropriating government funds for the railroad project.

In 1869, Charles Francis Adams, who would become head of the Union Pacific Railroad in the 1880s, described the Credit Mobilier business model this way: "The members of it are in Congress; they were trustees for the bondholders; they were directors; they were stockholders; they were contractors; in Washington they voted the subsidies, in New York they received them, upon the Plains they expended them, and in the 'Credit Mobilier' they divided them."[55] Yet those involved did not necessarily see this as improper. For Ames, spreading the wealth was a public-spirited way of ensuring Congress's continued support for a transcontinental railroad.

The web of corruption stretched from a future president of the United States, James Garfield, to Vice President Schuyler Colfax to House Speaker James Blaine to House Ways and Means Committee Chairman Henry Dawes to at least twenty-five other members of Congress who invested in Credit Mobilier either directly or through surrogates. "The men entrusted with the management of the Pacific Road," a contemporary reporter wrote, "made a bargain with themselves to build the road for a sum equal to about twice its actual cost, and pocketed the profits, which have been estimated at about THIRTY MILLIONS OF DOLLARS—this immense sum coming out of the pockets of the tax payers of the United States."[56] The take was over $600 million in 2018 dollars.

The story gained the attention of the press in 1872, a presidential election year, when the *New York Sun* published a list of Credit Mobilier's major shareholders.[57] In response, the House created a commission headed by Representative Luke Poland (R-VT). The Poland committee found evidence that "almost every important committee chairmen of the House of Representatives" as well as Senators William B. Allison and James Harlan of Iowa, James A. Bayard Jr. of Delaware, George S. Boutwell of Massachusetts, Roscoe Conkling of New York, John Logan of Illinois, James Patterson of New Hampshire, Henry Wilson of Massachusetts, and Vice

President Schuyler Colfax were involved. It recommended that Oakes Ames and Representative James Brooks of New York be expelled from the House.[58] Both were dead several months later, Ames from a stroke and Brooks from the effects of a fever he contracted in Asia.[59]

The whistleblower in this case, Henry Simpson McComb, was hardly innocent. Born in Wilmington, Delaware, he had received minimal formal education and had served as a Union colonel during the Civil War. After the war, he quickly rose to become president of the Mississippi Central Railroad, a company that stood to gain from a transcontinental railroad. He was one of the main investors and organizers of Credit Mobilier of America, but he fell out with Ames and the rest of the board after they refused his request for 375 shares of stock as compensation for his efforts in promoting investment in the railroad. When his protests of ill treatment were ignored, McComb sued Credit Mobilier, Ames, and others to get what he saw as his fair share of the spoils.[60]

In court, McComb submitted letters he had received from Ames in 1867 showing that Ames had engaged in what we would today call insider trading.[61] The most incriminating letter listed the individuals who had been selected to receive favorably priced stock to encourage their investment in the enterprise. Their public association with the project might then better inspire investor confidence in the entire venture (thereby increasing the profit margin for insiders). Ames had written McComb that he had placed the Credit Mobilier stock "where it will produce the most good to us."[62] If influential men in Washington were personally invested, the reasoning went, others would see it as in their interest to invest as well. In his letter, Ames explained why each person had been selected for favors and what each brought to the enterprise. Ironically, by choosing his beneficiaries so carefully, Ames thought he was upholding the public interest in seeing the transcontinental railroad become reality.

The problem with Ames's reasoning, of course, was that Ames was buying support from government officials, the very definition of quid pro quo corruption. Ames would later testify before Congress in 1873 that McComb tried to use them to blackmail him—just as Sheriff Jimmy O'Brien had endeavored to do with Boss Tweed.[63]

McComb strategically leaked the compromising letters to the *New York Sun*, which made the scoop public on September 4, 1872, under the headlines "The King of Fraud," "How Credit Mobilier Bought Its Way through Congress," and "Colossal Bribery." Republican-leaning newspapers at the time dismissed the charges as fake news, especially since the *New York Sun* was a vocal critic of the Grant administration.[64] The letters became a major issue in the 1872 presidential campaign. Many Americans saw in the correspondence graft and corruption rather than a public works infrastructure effort to better the nation. Nonetheless, many of the congressmen who were implicated in the 1873 investigation that ensued, including future president James A. Garfield of Ohio, escaped formal reprimand.[65] Vice President Schuyler Colfax was forced out of office, and his career was never repaired. McComb was never prosecuted but also never collected the money he thought was due him.[66] In the case of Credit Mobilier, the whistle got blown, and the extent of the exposed corruption shamed everyone.

The story broke a few years after the transcontinental railroad had become reality, on May 10, 1869, when the tracks of the Central Pacific were joined with those of the Union Pacific at Promontory, Utah. Yet this scandal was quickly eclipsed by bigger stories of graft on America's railroads. In February 1875, the *Chicago Daily Tribune* described misconduct in the Memphis, El Paso, and Pacific Railroad line as "the greatest instance of official corruption ever known in the Congress of the United States, or in any civilized government." Its headline trumpeted "a monster corruption fund with elevens of millions of dollars to bribe Congress."[67]

While efforts to buy influence were hardly new, Americans were unsettled by the scale of the markets and the private corporations that manipulated them. The new technologies involved were novel and threatening. Writing about the "Huntington Syndicate"—a powerful alliance of railroad magnates that included Collis P. Huntington, head of the Central Pacific Railroad—the *Chicago Daily Tribune* lamented, "All these different corporations will be melded into one. The men Huntington, Stanford, and Crocker will die, but the corporation will live. The country must rule it or it will rule the country."[68]

In his 1914 book *Drift and Mastery*, the journalist Walter Lippmann wrote that the Progressive Era's muckraking—the often

unscrupulous publishing of scandalous information about elites—
was a symptom of an age "when success had ceased to be easily
possible for everyone. . . . There has always been corruption in
American politics but it didn't worry people very much, so long as
the sphere of government was narrowly limited."[69] Historian Richard White concurs: "There was a sense that the 1873 crisis had revealed deep flaws, not just in the financial system, but in a larger
cultural order."[70]

Increasing economic inequality, dysfunctional government, and a
growing public sense that American democracy has been hijacked
by special interests were all features of American life in the late
nineteenth century. As the American state grew, so did the possibilities for corruption. In the first Gilded Age it took three principal
forms, all involving the self-enrichment of public servants. The
first variant involved fraud or false claims, the kind of transgression
Congress tried to address with the Lincoln Law. The second was
skimming or graft, when those holding public office enriched
themselves while actually building things such as public transportation or other infrastructure. Boss Tweed's New York was a labo-
ratory for that variety of misconduct. The third was a variant of
quid pro quo corruption, as seen in the Credit Mobilier scandal.
Public servants essentially received kickbacks in the form of discounted stock in exchange for continued government support and
financing. In the twenty-first century, we would call this insider
trading. Individuals used insider information to line their own
pockets through strategic investment.

In the nineteenth century, whistleblowers made Americans
aware of the downside of their developing economy. Large public
works and government contracts enabled the United States to harness the entrepreneurial spirit of the private sector to grow the
economy, develop infrastructure, and create jobs. They also presented unprecedented opportunities for graft and corruption. Even
when whistleblower motives were suspect, the public applauded
the exposure of elite greed. Whistleblowers thus helped post–Civil
War Americans to understand that economic growth as well as the
growth of the American state were not cost-free. The amounts of
money involved and the new financial instruments and institutions

needed to raise and manage those amounts of money were genuinely unprecedented. Whistleblowers made Americans aware of levels and kinds of graft they had never imagined. The exposure of such self-interested elite action undermined faith in American institutions. But American public servants shamelessly colluding with foreigners in their financial schemes for self-enrichment would have to wait for the twenty-first century.

CHAPTER THREE

Treason

T HE ANTAGONISM GENERATED BY the 1917 Russian Revolution had lasting repercussions for whistleblowing in America. The Soviet Union was the vanguard of the communist movement, which sought the overthrow of Western capitalism, including American constitutional democracy. How should we regard the activities of those Americans who served that movement more enthusiastically than they did the United States of America? Framed by the Cold War, attitudes toward national security dissenters would change dramatically over the course of the twentieth century.

Subversion and Espionage during World War I

Despite being a nation of immigrants, the United States often saw newcomers as threats to its security, leading it to impose measures that infringed on individual rights. The Alien Law of 1798 allowed the president to deport foreigners who endangered the nation's peace and safety. During World War I, some German Americans were accused of siding with the fatherland against their adopted home. In October 1917, former president Theodore Roosevelt warned of "Huns within our own gates and the allies of men whom our sons and daughters are crossing the ocean to fight."[1] Japanese

Americans were rounded up into internment camps during World War II—an action that was upheld by the Supreme Court in 1944 but later condemned by some justices in 2018. The ideological struggle between capitalism and communism, however, was different from the wars against Germany and Japan in that some communists were not Americans.

We need look no further than the Bolshevik perspective on the Russian war effort in World War I to see the inescapable tensions between communist ideals and the interests of liberal democracies. Marx and Engels had argued in the 1848 *Communist Manifesto* that "the working man has no country. We cannot take from them what they have not got."[2] It followed that a communist had no obligation to be patriotic and serve his or her country in wartime. Lenin's followers argued that fighting for Imperial Russia in World War I meant fighting for tsarism, when the tsar's interests in no way coincided with those of the working class.

When the Bolsheviks seized power in 1917, they quickly withdrew Russia from the war. The cost of that premature withdrawal was severe. The 1918 Treaty of Brest-Litovsk between Russia and the Central Powers shrank Russia to its seventeenth-century borders, but it gave the revolutionaries breathing room to consolidate their power. An example had been set. Since war served the interests of capitalists and capitalism, Lenin argued, working-class men and women should refuse to fight for their country and instead convert the war among nations into a class war against bourgeois governments—meaning European or American liberal democracies.

When the Communist International (Comintern) was created in Moscow in 1919 to organize Bolshevik supporters worldwide, it considered itself the nerve center of world revolution. From its very inception, the Comintern's dual mission was to spread the revolution and to defend the world's first socialist government. Lenin saw the Comintern as the international arm of the Russian Communist Party. The ultimate goal of foreign communist parties was therefore to assist the Comintern in waging war against existing democratic regimes. The 1920 Party Congress stipulated as a prerequisite for Comintern membership a commitment to create in one's own country a "parallel illegal organization" that would operate in secret until the decisive revolutionary moment.[3] Another resolution, adopted at the Third Congress of the Comintern in 1921, urged members to deploy both legal and illegal methods to achieve common goals.[4] Law was the enemy's weapon, a bourgeois smoke screen for continued exploitation of working people.

U.S. authorities were determined that communists not be allowed to do to the American war effort what they had done to Russia's. In June 1917, shortly after the U.S. entered World War I, Congress passed the Espionage Act, which prohibited any attempt to interfere with military operations or to support enemies of the United States during wartime. The Sedition Act of 1918, an amendment to the Espionage Act, prohibited the use of "disloyal, profane, scurrilous, or abusive language" about the U.S. government, its flag, or its armed forces. It was to apply only when the United States was at war, and expired in 1921. The Espionage Act had no expiration date and was strengthened in 1919 when the Supreme Court, in *Schenck v. United States*, unanimously upheld the constitutionality of both the Espionage Act and the Sedition Act.

Charles Schenck, the secretary of the Socialist Party of America, believed that military conscription violated the Thirteenth Amendment's prohibition on involuntary servitude. He had printed, distributed, and mailed leaflets urging prospective soldiers to resist the draft. For compromising the American war effort by encouraging insubordination, Schenck was convicted of violating the Espionage Act. He appealed to the Supreme Court, arguing that his First Amendment rights had been violated.

In a unanimous opinion written by Justice Oliver Wendell Holmes, the Supreme Court upheld Schenck's conviction. The First Amendment, Holmes wrote, was not to be extended to speech that actively encouraged betraying one's country in a time of need. As he memorably put it, "The most stringent protection of free speech would not protect a man in falsely shouting fire in a theater and causing panic." Rather, "the question in every case is whether the words are used in such circumstances and are of such a nature as to create a clear and present danger that they will bring about the substantive evils that Congress has the right to prevent."[5] Charles Schenck served six months in prison, and America now had the first judicial formulation of the "clear and present danger" test.

America's most prominent socialist, Eugene Debs, was also convicted under the Espionage Act for undermining the American cause in World War I. He ran as the Socialist Party's candidate for president in 1900, 1904, 1908, 1912, and 1920. It was a June 16, 1918, speech in Canton, Ohio, that landed him in hot water. The speech was similar to others he had given, but the district attorney for Northern Ohio, Edwin S. Wertz, had stenographers record Debs's remarks that day.[6]

Debs argued forcefully against American involvement in World War I. The Allies and the enemy, he said, had indistinguishable ends: both were fighting to enrich themselves.[7] He urged socialists to resist conscription and fight for genuine democracy instead. For Debs, America had become a plutocracy whose "Wall Street Junkers" had more in common with the Germans whom the United States was fighting against than they did with ordinary Americans. Debs urged his listeners to abandon the national war effort to uphold the higher cause of socialist justice.

It was no accident that Debs's position mirrored the Bolshevik internationalist call to arms in Russia. He thought that revolution was a glorious moment, worthy of emulation. The heroic Russians had set an example for the rest of the world. It is most illuminating to hear Debs speak for himself:

> Those Russian comrades of ours have made greater sacrifices, have suffered more, and have shed more heroic blood than any like number of men and women anywhere on earth; they have laid the foundation of the first real democracy that ever drew the breath of life in this world. And the very first act of the triumphant Russian Revolution was to proclaim a state of peace with all mankind, coupled with a fervent moral appeal, not to kings, not to emperors, rulers or diplomats but to the people of all nations. Here we have the very breath of democracy, the quintessence of the dawning freedom. The Russian Revolution proclaimed its glorious triumph in its ringing and inspiring appeal to the peoples of all the earth.[8]

That speech would eventually lead to ten charges of sedition against Debs, including attempting to promote the success of the enemies of the United States; attempting to cause insubordination, disloyalty, mutiny, and refusal of duty in the military or naval forces; attempting to obstruct the recruiting or enlistment in the service of the United States; uttering disloyal language about the form of government of the United States; uttering language intended to incite, provoke, or encourage resistance to the United States and to promote the cause of its enemies; and opposing the cause of the United States by words.[9]

After six hours of deliberation, the jury found Debs guilty on three counts: attempting to cause insubordination, disloyalty, mutiny, and refusal of duty in the military or naval forces; attempting to obstruct the recruiting or enlistment in the service of the United States; and uttering language intended to incite, provoke, or encourage resistance to the United States and to promote the cause of its enemies.[10] Debs celebrated his conviction as validating the socialist position that something was terribly wrong with American democracy.[11] When charged with sabotaging the war effort, he responded, "I have been accused of obstructing the war. I admit it. I abhor war. I would oppose war if I stood alone." Before his sentencing, he summarized his political orientation for the assembled: "While there is a lower class, I am in it. While there is a criminal element, I am of it. While there is a soul in prison, I am not free."[12]

Debs appealed his case all the way to the Supreme Court. The court ultimately upheld his conviction but refrained from considering the constitutionality of the Espionage Act itself.[13] A *Washington Post* editorial proclaimed, "The Decision of the United States Supreme Court . . . is welcomed by every patriotic American citizen who has faith in and admiration for the American republic."[14] Debs's response was nonchalant: "I told the Court when I was convicted that the law was despotic and have not changed my mind in the least. I am not concerned with what those be-powdered, be-wigged corporation attorneys at Washington do. I am going to celebrate tonight by taking Mrs. Debs to a picture show."[15]

The matter did not end with the Supreme Court's decision. Debs continued his campaign for social justice from prison. The Socialist Party demonstrated in Washington in April 1920 to demand Debs's release.[16] Life disenfranchisement, one result of his guilty verdict, did not stop him from running for president from prison under the campaign slogan "From the Jail House to the White House." President Warren Harding commuted his sentence in 1921 without a pardon. Five years later, Debs died in a sanatorium in Elmhurst, Illinois, with the knowledge that the movement to which he had devoted his life was on its deathbed. The 1925 national convention of the Socialist Party, which took place in Cleveland, was so poorly organized and sparsely attended that Debs judged the party to be "as near a corpse as a thing can be."[17]

Both Debs and Schenck wanted the United States to lose the war in order to build a better world. According to the *Oxford English Dictionary*, treason is the crime of betraying one's country, not any particular political leader or policy. Dissent itself does not constitute treason. Serving a foreign power does. Americans who want the United States to lose in war to precipitate regime change thus tread on traitorous ground.

Soviet Meddling and American Overreaction

The United States did not recognize the Union of Soviet Socialist Republics as a nation until 1933. Explaining the Wilson administration's position in a 1920 letter to the Italian government, Secretary of State Bainbridge Colby wrote that the United States could not possibly recognize the present rulers of Russia as a legitimate government because "the existing regime in Russia is based upon the negation of every principle of honor and good faith, and every usage and convention, underlying the whole structure of international law; the negation, in short, of every principle upon which it is possible to base harmonious and trustful relations, whether of nations or individuals."[18]

Joseph Stalin, who succeeded V. I. Lenin as general secretary of the Communist Party in 1924, accepted Marx's argument that the working man had no country and then took the logic a step further, directly equating the interests of the working class with those of the Soviet Union. A proletarian internationalist, he explained in 1927, is one "who unreservedly, unhesitatingly, and unconditionally is prepared to defend the USSR, because the USSR is the base of the world revolutionary movement." In 1948 he wrote: "Only he is a genuine internationalist who carries his sympathy, respect, recognition to the point of practical and maximum aid, support, and defense of the USSR by every means and in various forms."[19] The view that American communists answered to Moscow was Stalin's vision, not a creation of anticommunist conspiracy theorists.

After World War II, the United States created new institutions to defend American constitutional democracy against these new threats. The 1947 National Security Act and its amendments in 1949 crystallized America's transition from a country that focused on national defense during wartime to one that focused on national security at all times. Together, they significantly strengthened the powers of the executive branch through the founding of what are now familiar institutions: the Department of Defense (called the National Military Establishment from 1947 to 1949), the National Security Council, the Central Intelligence Agency, and the Joint Chiefs of Staff. The U.S. Army and Marines had previously been overseen by the Department of War and the U.S. Navy by the Department of the Navy. With the passage of the National Security Act, all branches of the military were overseen by the Department of Defense. The result was what Donald Robinson, in a 1974 essay, called "the routinization of crisis government."[20]

Was the development of the national security state necessary? The evidence we have in hand today conclusively confirms that the USSR actively cultivated an international network devoted to the overthrow of the United States. There were real spies, and they served Soviet rather than American interests. Harry Gold, a self-admitted spy who belonged only briefly to the Communist Party, gave the Soviet Union U.S. plans for the atomic bomb.[21] New archival revelations also show that individuals who were prosecuted for treason—Julius Rosenberg, Morton Sobell, and Alger Hiss, to cite three prominent examples—were almost certainly guilty as charged.[22]

The Soviet Union's long-term relationship with the American Communist Party (CPUSA) certainly provides evidence of treasonous activity. On January 22, 1920, for example, the Comintern transferred gold, jewels, and other valuables worth over a million rubles to the American communist and Harvard graduate John Reed for Communist Party work in the United States.[23] The Soviet Union continued to fund the party almost to the end, making its largest money transfers in the 1980s. A total of $3 million was transferred to it via Gus Hall, the party's general secretary, in 1988. The Soviets did not cut off the CPUSA until 1989, after Hall publicly criticized the Gorbachev reforms.[24] While Hall had always claimed financial independence, the Moscow daily *Izvestiya* revealed in 1992 that he had received $40 million in Soviet assistance between 1971 and 1990.[25]

Yet we can also see, with the benefit of hindsight, that the actual threat of subversion from within was greatly exaggerated. The number of bona fide American communists was always minuscule; even at its highest point, in the interwar period, CPUSA membership never exceeded seventy-five thousand, and of those, only a tiny fraction had any actual contact with Soviet intelligence or active involvement in propaganda or espionage.[26]

This small membership notwithstanding, the FBI infiltrated the American communist movement whenever possible. In 1980, deputy head of the CPUSA Morris Childs was outed as a Soviet agent who, with his brother Jack, had funneled money from the Soviet Union to the CPUSA for more than twenty years.[27] Morris traveled to Moscow to collect the money, while Jack met with Soviet couriers in New York City or Canada. We now know that the brothers also served as informants for the FBI.[28] Under the codename Operation Solo, Morris Childs was probably the first American spy to have face-to-face conversations with Nikita Khrushchev, Mao Zedong, and other senior communist leaders.[29]

Counterintelligence operations during the Cold War were built on the premise that America's enemies were the Soviet Union's friends. In a bipolar world, those who exposed America's secrets were by definition aiding and abetting the enemy. The COMINT Act of 1950 enshrined this principle in law. It punished "whoever knowingly and willfully communicates, furnishes, transmits, or otherwise makes available to an unauthorized person, or publishes ... any classified information ... concerning the communications intelligence activities of the United States."[30] Secrecy and security were always mutually reinforcing.

The COMINT Act framed the activities of Wisconsin senator Joseph McCarthy and those of the House Un-American Activities Committee (HUAC) as patriotic. McCarthy saw himself as blowing the whistle on subversives in the State Department.[31] His crusade, however, came at the price of ignoring Dwight Eisenhower's distinction between honest dissent and disloyal subversion. McCarthy's many lists and investigations ruined reputations but never produced a single conviction, perhaps because he made no distinction between youthful flirtations with communism and enduring commitment to the cause.[32] According to David Halberstam, McCarthy "illuminated the timidity of his fellow men."[33]

The director of the Federal Bureau of Investigation, J. Edgar Hoover, shared McCarthy's zeal. While such a long tenure would be unthinkable today, Hoover was appointed as the FBI's first director in 1935 and would serve in that position, under president after president, for thirty-seven years until his death in 1972.

We have recently learned new things about the extremism of Hoover's anticommunism. Documents declassified in 2007 show that he had a plan in place to suspend the writ of habeas corpus (the right to seek release from illegal detention), as Lincoln did during the American Civil War, and imprison American citizens he suspected of disloyalty. He spent years compiling a list of suspicious individuals, and at the time he drafted his plan, the list had grown to twelve thousand, 97 percent of whom were U.S. citizens. He envisioned placing these suspects in military prisons until they could be tried on charges of treason. Hoover sent his plan to the White House on July 7, 1950, twelve days after the outbreak of the Korean War.[34] Following the Soviet seizure of Eastern Europe, the rise of powerful communist parties under Moscow's sway in Italy and France, and the triumph of communists in China, Hoover saw the Korean War as but the latest chapter in communism's global quest for hegemony and the eventual overthrow of the U.S. government. Extraordinary measures were necessary to meet the existential threat.[35]

From Hoover's perspective, communists were eating away at the fabric of American life, infiltrating key American institutions in order to gain access to the nation's atomic, military, and industrial secrets. "There is a potential fifth column of 540,000 people," he told the Senate in June 1950. "Forty-eight percent of the party's membership" was "in the basic industry of this country, as in this manner, they would be able to sabotage essential industry in vital defense areas in the event of a national emergency." What Hoover found most infuriating was the way communists had succeeded in infiltrating the legal profession.[36] His numbers were surely exaggerated, but with the atomic spying cases—Klaus Fuchs, Harry Gold, the Rosenbergs—all concurrently making headlines, the threat certainly seemed real.

Like Hoover, the House Un-American Activities Committee found the loyalties of American communists at odds with American citizenship, in that the communists had pledged allegiance to another country. As the 1949 HUAC compilation *100 Things You Should Know about Communism* put it, "How can a Communist be identified? It is easy. Ask him to name ten things wrong with the United States. Then ask him to name two things wrong with Russia. His answers will show him up even to a child. . . . Communists will denounce the President of the United States but they will never denounce Stalin."[37] Another work in the same publication elaborated, "Are Communists traitors? This whole pamphlet is to help you make up your own mind on that. The facts speak louder than words."[38]

Ronald Reagan gave prescient testimony before HUAC in 1947. When the committee members asked for guidance on how they should proceed, Reagan recommended a return to first principles: "I believe that, as Thomas Jefferson put it, if all the American people know all of the facts they will never make a mistake. Whether the party should be outlawed, that is a matter for the government to decide. As a citizen, I would hesitate to see any political party outlawed on the basis of its political ideology. However, if it is proven that an organization is an agent of foreign power, or in any way not a legitimate political party—and I think the government is capable of proving that—then that is another matter."[39]

In Hollywood, Walt Disney had no hesitation in naming names when he caught even a whiff of subversion. He testified that he thought Disney Studios employee and union member David Hilberman was a communist because he "had no religion" and had studied theater in Moscow. When asked for his personal opinion of the Communist Party, Disney replied that he saw it as un-American:

> I don't believe it is a political party. I believe it is an un-American thing. The thing that I resent the most is that

they are able to get into these unions, take them over, and represent to the world that a group of people that are in my plant, that I know are good, 100 percent Americans, are trapped by this group, and they are represented to the world as supporting all of those ideologies, and it is not so, and I feel that they really ought to be smoked out and shown up for what they are, so that all of the good, free causes in this country, all the liberalisms that really are American, can go out without the taint of communism. That is my sincere feeling on it.[40]

Statements like Walt Disney's encouraged the blacklisting of writers, directors, and actors in the movie business. Attitudes on blacklisting were sharply divided along educational lines. A 1947 Gallup poll asked those who had heard of the Hollywood investigations whether the Hollywood writers who had refused to say if they were members of the Communist Party should be punished. Fifty-four percent of college-educated Americans said they should not be punished, against just 31 percent of grade school–educated citizens. The divide also fell neatly along class lines: 51 percent of white-collar workers found punishment unnecessary, versus just 35 percent of blue-collar workers.[41]

Many people who, during their youth, were captivated by communism soon found reasons to leave the party, sometimes because of its leaders' ideological intolerance and hair-splitting factionalism, and sometimes because they found its doctrines unrealistic and dehumanizing. But however quick their disillusionment, they could be forced to pay for their indiscretion years later. The Hollywood screenwriter Dalton Trumbo joined the Communist Party in 1943, when the U.S. and USSR were wartime allies. He became one of the Hollywood Ten, a group of ten film-industry figures who were called to testify before HUAC in 1947, refused to answer its questions, and were found in contempt of Congress. For declining to give the names of colleagues with communist sympathies, he was imprisoned for eleven months. After his release, he could no longer work in Hollywood and fled with his family to Mexico City.

Trumbo returned two years later and resumed writing, but under a pseudonym. His script for *The Brave One* won an Academy

Award in 1956, but he went unacknowledged. It wasn't until the 1960 release of *Spartacus*, directed by Stanley Kubrick, and *Exodus*, directed by Otto Preminger, that Trumbo could be publicly credited for his work. In 1975, a year before his death, he was officially recognized as the Oscar-winning screenwriter of *The Brave One*. In 2011, thirty-five years after his death and nearly sixty years after the picture's release, the Writers' Guild finally acknowledged Trumbo's second Oscar, for *Roman Holiday* (1953). The credit now reads: "Screenplay by Dalton Trumbo and Ian McLellan Hunter; Story by Dalton Trumbo."[42]

The anticommunist crusading coming out of Washington and Hollywood undoubtedly helped shape public sentiment. Gallup polls from the time reveal overwhelming voter approval for the anticommunist orientation of the Cold War establishment. An April 1947 poll, for instance, showed that 61 percent of Americans believed "membership in the Communist Party in this country should be prohibited by law." Only college-educated Americans thought otherwise. These attitudes hardened over time: by November 1949, 68 percent of Americans thought the Communist Party should be banned, and even a majority of college-educated Americans (54 percent) agreed. Seventy-seven percent of Americans thought Communist Party members should be required to register with the Justice Department.[43]

In August 1948, 63 percent of Americans supported the passage of the Mundt-Nixon bill, which would permit membership in the Communist Party but require every party member to register with the Justice Department. Fifty-six percent thought party members were loyal to Russia rather than the United States, and 73 percent believed that in the event of war between the two powers, Communist Party members would side with Russia. In 1949, 73 percent of Americans also thought that members of the Communist Party should not be allowed to teach in American schools, and 72 percent approved of the loyalty oaths that the University of California required its professors to take—even after they were told how strongly faculty members at this and other institutions opposed the procedure.[44] Public support enabled McCarthyism.

On balance, Soviet subversive activities on American soil were a real problem, but the American response was incommensurate to

the threat. New archival evidence shows that the Truman administration was most successful in rooting out spies at exactly the same
moment that fears of communist infiltration were at their highest.
Just as McCarthy was telling the American people that spies were
everywhere, Russians stationed in America were complaining to
their superiors that they had no agents.[45]

The Two Daniel Ellsbergs

The case of RAND Corporation military analyst Daniel Ellsberg illustrates the high price of secrecy in the service of security. When
government is given a blank check to do whatever is necessary to
protect its citizens, that trust is all too easily abused. Secrecy is a
vital resource in securing freedom, but when it is deployed cynically
as a political weapon, it can wind up undermining both freedom and
the right to privacy.

Ellsberg's career gave him almost unparalleled expertise and in-
sight into the dynamics of the Vietnam War. He served as an infan-
try officer in the U.S. Marine Corps from 1954 to 1957 and then
earned a PhD in economics from Harvard, writing a dissertation titled "Risk, Ambiguity, and Decision." He went on to become a strategic analyst at RAND, consultant to the Commander-in-Chief
Pacific (CINCPAC) in 1959 and 1960, and later a consultant to the
State and Defense Departments. On August 4, 1964, the day of the
Tonkin Gulf incident, an alleged second North Vietnamese attack
on the USS *Maddox* that fueled further U.S. involvement in the
conflict, Ellsberg transferred from RAND to work as a special assistant to John T. McNaughton, the assistant secretary of defense for
international security affairs. He remained in this role at the Office
of the Secretary of Defense (OSD) until mid-1965, when he joined
the State Department to analyze the progress of "pacification" in
South Vietnam under General Edward Lansdale. Before returning
to RAND in June 1967, Ellsberg traveled throughout South Vietnam and joined American patrols in the disputed hamlet of Rach
Kien, seeing firsthand the frustration and futility of the U.S. Army's
involvement.

There were large discrepancies between how secretary of
defense Robert McNamara, Ellsberg, and other high-ranking

government officials saw the situation in Vietnam and what they reported to the American public. In the fall of 1966, McNamara visited Harvard Business School (his alma mater) at the invitation of the political scientist Richard Neustadt. McNamara told Neustadt and other Harvard faculty members that the war was not going well and that future scholars would want to know why.[46] A year later, McNamara concluded that U.S. policies in Southeast Asia had failed and that lessons needed to be learned from that experience to avoid a replaying of history. In June 1967, he commissioned a comprehensive historical study, co-led by Ellsberg's former boss John McNaughton, to evaluate America's political and military involvement in Southeast Asia from 1945 through 1968.[47] Officially titled "The History of U.S. Decision-Making in Vietnam from 1945–1968" and sometimes referenced internally as the Report of the OSD Vietnam Task Force, it contained, when finished, some seven thousand pages of analysis and documents. Later it would acquire the name by which most people know it today: the Pentagon Papers.

The Pentagon Papers included discrete sections for each administration from Truman to Nixon, with each divided into two subsections: "Justification of the War: Public Statements" and "Justification of the War: Internal Documents."[48] By its very structure, in other words, the study acknowledged that the government was saying one thing to the public and another internally. The Pentagon Papers revealed that the Johnson administration had known early on, despite public declarations to the contrary, that the Vietnam War was unlikely to be won. They also showed extensive covert operations unknown to the public.

The gap between public statements and reality was especially apparent in Ellsberg's interactions with secretary of defense McNamara. In his 2002 book *Secrets*, for example, Ellsberg recalled an informal conversation with McNamara on a return flight to Washington in October 1966, in which McNamara agreed with him that after putting "more than a hundred thousand more troops into the country over the last year … the underlying situation is really *worse*." But as soon as he got off the plane, McNamara told reporters just the opposite: "Gentlemen, I've just come back from Vietnam, and I'm glad to be able to tell you that we're showing great progress in every dimension of our effort."[49]

McNamara's successor, Clark Clifford, received the finished study in January 1969, five days prior to Richard Nixon's inauguration as president. By that time, large differences in opinion existed between McNamara, who had left the administration convinced of the war's futility, and President Lyndon Johnson, who was considering requests for ground troop escalation as late as March 1968.[50] Because the disagreement was so strong, McNamara had kept the expanding Pentagon Papers archive hidden from many government officials, including secretary of state Dean Rusk and President Johnson, for fear they might suspend the project or destroy the archive due to the sensitivity of its contents and its implications for future policy.

Because Ellsberg had worked for a time on the Pentagon Papers, he had access to the completed work, which was marked "Top Secret—Sensitive." ("Sensitive" meant it could embarrass the U.S. government were it ever made public.) Reading in full the first volumes of the study crystallized Ellsberg's perspective on the Vietnam War. As he recounts in his memoirs, he decided that "I'm not going to be part of this lying machine, this cover-up, this murder, anymore." He says his point of no return came while attending a War Resisters International conference at Haverford College in August 1969, as he listened to Randy Kehler speak about his imminent arrest for his refusal to be drafted. "I was ready to change my own relation to the situation, ready even to change my life," Ellsberg wrote, "if there was reason for it."[51]

Ellsberg's first step was to copy the Pentagon Papers. A friend at RAND, Tony Russo, had pushed him to make the study public. Russo's girlfriend ran an ad agency that had a Xerox machine. When he left work in the evening, Ellsberg would take a volume from his safe, put it in his briefcase, and walk out. Since the security guards at RAND knew him, they did not check his briefcase as he left the building. Russo and Ellsberg would copy through the night at Russo's girlfriend's office. The next day, Ellsberg would return to work with the volume in his briefcase, return it to his RAND safe, and then repeat the process that evening.[52] He even involved his son Robert and daughter Mary, thirteen and ten at the time, in his clandestine enterprise. Robert assisted with Xeroxing, and Mary was given the task of cutting "Top Secret—Sensitive" off the top and bottom of each page.[53]

Once he had the full study in hand, Ellsberg first quietly attempted to convince the chair of the Senate Foreign Relations Committee, William Fulbright, to release selected portions through hearings on the Senate floor under congressional privilege. This would have protected Ellsberg from prosecution. While sympathetic to Ellsberg's concerns, Fulbright was not inclined to release top secret documents, even for the best of reasons, so he instead asked secretary of defense Melvin Laird to obtain the study for him officially. That put the word out in Washington that there was a leak, which stepped up the pressure on Ellsberg to get the materials into the right hands before he was stopped by the FBI.[54]

Despite finding officials in Washington reluctant to share anything in the Pentagon Papers with the public, Ellsberg continued to seek to use his insider influence to change U.S. policy. He met with national security advisor Henry Kissinger in August 1970 at Kissinger's San Clemente office. Ellsberg simply urged him to read the report—or at least the summary at the beginning of each volume. Kissinger asked whether the volumes really contained anything new. Noting that Senator Fulbright did not seem to be moving in the right direction either, Ellsberg met with him again in December 1970 and was disappointed when Fulbright, like Kissinger, wondered aloud whether there was anything new in the report. He asked Ellsberg to "give him an example of a revelation that would make a big splash."[55]

Ellsberg then turned to Senators George McGovern and Charles Mathias. Both were lukewarm about getting involved. Despite his opposition to the war, McGovern was said to be "indignant" that Ellsberg thought a senator should break the law when he himself would not.[56] Only after it was obvious that his efforts to influence events as an insider had failed did Ellsberg go to the *New York Times*.[57]

By this time, a year had passed since Ellsberg first sought to share the report with Congress, and more and more people knew that he had spirited it out of RAND. After speaking publicly

against the war and about a secret study in which he had been involved, he was starting to become fearful about the security of his
set of documents. Ellsberg had left his job at RAND and was now
working as a research fellow at MIT. Just in case his copy of the report was confiscated, he made additional copies at a commercial
shop in Harvard Square and stored them at the homes of friends
and relatives.[58]

In early March 1971, he contacted *New York Times* correspon-
dent Neil Sheehan, who was interested in Ellsberg's materials but
couldn't promise that his paper would do anything with them until
he knew more about their content. Ellsberg invited him to come to
his apartment in Cambridge to read and take notes. He even gave
Sheehan access to the place when he and his wife were out of town.
Unbeknownst to Ellsberg, though, Sheehan made his own copy of
the report, and the staff of the *New York Times* was feverishly at
work processing the reams of information. When the *Times* ran its
first story on the Pentagon Papers, revealing that Ellsberg was the
leak, Ellsberg himself was taken completely by surprise.[59]

Since he had met with Ellsberg and discussed the Pentagon
Papers, national security advisor Kissinger responded to the breaking news in predictable fashion. He led with an ad hominem attack,
describing Ellsberg as "always a little unbalanced" and as having
changed from a supporter to an opponent of administration policies after abusing drugs.[60]

The *Times* published the first excerpts in its Sunday edition on
June 13, 1971, under the headline "Vietnam Archive: Pentagon
Study Traces Three Decades of Growing US Involvement." Television coverage amplified the message. The Nixon administration
immediately filed a restraining order that barred the paper from
any further publication on national security grounds. The *Times*
agreed to stop the presses.

Ironically, the government's efforts to stop the publication of
the Pentagon Papers increased their notoriety and gave Ellsberg additional credibility. When the Justice Department got an injunction
to stop the *Times*, Ellsberg simply passed copies to the *Washington
Post*. When the *Post* received its own injunction, Ellsberg gave copies
to the *Boston Globe* and *St. Louis Dispatch*. In the end, twenty different newspapers published parts of the Pentagon Papers, even

though the White House publicly insisted that their actions were doing irreparable harm to national security.[61]

After two lower courts sided with the *New York Times* in maintaining that the U.S. government had not met its heavy burden of justifying prior restraint, and two courts of appeal then issued conflicting opinions, both the *Times* and the U.S. government appealed the case to the Supreme Court. The issue at stake was whether the government was authorized to suspend the First Amendment in this particular instance and enforce prior restraint, which *Near v. Minnesota* (1931) had ruled presumptively unconstitutional. On June 30, the Supreme Court upheld the right of the *New York Times* and *Washington Post* to publish the Pentagon Papers, with six justices concurring and three dissenting. In the majority's view, the Nixon administration had not given sufficient evidence that "a grave and irreparable danger" would result from making the information public. A ruling with significant implications, *New York Times Co. v. United States* confirmed that the burden of proof for suspending First Amendment rights was on the U.S. government.

The newspapers were protected, but Ellsberg was not. He was charged under the Espionage Act with conspiracy, espionage, and theft of government property—becoming the first person in the act's history to be charged without being accused of having passed secrets to a foreign power. On June 28, 1971, he surrendered to federal authorities at the U.S. Attorney's Office in Boston.

And then the real circus commenced. Perhaps to better understand what Ellsberg's next move might be, in August 1971 the White House asked the CIA to perform a psychological study of him. But then the White House rejected the study as unsatisfactory because it claimed that Ellsberg was motivated by "what he deemed a higher order of patriotism." The study described him as an "extremely intelligent and talented individual" who "saw himself as having a special mission and bearing a special responsibility." It added: "There has been a notable zealous intensity about the subject throughout his career. Apparently finding it difficult to tolerate ambiguity and ambivalence, he was either strongly for something or strongly against it."[62]

Nixon official John Ehrlichman told Congress, and Kissinger told the press, that Ellsberg had secretly given the Pentagon

Papers directly to the Soviet Union.[63] Perhaps they genuinely believed this, but no evidence to support the allegation has ever
emerged. That did not stop the media from repeating the charge
endlessly, fueling the impression that Ellsberg was a Soviet spy.
Ehrlichman and Kissinger believed they were conducting damage
control in the service of the United States, albeit at a cost to the
truth. Since government officials have access to classified information that newspapers do not, it is hard for journalists to counter
claims that leaks of classified information have compromised U.S.
security unless other official sources weigh in to contradict them.

Members of the special White House investigating unit (the
"Plumbers' Unit") who had rejected the first CIA profile later
broke into Ellsberg's psychiatrist's office in Los Angeles to look for
other incriminating evidence.[64] We now know that the White
House had created the Plumbers, its own investigative body, after
it became convinced that the FBI was not pursuing the Ellsberg
leak with proper zeal. The Plumbers' pursuit of what they thought
had to be the real goods on Ellsberg ultimately led federal judge
Matthew Byrne to dismiss the charges against Ellsberg on May 11,
1973, because of "improper Government conduct."[65] It was disclosed during the trial that Ehrlichman had met twice with Byrne
to discuss the possibility of Byrne's becoming FBI director; Byrne
said he rejected consideration of the opportunity while the trial
was ongoing.[66]

Did Daniel Ellsberg compromise U.S. security in exposing
how the government had misrepresented the situation in Vietnam?
He did not urge Americans to dodge the draft. He did not conspire
to overthrow the government. He did not pass secrets directly to
the enemy. His sin was the release of classified information that exposed the gap between political rhetoric and reality.

Since the Pentagon Papers were historical rather than studies
of operations in process, it is hard to argue that their public revelation did real damage to national security, especially since Ellsberg
intentionally held back documents so as not to compromise ongoing peace negotiations.[67] He told the *New York Times* in 2011 that
he omitted materials because he thought that Nixon would use
their release as an excuse for breaking off negotiations with North
Vietnam. In a 1989 *Washington Post* op-ed, the prosecutor of the

Ellsberg case and former dean of Harvard Law School, Erwin Griswold, recanted his original claim that the public release of the Pentagon Papers would gravely harm national security. "I have never seen any trace of a threat to the national security from the publication," he wrote. "Indeed, I have never seen it even suggested that there was such an actual threat." He also warned of the dangers of overclassification. "It quickly becomes apparent to any person who has considerable experience with classified material that there is massive over-classification and that the principal concern of the classifiers is not with national security, but rather with governmental embarrassment of one sort or another."[68] In June 2011, on the fortieth anniversary of the initial release of the Pentagon Papers, the full study was finally declassified and released by the National Archives.[69]

After reading the Pentagon Papers in their entirety, the political philosopher Hannah Arendt found herself haunted by their "remoteness from reality." The gap between official statements and reality forced those carrying out government policies "to disregard altogether the distinguishing line between truth and falsehood in order to be able to survive." Americans were fighting and dying for prestige, not for power or profit. When the public is manipulated so completely, Arendt tells us, the very notion of truth evaporates. The self-deception of people in power crowds out perspective, common sense, and respect for basic diplomatic relationships.[70] By extension, that is why national security whistleblowing speech needs rigorous First Amendment protection.

In his 2017 book *The Doomsday Machine*, Ellsberg reveals that from the fall of 1969 to his departure from RAND in August 1970, he copied *everything* in his top secret office safe, "of which the seven thousand pages of the Pentagon Papers were but a fraction." In 1961, long before he became outraged about policymakers' conduct of the Vietnam War, Ellsberg was shocked to learn of general nuclear war gaming involving an American first strike on China, the Soviet Union, and its Warsaw Pact allies that would have left an estimated 600 million dead—"a Hundred Holocausts." His life purpose from that day forward, he writes, was "to prevent the execution of such a plan." He made the decision to release the Pentagon Papers first, he tells us, so that the press would focus proper

attention on the Vietnam War debacle. The bad news on America's
nuclear posture could be revealed after the war's end. Ellsberg entrusted the nuclear documents to his brother Harry, who first bur-
ied them in a box inside a plastic garbage bag under the compost
pile in his backyard in Hastings-on-Hudson, New York. As the
media frenzy intensified, Harry made the fateful decision to transfer them to the local trash dump, where they were destroyed by a
tropical storm in the summer of 1971.[71]

Ellsberg first submitted the first third of what would become
The Doomsday Machine to a publisher in 1975, and he followed up
in the 1990s by submitting the manuscript to seventeen other publishers. No one wanted to take it on. Decades later, Bloomsbury
saw things differently.[72]

Ellsberg presents himself in *The Doomsday Machine* as a whistleblower on America's stance toward nuclear deterrence. As the nuclear club expanded in the years after he left RAND, nothing in
America's deterrence strategy changed, and Ellsberg considers this
madness. We still possess nuclear weapons in numbers large enough
to destroy life as we know it, nobody has pledged no first use, and
both the Russian and the American arsenals are deteriorating, raising the probability of accidents or of weapons falling into the wrong
hands. Prior to publication of *The Doomsday Machine*, Ellsberg spoke
out on these issues in multiple public forums.[73]

Ellsberg's points are all well taken, but with the possible exception of his revelations regarding the delegation of launch authority
to theater commanders, none of this is new information. Decades
after Ellsberg first tried to publish his information, when all the documents on which he relied to make his case have been declassified,
Ellsberg no longer qualifies as an insider exposing wrongdoing to
the public, although he has certainly trained an important spotlight
on Washington's ongoing failure to reduce the risk of accidental nuclear war. Arguments about the best way to ensure second-strike capability require thinking through first-strike scenarios, so those
possessing nuclear weapons cannot be faulted for striving to see
that deterrence holds. As Harvard professor Graham Allison re-
minds us, there is an entire strategic studies literature devoted to
evaluation of alternative nuclear postures.[74] It is certainly true that
the risk of nuclear weapons falling into the wrong hands has vastly

grown since the Soviet Union's collapse, and that Russia and the United States continue to possess arsenals that could end the world as we know it. These are deeply worrying facts, as organizations like the Nuclear Threat Initiative and former cabinet members like Henry Kissinger, Bill Perry, and George Shultz have been tirelessly warning us.[75]

Watergate

While Ellsberg was making decisions that would change his life, Special Agent Mark Felt, who would ultimately rise to the number two position in the FBI, was secretly feeding *Washington Post* reporter Bob Woodward off-the-record material that would eventually bring down Nixon's presidency. In their book about the Watergate scandal, *All the President's Men*, Woodward and coauthor Carl Bernstein would give Felt the nickname Deep Throat, after a pornographic movie released in 1972. Deep Throat's identity would remain a mystery until Felt revealed himself three years before his death.

As a fervent supporter of FBI director J. Edgar Hoover, Felt valued an autonomous FBI and wanted to preserve the bureau's integrity by liberating it from political manipulation. That belief motivated him to leak classified FBI information to the press.[76] In the 2006 update of his 1979 memoir, *A G-Man's Life* (which had not originally revealed his identity as Deep Throat), he reflects, "It's impossible to exaggerate how high the stakes were in Watergate. We faced no simple burglary, but an assault on government institutions, an attack on the FBI's integrity, and unrelenting pressure to unravel one of the greatest political scandals in our nation's history. ... Did my obligation as an FBI official to work within channels supersede my duty as an American citizen to expose the truth?"[77] Felt's motives, however, were not entirely pure; some of his leaks served to undermine his boss, acting FBI director L. Patrick Gray, whom Felt aspired to replace.[78]

Felt's early years at the bureau had trained him well in Nazi counterintelligence operations. He taught Woodward to follow a countersurveillance protocol to eliminate any chance of their being followed. If Woodward wanted to schedule a meeting, he was to place a flowerpot with a red construction flag on the balcony of his apartment. If Felt had information for Woodward, he would circle page 20 in the copy of the *New York Times* that was delivered to Woodward's apartment and draw the hands of a clock on the lower part of that page to indicate the time of their meeting, typically in the middle of the night in a parking garage in Rosslyn, Virginia. Woodward would exit his apartment through the back-alley stairway, then take two separate cabs and walk the last few blocks to avoid being followed.[79]

The information Felt was leaking about the Watergate scandal revealed obstruction of justice in the Nixon administration that went all the way up to the White House. The operatives who broke into Democratic National Committee Headquarters at the Watergate office complex were small parts of a much larger subversive operation approved at the highest level. Under such circumstances, whistleblowers have very limited options for lodging an internal complaint. Felt was thus forced to lead a double life. Nixon's aides had heard rumors that Felt was leaking information to reporters, and he had to throw them off his trail. When Gray confronted him about the rumors in January 1973, Felt denied leaking "anything to anybody." Despite Nixon's urging, Gray decided not to give Felt a lie-detector test, citing loyalty to his fellow bureau employees, but that didn't stop Felt from using the technique on at least one subordinate in an effort to cover his tracks by maintaining a rule-follower reputation within the organization. After Woodward and Bernstein published a story about illegal wiretaps, for example, Felt wrote an FBI memo reminding "all agents of the need to be most circumspect in talking about this case with anyone outside the Bureau."[80]

As Deep Throat continued to pass information, the *Washington Post*'s coverage of the controversy encouraged a growing public outcry. Felt directed Woodward and Bernstein to the money trail that the five Watergate burglars had left behind. As they traced the chain of payments back to the $300,000 fund from the Committee to Re-elect the President (CRP), more and more top officials in the Nixon administration and the president himself were implicated: Donald Segretti, a political operative in CRP; G. Gordon Liddy and former CIA operative E. Howard Hunt of the "White House Plumbers," who took over Segretti's Watergate break-in operation;

and Herbert Kalmbach, Nixon's personal lawyer, who had paid Se-gretti.[81] By late July 1974 it had become clear, via an Oval Office tape recording that Nixon was forced to hand over to Special Prosecutor Leon Jaworski, that the president had been complicit in criminal obstruction of justice and abuse of power. The "smoking gun" tape revealed that Nixon had been privy to the cover-up since June 1972, immediately after the break-in had occurred—and that he had suggested using the CIA to hinder the FBI's investigation into the matter. This revelation validated Felt's view that the Nixon administration had politicized the agency. After the House of Representatives approved articles of impeachment and a group of Republican senators informed him they would vote to convict if the impeachment went to the Senate, Nixon decided to resign on August 8, 1974.[82]

Felt retained his anonymity for over thirty years, rising to second in command at the FBI during the Watergate investigations. He was disappointed when President Nixon appointed William D. Ruckelshaus to head the bureau instead of him. (Nixon's original nominee, acting director Gray, withdrew from consideration after his ties to the Watergate transgressions—which Felt had helped expose—doomed his confirmation hearings.) It was Ruckelshaus who followed through on the evidence, by then quite strong, that Felt was leaking information to the press, finally forcing Felt's resignation in June 1973. Author Michael Dobbs writes, "It is impossible to disentangle Felt's sense of outrage over what was happening to the country from his own desire to scramble to the top of 'the FBI Pyramid.' "[83]

Resignation led to public disgrace for Felt. While he had been providing information to Woodward, Felt had also authorized warrantless surveillance in FBI investigations of the terrorist organization the Weather Underground. He was convicted of a felony in 1980 for these illegal operations, and pardoned by President Ronald Reagan in 1981.[84]

Despite being hailed as an American hero under the Deep Throat alias, Felt chose to remain anonymous for most of his life. Both Woodward and Felt kept their promise of nondisclosure for three decades, and it was only in early 2005 that Felt, at the age of ninety-one, finally agreed to go public. The story broke on the *Vanity Fair* website on May 31, 2005; Felt revealed his identity in an article titled "I'm the Guy They Called Deep Throat."[85] Partly because of Felt's ambivalence about what he had done, and partly because Woodward did not wish to reveal his source, the two men, formerly close friends, had fallen out of touch. Woodward had drafted a manuscript in anticipation of the day Felt's identity might be made known, and when that day came, he reestablished connections with Felt to interview him and bring the work to completion. Yet Woodward's book on Felt, *The Secret Man*, did not turn out as he had hoped. Felt, suffering from severe memory loss, no longer remembered Watergate, and Woodward's frustration is palpable throughout.[86]

The Pendulum Swings Back

Ellsberg's and Felt's stories demonstrate the obstacles to whistle-blowing on government wrongdoing when the government can invoke national security and executive prerogative. Ellsberg found no other insiders who were concerned enough about government deceit to give him any help, and so was forced to engage the American people directly via the press. Felt could not complain to his superiors because the entire chain of command, right up to the president, was involved in an extensive cover-up; he had to turn to the media as well. Had he not remained anonymous for three decades, he would have lost his livelihood.

Yet the American people's reaction was very different from that of government elites. The Watergate scandal, paired with the loss of the Vietnam War, fostered skepticism and doubt toward elected officials. The Pew Research Center found that trust in government plummeted in the 1960s during the Vietnam years and again in the 1970s in response to Watergate.[87] Congress was forced to respond with legislation. The Sunshine Act of 1976 required that all government meetings be open to public review, with ten specific exemptions, including national defense. The 1978 Ethics in Government Act required government officials to release their financial and employment histories to the public. The 1978 Presidential Records Act transferred legal ownership of presidential records to the public.

Despite the substantial expansion of intelligence institutions, from the creation of the CIA to the founding of the NSA, congressional oversight of intelligence operations did not exist until the Watergate scandal undermined public trust in the White House. The Senate Select Committee to Study Governmental Operations with Respect to Intelligence Activities, chaired by Senator Frank Church, was set up in 1975 to investigate the consequences of this oversight gap. Most of the Church Committee's reports were classified, but fifty thousand pages were declassified in 1992. The committee highlighted how ambiguity and confusion about what was permissible created opportunities for the abuse of power. It revealed that the CIA had been plotting to assassinate foreign leaders and that the NSA had intercepted the telegrams and phone calls of American citizens.

Congress and the executive branch responded to public outrage over these findings in multiple ways. In 1976, President Ford issued Executive Order 11905, banning direct U.S. government involvement in the assassination of foreign leaders. President Carter strengthened that order in 1978 with Executive Order 12036, which banned indirect U.S. involvement in the assassination of foreign leaders.

Congress changed the rules of the surveillance game with the 1978 Foreign Intelligence Surveillance Act (FISA), which placed strict limits on the collection of intelligence on American soil. The act's greatest restrictions were on wired communications. In the 1970s, most international communications were conducted by satellite, while domestic calls were transmitted over wires. Protecting the privacy rights of Americans, therefore, largely meant restricting warrantless surveillance of wired communications, and the law was given some real teeth. Violations are punishable with a $10,000 fine and up to five years in prison. But FISA was not designed to function effectively in the digital, cellular world that would follow, where communications travel via fiber-optic cables and wireless networks.[88]

For all wiretap cases, the law required a search warrant from the Foreign Intelligence Surveillance Court (FISC), whose confidential sessions were to be held at the Justice Department. According to FISC's website, "The Court entertains applications made by the United States Government for approval of electronic surveillance, physical search, and certain other forms of investigative actions for foreign intelligence purposes." The court is composed of eleven federal district court judges who are appointed by the chief justice of the United States. Each judge serves for up to seven years and typically sits for one week at a time on a rotating basis. The judges' terms are staggered so that continuity on the court is ensured.[89]

Just as nineteenth-century whistleblowers opened American eyes to the way the country's economic development intersected with corruption, twentieth-century dissenters exposed the potential tensions between national security and free speech. "The Soviet Union threatened nothing less than the displacement of the United States from the vanguard of history," wrote Gordon Wood. "For the first time since 1776, Americans were faced with an alternative revolutionary ideology with universalist aspirations equal to their own."[90] At issue were competing visions of the best social system. At the most basic level, American principles were at stake. But the effort to save the nation from enemy spies and propagandists cast a very wide net. The country's rise to superpower status was accompanied by security practices that undermined freedom of expression and the right to privacy.

The implicit equation of leftist dissent with treason thus came with collateral damage. The superpower struggle made legitimate criticism of capitalism's excesses sound like communist propaganda. During the Cold War, those who voiced skepticism about the unfettered free market's ability to advance the common good became the enemies of the United States. The Cold War era thus refashioned how America thought about whistleblowers, and those sentiments lingered after its end. Those promoting free markets or the national security of the United States were presumed beyond reproach. Whistleblowing on national security processes became taboo. Dissent became treason.

CHAPTER FOUR

Business

W HEN RONALD REAGAN PROCLAIMED in his first inaugural address, "Government is not the solution to a problem. Government is the problem," the president was announcing a new agenda that, for many, would become almost a secular religion. Free-market solutions to public problems were to be preferred whenever possible. In the decades that followed, regardless of which party was in charge, whatever could be privatized was, muddling public and private interests in a way that raised the stakes for whistleblowing. National security was no exception.

The privatization mantra reinforced Americans' long-standing suspicion of concentrated government power. Faith in the transformative power of free markets has been a feature of American political life since the founding. The collapse of communism in 1991 as an alternative form of economic organization only strengthened the American inclination to rely on the private sector whenever possible. In the beginning of the twentieth century, big government was bureaucratic government. Today, government can be "big" in terms of spending and hand most of its work over to contractors. For much of the twentieth century, business and government were adversaries. Today, the wall between them has become a revolving door, and both share common interests.

The staggering amount of money one may earn as a private-sector employee doing the government's business makes it difficult to resist cashing in after years of poorly paid public service. In 2014, six of America's ten richest counties skirted the Beltway.[1] The number of active lobbyists with prior government experience increased nearly fourfold between 1998 and 2012, and in that same period, revenue from lobbying increased from $703 million to $1.32 billion.[2] In 1970, only 3 percent of senators and congressmen left office to become lobbyists. Today more than 50 percent do so. As Zephyr Teachout points out, "The likely career path of a congressperson is to become a lobbyist."[3]

The revolving door between government and business, which grew exponentially after the Reagan revolution, added to the complications for would-be whistleblowers. For a whistleblower to call attention to self-interested acts of business-government collusion often meant forfeiting a livelihood in both the private and the public sectors. Even when their complaints were validated, whistleblowers risked becoming targets of retaliation, paying a price for stirring up trouble. The free-market fundamentalism that fueled the privatization impulse made pointing out the private sector's excesses a career-ending proposition, especially once the war on terror was in full swing. Under these circumstances, the importance of whistleblower protection grew.

But who qualifies for protection? Since contractors performing government work are not government employees, their eligibility under whistleblower protection laws was often ambiguous. This regulatory gray zone made the price of speaking out even higher.

Eisenhower's Warning

The roots of today's contractor-industrial complex may be found in President Dwight D. Eisenhower's establishment—almost against his will—of America's first peacetime defense establishment, to which he gave the name "military-industrial complex." As he ominously noted in his 1961 farewell address, "We have been compelled to create a permanent armaments industry of vast proportions. . . . We annually spend on military security more than the net income of all United States corporations." This massive concentration of federal power, he noted, was "imperative," yet it also carried the potential for great abuse. The United States must always "guard against the acquisition of unwarranted influence, whether sought or unsought, by the military-industrial complex."[4] Many factors increased this risk. The existence of a clear and present danger in Soviet power seemed to demand the capacity for emergency response. Anti-communist hysteria in the U.S.—overblown despite the existence of a real threat—fed the public's sense that a large peacetime military establishment was necessary in this changed world and set new precedents for unfettered presidential power.

At the time of Eisenhower's farewell address, the military accounted for more than half of all government spending and more than 10 percent of America's gross domestic product.[5] Unwarranted influence, for Eisenhower, had more to do with the military's relationship to society and the economy than with the size of the standing army. He was legitimately concerned that the economy could become subservient to military imperatives. Documents released in December 2010 by the National Security Archive reveal how deliberately Eisenhower chose his words. Earlier drafts of his speech had referred to a "war-based industrial complex" and a "vast military-industrial complex" before the adjective was dropped and he settled on the unadorned "military-industrial complex."[6] The speech was under development for months and underwent twenty-nine drafts; other major speeches, like the State of the Union, typically went through fewer than half as many rounds.[7] Eisenhower struggled throughout his presidency to rein in military spending. It was an issue he cared about deeply, but the Cold War led his successors in the opposite direction.

Defense companies had seen the link between a dangerous world and their continued profitability from the start of the Cold War. The Lockheed Corporation's chief executive officer told a Senate committee in 1947 that U.S. military funding must be "adequate, continuous, and permanent."[8] Once those needs were fulfilled and a codependent relationship was established, questioning just how well Lockheed might be serving the interests of the United States became unwelcome.

Six-Hundred-Dollar Toilet Seats

It was for asking such questions that, in 1969, President Richard M. Nixon fired Ernest Fitzgerald. Fitzgerald was a Defense Department auditor who told Congress about a \$2 billion cost overrun associated with Lockheed's C-5A Galaxy, a large strategic airlifter designed to transport heavy loads around the globe on short notice.[9] Lockheed had won the C-5A contract in 1965 with a proposal to build a fleet of 115 C-5As at \$16 million each, for a total cost of \$1.9 billion. After the contract was awarded, the cost per plane quickly mushroomed to \$40 million.[10] When costs balloon in such unanticipated fashion, who should pick up the tab, the U.S. taxpayer or the company incurring the cost overruns? Lockheed had to hire more employees, pay men overtime, and even outsource some of the work to England. From its perspective, the overruns were "within the normal range," and the U.S. taxpayer should cover the gap between budgeted and actual costs.[11]

Based on the performance measurement reports Lockheed sent to the U.S. Air Force, however, Fitzgerald could sense that something was amiss.[12] In January 1966 he made a routine trip to Marietta, Georgia, where the planes were being built, and confirmed that the massive cost overruns were wasteful. He reported his findings to his superiors at the Defense Department, and somehow Congress got wind of it.

Some believed that Senator William Proxmire (D-WI), a prominent critic of wasteful government spending, had seen the correspondence between Fitzgerald and the Office of the Secretary of Defense in which they had discussed the cost overruns. His request that Fitzgerald testify before Congress did not please the air force, which first refused to allow him to appear and even intercepted a personal letter from Senator Proxmire addressed to Fitzgerald.[13] After Proxmire found this out and predictably protested, the air force relented but urged Fitzgerald not to testify. Robert C. Moot, comptroller of the Defense Department, also urged Fitzgerald to decline.[14] But Fitzgerald chose to speak, first testifying before Senator Proxmire's Subcommittee on Economy in Government in the fall of 1968. He eventually spoke more than fifty times before congressional committees.[15]

Fitzgerald's increasingly numerous complaints to superiors about wasteful spending earned him his first poor performance rating in March 1968, prompting him to write a letter that August to Colonel Henry M. Fletcher Jr., director of procurement policy in the Office of the Secretary of Defense, in which he protested the department's failure to act on his findings. "Vast cost growth has taken place, and analyses have identified avoidable correctable causes," he wrote. "Proposed corrective actions have been blocked by government management people."[16] (Lockheed throughout viewed contract waste as a management problem that only management could solve.)[17]

By January 1969, the cost of the project had more than doubled, to $4 billion. Lockheed tried to mitigate the size of the gap between budgeted and actual costs by claiming that its original estimates had been in error. At a hearing that month, Fitzgerald revealed that the air force had ignored the cost of spare parts for the planes. Those costs alone had increased anticipated expenditures in 1965 from $300 million to over $1 billion.[18]

The Nixon administration decided that Fitzgerald was not a team player and had to go. With the Vietnam War in high gear, officials worried that the information he had "leaked" would damage the military's image. He was fired in fall 1969 in what the administration called a "reorganization" and told that his promised civil service tenure had been a computer error.[19]

The White House tapes later revealed that it was Nixon himself who fired Fitzgerald. "I said, 'get rid of that son of a bitch,'" he was recorded telling his aides.[20] The tapes also feature a revealing discussion of the Fitzgerald case in the Oval Office on January 31, 1973. Domestic advisor John Ehrlichman identified Fitzgerald as "the guy that, uh, ratted on the C-5A overruns. . . . He was a, he was a thorn in everybody's side you see." Nixon interrupted, "Yeah, well the point was not that he was complaining about the cost overruns, but that he was doing it in public." Ehrlichman agreed. "That's the point. And cutting up his superiors." To which the president responded, "That's right. . . . And not, frankly, not taking orders."[21]

The White House's subsequent actions underscore the cost of appearing disloyal. In a January 20, 1970, confidential White House memorandum to chief of staff Bob Haldeman, deputy assistant to the president Alexander Butterfield described the stakes: "Fitzgerald is a top-notch cost expert, but he *must* be given very low marks in loyalty; and after all, loyalty is the name of the game.... We should let him bleed, at least for a while. Any rush to pick him up and put him back on the federal payroll would be tantamount to an admission of earlier wrongdoing on our part."[22]

Fitzgerald's options were severely limited. He thought at first he could simply end his government career and get hired in the private sector at a higher salary, but he quickly found that no one would hire him. So he sued to get his Pentagon job back, in a case that ultimately went all the way to the Supreme Court. Nixon was the one who fired him, but the Supreme Court ruled that the president has absolute immunity from civil damages for actions taken in his capacity as president.[23]

It took four years and $1 million in legal fees before Fitzgerald was reinstated to the civil service.[24] But he was excluded from working on purchases of big weapons systems, his specialty. So in 1974, after Nixon's resignation, he sued again. The Watergate scandal had sensitized Congress and the American people to the consequences of corrupt power. Ralph Nader had been promoting the importance of whistleblower protection. According to Nader, "Whistleblowing, if carefully defined and protected by law, can become another of those adaptive, self-implementing mechanisms which mark the relative difference between a free society that relies on free institutions and a closed society that depends on authoritarian institutions." Senator Proxmire became an ally in promoting new legislation to prevent abuses of power, writing in "The Whistleblower as Civil Servant," a chapter contributed to a book edited by Nader, that "every federal employee should have the right to file a civil action in a federal court against the federal government for damages that result from the unjust actions of his former superiors."[25]

The Civil Service Reform Act of 1978 was one product of the changed environment after the Watergate scandal. It abolished the U.S. Civil Service Commission and replaced it with three new agencies: the Office of Personnel Management, the Federal Labor Relations Authority, and the Merit Systems Protection Board. The MSPB was to hear complaints from government employees about alleged discriminatory practices and refer potential instances of abuse to a newly established investigative unit, the Office of Special Counsel. In this way, the Civil Service Reform Act established a modicum of whistleblower protection for all civil servants except employees of the FBI and, by extension, anyone working in national security.[26] The new law indirectly strengthened Fitzgerald's cause by highlighting the importance of whistleblower protection in preventing government waste and fraud.

In 1982, after eight years of litigation, Fitzgerald emerged victorious for a second time and was able to reclaim his old job. He continued to report cost overruns and military contractor fraud, including a newsworthy discovery in the 1980s that the air force was being charged $400 for hammers and $600 for toilet seats. He finally retired from the Defense Department in 2006.[27]

Fitzgerald's life of whistleblowing received bipartisan praise. Senator Charles Grassley (R-IA) declared his efforts "one of the few major victories the taxpayers have had this decade." Congresswoman Barbara Boxer (D-CA) called him "a true American hero." Senator Proxmire said of his efforts, "He's one of the very few people in government who has made a difference, and he's done it in an astonishing way."[28]

Some of Fitzgerald's colleagues at Lockheed and in the air force thought differently. Assistant secretary for financial management Richard Carver, who was Fitzgerald's boss from 1984 to 1988, described him as having "the capacity to really irritate people. He has a kind of antagonistic way of doing things." From the perspective of the average air force employee, "Ernie is more interested in headlines and raising heck than he is in getting the job done."[29] In Lockheed's view, he was overlooking the inevitable costs of developing new weapons. It always takes several iterations and some mistakes to get things the way you want them, and it is naïve not to acknowledge those realities.

Rather than naïve, Fitzgerald saw himself as upholding important American values: "The founders of our country taught us to distrust concentration of power in individual hands. As for privileged, unaccountable power, these same founders resorted to violent revolution to be free of it. Now we are again confronted with great concentrated, unaccountable, privileged power. True, it is native power and appears benign or even benevolent to most citizens. This protective coloring makes it all the more dangerous, and citizens must learn to control the military spending juggernaut before they are robbed of their resources and their freedoms."[30]

Throughout his seventeen-year career as a cost analyst, Fitzgerald's continual whistleblowing brought a consistent response from the air force. It demoted him, limited his access to information, and investigated his private life. Yet he carried on identifying wasteful practices, despite incessant efforts to silence him, over his entire career as an auditor. Whistleblowing, he wrote, was "committing the truth."[31] And there were people in prominent positions in Washington who celebrated his single-mindedness. The 1986 amendments to the False Claims Act advanced Fitzgerald's cause, extending the act's coverage to virtually any program reliant on government funds, not only defense contracts. They held defendants liable for acting with "deliberate ignorance" or "reckless disregard" of the truth and lengthened the statute of limitations from six years to ten.[32] The amendments also ramped up whistleblower protection, providing for whistleblowers who had been fired to be reinstated to their jobs with double back pay and interest on back pay, as well as compensation for discriminatory treatment and legal fees.[33] After these changes, whistleblowers who exposed fraud against the government were entitled to between 15 and 30 percent of any money recovered by the government in a qui tam suit.[34]

Top Secret America

Along with their many other consequences, the attacks on the World Trade Center and the Pentagon on September 11, 2001, significantly expanded the problem of unwarranted influence. Washington responded to the terrorist attacks on U.S. soil by throwing no-questions-asked money at the problem. Just days after September 11, Congress approved an emergency outlay of $40 billion to address the threat—twice what President Bush had requested. By the end of the month it had authorized another $40 billion for the "Global War on Terror."

Spending on the war on terror fell into a classified no-man's-land that made it impossible to keep track of funds and oversee their use. A CIA legal counsel told Dana Priest of the *Washington Post* that "there was a flood of money and also a flood of authorities, a flood of responsibilities that we were directed to undertake, obviously immediately. It overwhelmed the structure that was in place."[35] Cofer Black, the former director of the CIA Counterintelligence Center, testified to the Senate Intelligence Committee, "This is a highly classified area. All I want to say is that there was 'before' 9/11 and 'after' 9/11. After 9/11 the gloves come off."[36] Dana Priest and William Arkin have called this new world "Top Secret America." In their book with that title, they make the post-9/11 intelligence community exhibit A in discussing unprecedented government spending on high-priority work that largely gets funneled out to private companies.

In the world of Top Secret America, they write, President Barack Obama would inherit what "had really become two governments. The one with which Americans were familiar operated more or less in the open. The other was a parallel top secret government whose parts had mushroomed in less than a decade into a gigantic, sprawling universe of its own, visible only to a carefully vetted cadre—and its entirety, as Pentagon intelligence chief James Clapper admitted, visible only to God." Arkin calculated that this cadre of holders of top secret security clearance numbered 854,000 individuals in 2010, roughly 1.5 times the entire population of DC.[37] Of those 854,000, he estimated that some 265,000 are contractors—private-sector employees. "Private contractors working for the CIA," Priest and Arkin reported in the *Washington Post*, "have recruited spies in Iraq, paid bribes for information in Afghanistan and protected CIA directors visiting world capitals. Contractors have helped snatch a suspected extremist off the streets of Italy, interrogated detainees once held at secret prisons abroad and watched over defectors holed up in the Washington suburbs. At Langley headquarters, they analyze terrorist networks. At the agency's training facility in Virginia, contractors are helping mold a new generation of American spies."[38]

Another way to grasp the scope and reach of Top Secret America is to be aware that the intelligence community, as defined by the Office of the Director of National Intelligence, encompasses twelve other entities above and beyond the FBI, CIA, NSA, and

Department of Homeland Security. These include parts of the Treasury Department, the State Department, and the Department of Energy.[39] Budgetary figures for the intelligence community are released to the public only as an aggregate figure for the entire National Intelligence Program (NIP). While we can't see which agencies receive what funding, the total budget has been rising steadily since the first figures were made available. To place these spending increases in a larger context, from FY 2006 to FY 2017, aggregate NIP appropriations (nominal $) increased 33.5 percent (from $40.9 billion to $54.6 billion), while total discretionary outlays (nominal $) increased 18.1 percent (from $1,016.6 billion to $1,200.2 billion) in the same period.[40]

As the expansive intelligence community has come to rely more heavily on contractors, the picture for whistleblowers has grown more complicated. Privatization adds an additional layer of secrecy to operations that are already top secret. It expands opportunities for corruption hidden from public view and camouflaged by the norms of confidentiality that are standard features of any government contract with private business. And it churns through big chunks of taxpayer money. At the Department of Homeland Security, for example, a 2008 survey found that contractors made up 29 percent of the staff but 49 percent of the budget.[41] The Office of the Director of National Intelligence has reported that it pays contractors 1.66 times as much as a federal employee ($207,000 annually for a contractor employee versus $125,000 for a federal employee) to do the same work.[42] Defense secretary Robert Gates confessed to Dana Priest that he had no idea how many contractors were working for the Office of the Secretary of Defense, an institution he led at the time of the interview.[43]

Some maintain that contracting saves money, but this is hard to prove when the number of contractors in play at any given moment is a moving target. Contractors also increase security risk, since they are doing everything from interrogation (until CIA director Leon Panetta banned it) to systems administration (Edward Snowden's job as a contractor).[44] They are also dying for their country. In June 2010, eight of the twenty-two stars chiseled into the marble wall at CIA headquarters honoring the fallen were those of contractors.[45]

Despite ambiguity about its efficacy, "when in doubt, out-source" became a bipartisan mantra in the twenty-first century. Iraq and Afghanistan were America's first contractors' wars: at times in both conflicts, they outnumbered men and women in uniform. The transformation can be tracked through spending patterns. In 2000, the Department of Defense spent $133.2 billion on contracts. By 2008, that figure had grown to $391.9 billion, an almost threefold increase. In 2000, the State Department spent $1.3 billion on contracts, and in 2008, $5.6 billion, a 431 percent increase. In 2000, USAID spent $478.6 million on contracts. By 2008, that figure had climbed to $3.3 billion, a nearly sevenfold increase. The Department of Homeland Security, established in 2003, awarded $13.7 billion in contracts in 2008. With Obama's withdrawal from Afghanistan and Iraq, these figures declined, but the legacy of outsourcing and the hollowed-out government it tends to leave in its wake endure.

Top Secret America reflects the abiding belief that if the government invests enough money in a problem and unleashes the private sector to devise innovative solutions to it, taxpayer money will by definition be well spent. There is little incentive for elites to challenge any aspect of this procedure, for fear of getting blamed when security fails, as even the best systems inevitably must. This system is not the creation of any one party; both Democrats and Republicans shared the belief that market solutions necessarily deliver better outcomes than government ones.

Not surprisingly, there was big money to be made in this high-alert world. In the first decade of the twenty-first century, revenues for U.S.-based defense contractors soared. The big five defense contractors saw unprecedented profits, but small companies also benefited from the 9/11 security-spending boom. For example, Predator drones are made by General Atomics Aeronautical Systems, which over the last decade went from eight employees to fifty-three hundred. The ITT Corporation, which supplied radio jammers, went from twenty-five employees to five hundred.[46] Fighting terrorism was good for start-ups and big business alike.

Companies whose executives could imagine what government might need next to thwart America's enemies possessed enormous power. The Lockheed Corporation became Lockheed Martin in

1995, and if any defense contractor possesses what Eisenhower called "unwarranted influence," it is Lockheed Martin. The company spends $15 million a year lobbying Congress and contributing to campaigns. Writing in the *New Yorker*, Jill Lepore reports that Lockheed contributed to "fifty-one of the sixty-two members of the House Armed Services Committee, twenty-four of the twenty-five members of that committee's Subcommittee on Tactical Air and Land Forces—in all, to three hundred and eighty-six of the four hundred and thirty-five members of the 112th Congress."[47] Domestically, Lockheed Martin also sorts your mail, tallies your taxes, cuts Social Security checks, counts people for the U.S. Census, runs space flights, and monitors air traffic. Abroad, it has supplied interrogators for U.S. military prisons in Guantánamo Bay, trained police in Haiti, run a postal service in Democratic Republic of Congo, and helped write the Afghan Constitution.[48] In 2004, nearly 80 percent of its revenues came directly from the U.S. government.[49] It received more federal dollars in 2008 than the Environmental Protection Agency, the Department of Labor, or the Department of Transportation.[50]

After 9/11, Top Secret America expanded without real constraints on its reach and power. It was big, privatized, and largely off-limits to whistleblowers, since all of its activities were classified. When the security state overstepped the bounds of the permissible, the odds were stacked against anyone being able to do something about it.

The Deepwater Disaster

One of the government's first moves after 9/11 was to ramp up the Coast Guard to fortify homeland security. The Deepwater Program, launched in 2002, was a twenty-five-year plan—the most comprehensive in the service's history—to modernize and update the Coast Guard's boats and aircraft. Rather than do it piecemeal, the Coast Guard decided to bundle all the required work, with the idea that the multibillion-dollar price tag would garner sustained attention from Congress and the White House.[51] It then delegated overall management of the project to a contractor. Integrated Coast Guard Systems (ICGS), a joint venture of Lockheed Martin and Northrop Grumman, was assigned the task of choosing who should perform the work as well as evaluating how well the project was progressing. ICGS chose its two parent companies to do most of the work.

The circular arrangement meant that Lockheed and Northrop were responsible for planning, constructing, and delivering the new boats and helicopters and also for evaluating their own performance. "People say that this is like the fox watching the henhouse," a retired past commander of the Coast Guard's Engineering and Logistics Center, Captain Kevin Jarvis, later commented to CBS News. "It's worse than that. It's where the government asked the fox to develop the security system for the henhouse. Then told 'em, 'You're gonna do it. You know, by the way, we'll give you the security code to the system and we'll tell you when we're on vacation.' "[52]

The Deepwater contract launched a madly spinning revolving door between government and the private sector. Of the seven top U.S. Coast Guard officers who retired after 1998, four migrated to Lockheed and Northrop. Michael P. Jackson, deputy secretary of transportation and later deputy secretary at the new Department of Homeland Security, which assumed responsibility for the Coast Guard in 2003, announced the award at the Transportation Department in 2002. He praised it as a model for unleashing the innovative potential of contractors to shape how government pursues its core mission.[53] The Coast Guard assigned just seven inspectors to oversee the work, when twenty would be the norm on a project of this size. The strategy was to extend forty-nine existing 110-foot Island-class patrol boats to 123 feet by cutting each boat in half and welding another 13 feet of hull into the middle. This was meant to improve the boats' capabilities until they could be replaced with new Deepwater fast-response cutters (FRCs) in 2018.[54] As Lieutenant Benjamin Fleming, the Coast Guard's representative at the shipyard in Lockport, Louisiana, told the *New York Times* in 2006, "In theory, we were going to drive a 110-foot cutter up to the pier, drop it off and come back in 34 weeks to pick up a 123-foot cutter. . . . We were putting a lot of trust and faith in our partners."[55] Mere weeks after they were delivered, eight of the boats had buckling floors and surfaces that should have been flat but were instead curved. Because of these severe structural problems, all eight boats were deemed unseaworthy and had to be pulled out of service. With problems too serious to fix, they were parked at the Coast Guard's Baltimore yard to await decommission.[56]

The boats also had problems with their electronics. The radio on one of the smaller boats would be constantly exposed to the elements but was not waterproof. The classified communications on board had not been properly protected from surveillance. Cameras that were to provide 360-degree surveillance had blind spots. Michael DeKort, Lockheed Martin's lead engineer for electronics on the revamped 123-foot patrol boats, reported these shortcomings repeatedly to his supervisors, but his warnings fell on deaf ears.[57]

After complaining all the way up the chain of command and getting nowhere, DeKort did something unprecedented. In desperation, he uploaded a whistleblower video on YouTube in August 2006 that received significant media attention.[58] DeKort was fired just days after the video was posted, although Lockheed says he was told earlier in the year that he was out of a job.[59]

In September 2006, DeKort filed a qui tam whistleblower lawsuit against Lockheed Martin on behalf of the U.S. government to recover damages for the waste of taxpayer money. A July 2007 Department of Homeland Security inspector general report (DHS IG) validated many of DeKort's concerns but also raised new questions.[60]

In order to respond to these questions, DeKort felt he had to reveal classified information he had pledged as a Lockheed employee to keep confidential. On the Project on Government Oversight (POGO) blog, which for a while became his vehicle for presenting his perspective to the world, DeKort wrote, "Unfortunately, the DHS IG has forced my hand. Now, I am forced to disclose information relative to these matters that I had previously agreed not to disclose. I am breaking my promise because individuals and organizations have obliterated the trust I had in them on behalf of our country. . . . They all have to cover their poor performance. . . . Government officials and the world's largest defense companies put the country at risk post-9/11, wasting hundreds of millions—maybe billions—of taxpayer dollars, all to avoid admitting their mistakes."[61]

Some critics suggested that DeKort was suing to recover damages because he had become unemployable. The silence of his former employers makes it difficult to assess the validity of this claim. What is clear, however, is that DeKort paid a steep price for his outspokenness. Criticized in the POGO blog comments section for his failure to pledge that he would not benefit financially from a successful claim, DeKort responded, "I moved my family three times in the past 6 years because of Lockheed issues. This whole thing has been trying on my family. We have sacrificed a lot and hung in there to be the only party who is aggressively pursuing recovery. I will certainly not give up all of any recovery I get to the national debt. My lawyer will recover what he should; I will pay my taxes, donate to charity, help out family members and friends and then take care of my family."[62]

By all accounts, the results of the Deepwater innovations were catastrophic. Four years into the program, the Coast Guard had fewer operational boats and ships than it had when Deepwater was first launched, and by the time the Department of Homeland Security brought the project back in house, what had originally been a $17 billion program was projected to cost $24.2 billion. The Government Accountability Office estimated in July 2011 that its cost had exceeded $29 billion. Former ICGS officials have told multiple media outlets that Lockheed and Northrop not only failed to secure the best price for the government but knowingly built defective ships.[63]

DeKort's qui tam suit against Lockheed was settled in December 2010 for an unspecified amount. He continued the case against ICGS and Northrop Grumman. The aim was to recover the $96.1 million the Coast Guard believed it was owed.[64] On July 16, 2012, the Fifth Circuit Court of Appeals upheld a ruling in favor of ICGS and Northrop Grumman, ending the case.[65] DeKort found employment in Pittsburgh, where his wife's family is from, and pursued his lawsuits from there.[66] Both Lockheed and Northrop remain eligible to bid for Coast Guard contracts, since the U.S. government is obligated to its taxpayers to find "best value."[67]

Blowing the Whistle on Abu Ghraib

The horrific pictures from Baghdad's Abu Ghraib prison exposed a huge gap between American ideals and wartime practices. Interrogation in a war zone had traditionally been a task reserved for government employees. But in Iraq and Afghanistan, America's first contractors' wars, everything was available for outsourcing. Twenty-seven of the thirty-seven interrogators at Abu Ghraib were contractors. America especially needs a conscience in wartime, but people at war are least inclined to acknowledge this need. As some would learn the hard way, whistleblowing in such circumstances is an unappreciated gift.

U.S. military police officer Joseph Darby learned the personal costs of whistleblowing in wartime. While stationed at Abu Ghraib on January 13, 2004, Darby handed evidence of ongoing abuse of prisoners to an agent of the U.S. Army Criminal Investigation Command. He had asked a photographer friend, prison guard Charles Graner, if he had any good pictures he could send home. Graner cheerfully turned over his complete collection on two CDs. The CDs included photos of prisoners in various states of torture and humiliation. Some showed prisoners who had been forced to strip off their clothes and assume a variety of sexual positions while U.S. soldiers and contractors posed with them. Darby said he doesn't think Graner realized what was on the CDs, but that it didn't really matter. He copied the disks and returned the originals to Graner, who turned out to have been the ringleader of the group that staged the photos.[68]

It took Darby three weeks of soul-searching to decide what to do with the photos. He drafted a letter and addressed it to the army investigation office, where soldiers can report criminal acts such as sexual harassment and theft, rather than to his superior officers.[69] The reason was simple. "In the past," he said, "every time something came to them, it got covered up."[70] Later, some would see this as an unforgivable breach of the chain of command.[71]

Darby had intended to be an anonymous whistleblower. Like the other soldiers who had witnessed abuses, he was reluctant to out his fellow soldiers. "I had the choice between what I knew was morally right and my loyalty to other soldiers," he said. "I couldn't have it both ways."[72] He knew how violently his peers at Abu Ghraib would respond to his ratting on a fellow soldier.

But he did not remain anonymous for long; there was political capital to be gained from hailing him as a hero. The *New Yorker* writer Seymour Hersh was the first to reveal Darby's name, but as Darby told *Mother Jones* feature writer Justine Shorrock, "Who reads the damn *New Yorker*?" But when secretary of defense Donald Rumsfeld in a Senate hearing thanked Darby by name for alerting the "appropriate authorities" and "for his courage and his values," Darby's life was instantly and irreparably changed. He was sitting in the mess hall of Abu Ghraib when the CNN broadcast carrying Rumsfeld's testimony came on the television. Suddenly, four hundred eyes were on him. At the time he had reported the photos, Darby thought he was providing an anonymous tip and would never be identified; he never dreamed it would lead to a national scandal or that he would receive full credit for putting the chain of events in motion. He would later receive a letter from Rumsfeld, written not to thank him but to request that he stop talking about how his identity was exposed despite receiving assurances from military personnel that he could remain anonymous.[73]

Following his exposure by Rumsfeld, Darby was quickly removed from Iraq. His wife met him stateside upon arrival, and the couple was whisked away to an undisclosed location, where they received 24/7 protection for the next six months. Everywhere Darby went, he was accompanied by bodyguards.[74] During this witness-protection period, he met with Major Chung, the provost marshal for his unit based in Cumberland, Maryland, and told him, "I just want to go home." Chung responded, "You can't go home. You can probably *never* go home." He was right. As Darby told *GQ*, "I've only been back to my town twice: for my mother's funeral and for a wedding. . . . I'm not welcome there."[75]

Some of his fellow soldiers considered Darby's actions borderline treasonous. As a commander of the VFW post in Darby's hometown, Colin Engelbach, told *60 Minutes*, "But do you put the enemy above your buddies? I wouldn't."[76] "People aren't pissed because I turned someone in for abuse," Darby told Justine Shorrock of *Mother Jones*. "People are pissed because I turned in an American soldier for abusing an Iraqi. They don't care about right and wrong."[77] Asked by Anderson Cooper of CNN if he'd do it again, Darby responded, "Yes. They broke the law and they had to be punished." "And it's that simple?" Cooper asked. "It's that simple," Darby replied.[78]

The evidence Darby provided led to the prosecution of eleven soldiers for violations of the Geneva Convention. Prosecuting the contractors proved more difficult. Their legal status under the Geneva Convention is ambiguous, leaving their conduct to be overseen by company policy. Since no company has an interest in confirming that its employees have committed human rights abuses, private-sector misconduct is highly likely to go unpunished. The Virginia-based contractor Engility has paid $5.28 million to settle with former Abu Ghraib inmates. In the case of the Abu Ghraib interrogators, as of March 2019, a civil suit against CACI International was still ongoing. According to the *Washington Post*, it is the first civil case against U.S. contractors to reach a point where a judge is hearing allegations of misconduct.[79]

The Darby case shows that praise from the powerful does not guarantee that a whistleblower will be protected from retaliation. Ordinary people dislike a snitch, the national security community dislikes leakers, and Darby had no laws to protect him. Whistleblowers are essential to democracy, but human self-interest encourages groupthink. The external incentives for truth telling are often low, if not nonexistent.

Contract Graft in Wartime

Bunnatine ("Bunny") Greenhouse overcame many obstacles before becoming the U.S. Army Corps of Engineers' principal assistant responsible for contracting (PARC), a position in the Senior Executive Service in which she was responsible for oversight of major contracts. She grew up on the Black side of segregated Rayville, a small cotton-picking town in the Louisiana delta, the daughter of poor and uneducated parents, Chris and Savannah Hayes, who had high expectations for all of their children. Greenhouse's older sister became one of the first Black professors at Louisiana State University, with a doctorate in linguistics and English literature; her older brother became a professor at Southern University in Baton Rouge; and her younger brother was named one of the fifty best athletes in the National Basketball Association.[80]

Greenhouse was valedictorian of her high school class and graduated magna cum laude with a degree in mathematics from Southern University in just three years. She earned three master's degrees—in business management from the University of Central Texas, in engineering from George Washington University, and in national resources strategy from the National Defense University. After finishing her education, she taught math in her hometown high school for sixteen years and then began a career as an army procurement officer, starting at one of the lowest pay grades, GS-5.[81]

In 1997, after Greenhouse had received regular promotions, Lieutenant General Joe Ballard offered her a civilian leadership position in the Corps of Engineers, making her the first Black person to hold the position of principal assistant responsible for contracting. He called her "one of the most professional people I've ever met." The new job put her in the Senior Executive Service, the top level of government employees, and had her overseeing the management of billions of dollars.[82]

Right before the invasion of Iraq, the corps wanted to award a no-bid "emergency" contract worth $7 billion to Kellogg, Brown and Root (KBR)—a Halliburton subsidiary—to repair Iraq's oil infrastructure.[83] Greenhouse thought the plan was absurd. She objected to KBR using its own cost projections for a multiyear no-bid contract and did not buy the assertion, written into the contract, that a five-year deal was necessary because of "compelling emergency." Greenhouse also saw evidence of a clear conflict of interest: before becoming the vice president of the United States, Dick Cheney had served as CEO of Halliburton. She recommended that the contract be limited to a year and that other companies be allowed to bid on it.[84] Yet when she received the final draft of the contract, her recommendations had been ignored, perhaps because a reliable fuel supply is critical to any military operation, so the incestuous relationship was comforting.

Greenhouse wrote her reservations on that draft in ink, and her notations became public after the contract was released through a Freedom of Information Act request in 2004.[85] In the ensuing furor, Greenhouse gave interviews to the media, and the FBI opened an investigation into "alleged price-gouging" and overbilling. After Greenhouse accused KBR of price gouging, a Pentagon audit found that "KBR apparently overbilled the government $61 million for fuel in Iraq." But the audit was stopped after the corps granted KBR a waiver from explaining the charge, saying that its pricing had been dictated by an Iraqi subcontractor.[86]

Greenhouse was incensed. She thought not only that the waiver was wrong but that her superiors had done an end run around her, drawing up and approving the waiver while she was out of the office.[87] Yet they did not stop there. In October 2004, they tried to demote her and remove her from the position she held.[88] A strong motivation for demoting her was her objection to the Halliburton contracts. On discovering this, the acting secretary of the army, Les Brownlee, insisted that the corps wait until an investigation of Greenhouse's allegations was completed before taking action.[89]

With her removal stalled, Greenhouse was invited to testify before the Senate Democratic Policy Committee in June 2005—the only congressional body that expressed interest in her charges.[90] Since the committee was partisan, her superiors told her she would be ill advised to do so. But she told the committee, "I can unequivocally state that the abuse related to contracts awarded to KBR represents the most blatant and improper contract abuse I have witnessed during the course of my professional career."[91] Three weeks later, the corps informed her that she would be removed from office.[92] She was demoted and stripped of her top secret security clearance and her membership in the Senior Executive Service, and her pay was cut by $2,000.[93] "They stuck me in a little cubicle down the hall, [and] took my building pass," she said. "It's all about humiliation."[94]

Her superiors alleged she had been demoted for poor job performance.[95] Lieutenant General Carl A. Strock said her removal was "based on her performance and not in retaliation for any disclosures of alleged improprieties she may have made." This stood in stark contrast to the stellar reviews she had received as PARC. Greenhouse was rated near or at the highest possible level in job reviews three years in a row; her supervisors described her as "effective, enthusiastic, energetic, tenacious, selfless . . . the epitome of fairness in Corps contracting" and praised her work ethic.[96]

Some coworkers did say, however, that Greenhouse had been having trouble on the job, and a former boss explained to NBC News that while she had great integrity, she also had detractors because she was "a stickler for the rules."[97] Another factor in the conflict may have been Greenhouse's race and gender. More than one corps employee mentioned hearing racist remarks made about Bunny Greenhouse, and she had even filed a complaint with the Equal Employment Opportunity Commission alleging race and gender discrimination. Soon enough, her annual performance reviews went from five stars to harsh critiques.[98]

Regardless of the peripheral motivations for removing Greenhouse from her job, it was clear that her whistleblowing was at the center of it. Her lawyer, Michael Kohn, stated that her removal constituted "blatant discrimination" and violated the earlier agreement with the army to suspend her demotion until the inspector general had finished his investigation. When Kohn called Dan Meyer, director of whistleblowing and transparency in the DOD Inspector General's office, on August 24, 2005, Meyer was shocked to hear that the corps had proceeded against Greenhouse; he said he would open a civilian reprisal investigation.[99] Kohn took this even further: he wrote to secretary of defense Rumsfeld that "the circumstances surrounding Ms. Greenhouse's removal are the hallmark of illegal retaliation," to which Rumsfeld never replied.[100] A group of Democratic senators joined Kohn and asked Rumsfeld to reinstate Greenhouse pending an investigation, but her situation failed to improve, and her clearance and status were not reinstated.[101]

After Greenhouse returned multiple times to testify to Congress, the humiliation escalated to physical intimidation.[102] A day before her sixty-sixth birthday, she stumbled on a trip wire that had been set up in her office, injuring her left kneecap. After that incident, she asked if she could telecommute or move to another agency. Her superiors refused. She filed a Title VII discrimination complaint.[103] Greenhouse retired from government on July 22, 2011; a few days later, she won a $970,000 settlement for lost wages, compensatory damages, and legal fees. "No settlement is going to make me whole," she remarked.[104] At the time, Greenhouse maintained she was happy to move on but sad that her career in government had ended so abruptly after twenty-nine years. Testifying before the House Oversight Committee in support of the 2009 Whistleblower Protection Enhancement Act, Greenhouse described the hostility she faced as "blatantly tied to my race and gender."[105]

The attacks of 9/11 were a wake-up call for Americans and the security state. The system had failed to detect an imminent threat, and steps were taken to ensure that the catastrophe would never be repeated. An entirely new government department was created, the Department of Homeland Security. Unprecedented resources were channeled to the intelligence community, which in turn outsourced much of the work to the private sector. Democrats and Republicans alike endorsed the security state's expansion. The digital age brought new opportunities for whistleblowing as well as for surveillance in the name of national security.

The Bush administration's war on terror went hand in hand with a war on leaks. The absence of consistent whistleblower protection for national security employees meant that those who could not get their concerns addressed within their organizations had no way to alert the public other than to leak information to the press. Employees who reported potential violations in this way were charged with aiding and abetting the enemy. Those tasked with upholding the security of the United States were given the benefit of the doubt.

The First Amendment upholds freedom of the press and freedom of speech, but the Supreme Court has also acknowledged that the requirements of national security place limits on free expression. As Justice Holmes famously argued in *Schenck v. United States* (1919), a person does not have the right to falsely shout fire in a crowded theater. Yet secrecy imposed for national security reasons can make it impossible for the public to know whether what is being shouted is true or false. The claim that Saddam Hussein had weapons of mass destruction, used to justify the invasion of Iraq, turned out to be false. The Bush administration never provided firm evidence to support this claim, allegedly for fear of compromising intelligence sources, but in reality, we now know, it was because the administration did not have that evidence in hand.

The 9/11 attacks thus changed the business of government in ways that had deep repercussions. With two wars raging and the contractor-industrial complex in high gear, those who spoke out in an effort to contain the negative consequences of privatization paid dearly for committing the truth.

Contracting abuses are, of course, nothing new. But the scope and scale of contracting activity and the security state it serves were unprecedented. With self-interest and state interests commingled by the privatization of government activity, the opportunities for corruption grew exponentially.

Wartime contracting was a national security concern, and many Americans were for a time content to avert their gaze so that the wars might be won and the homeland kept secure. National security whistleblowing is by definition a perilous endeavor, all the more so when there are vast sums of money involved. Government by contract, when the business of government is business, only amplifies this challenge.

PART II

The Internet Age

CHAPTER FIVE

Secrecy

A S A CANDIDATE FOR president, Barack Obama promised to rein in the Bush team's global war on terror, but President Obama largely maintained previous antiterrorism policies despite having called them unconstitutional. These similarities prompted George W. Bush's former press secretary Ari Fleischer to remark in 2013: "Drone strikes. Wiretaps. Gitmo. Renditions. Military Commissions. Obama is carrying out Bush's fourth term."[1] Those who criticized this continuity were swiftly silenced. Edward Snowden was the seventh person the Obama administration charged with violating the 1917 Espionage Act. Previously, only nine individuals had been prosecuted over the course of the act's existence.[2]

The Obama White House defied its supporters' expectations. Both the *Washington Post* and the *New York Times* repeatedly criticized the administration for its pursuit of leakers. In a 2013 report titled "The Obama Administration and the Press," for example, Leonard Downie, former executive editor of the *Washington Post*, described this relentless pursuit as unprecedented and claimed it was having a chilling effect on media coverage of the administration. *New York Times* Washington bureau chief David Sanger, who has worked in Washington for two decades, called the Obama team "the most closed, control-freak administration I have ever covered."[3]

The principles of open government and public accountability that many whistleblowers seek to promote were under fire in the Obama years. Senator and presidential candidate Obama had been a committed advocate of greater transparency, but President Obama did not practice it despite impressive rhetoric to the contrary, beginning with a presidential memorandum mandating transparency and open government on his first day in office.[4] Although he began his second term with a fireside Google Hangout in which he declared, "This is the most transparent administration in history," the record speaks for itself.[5] In late 2010 his administration almost let the Whistleblower Protection Enhancement Act die in the Senate before activists resuscitated it. Dodd-Frank mandated a new whistleblower office at the SEC that almost did not get off the ground on Obama's watch.[6] Senator Obama had supported the Free Flow of Information Act, a bill designed to give federal protection to journalists refusing to reveal their sources, but President Obama did nothing to move it through Congress. Senator Obama championed the Federal Funding Transparency and Accountability Act, but President Obama did little to uphold the spirit or letter of that law. As a Senate candidate, Obama called the Patriot Act "shoddy and dangerous"; as a senator in 2006, he voted for it. As president, he supported its reauthorization in 2011.[7]

The administration also sought to curtail public discussion of intelligence operations. In October 2011 it instituted the Insider Threat Program, which requires federal employees to report colleagues who are behaving suspiciously and thus could be sources of unauthorized leaks. In 2013, it blocked the publication of a whistleblowing book about the "Fast and Furious" gun-smuggling sting operation for fear that it would damage morale within the law enforcement community.[8] In March 2014, director of national intelligence James Clapper banned all intelligence community personnel from contact with journalists or academics.[9] That ban made the research for this book sometimes challenging.

The gap between the Obama administration's words and deeds presents a puzzle. The same administration that championed open government and transparency had a zero-tolerance policy for leakers of national security information. Both the Obama White House and Congress saw "national security whistleblowing" as a contradiction in terms. Any security breach required punishment, regardless of what was revealed. The administration prosecuted purported national security whistleblowers, whose activities were by definition suspect, and the American people seemed to agree.

The Bipartisan War on Leaks

After a long struggle to make it public, on December 9, 2014, the Senate Intelligence Committee released its heavily redacted, 528-page report condemning the Central Intelligence Agency's torture of suspected terrorists and its consistent efforts to hide its programs from congressional overseers. With a few noteworthy exceptions (including former prisoner of war and Republican senator John McCain), the reaction followed partisan lines. The Left said the report showed that CIA programs betrayed American values while failing to deliver results. The Right insisted that CIA actions were both successful and necessary. While the debate raged and long after it had died down, John Kiriakou, the whistleblower who brought the CIA's secret enhanced interrogation program to the attention of the American people, remained in jail.

The sixth individual the Obama administration prosecuted under the Espionage Act, Kiriakou was a former CIA agent who in a 2007 interview with ABC News publicly confirmed the CIA's use of waterboarding in its interrogations and called it torture. He received a thirty-month prison term for violating his oath of silence and revealing the name of a covert intelligence agent to a reporter investigating the interrogations.[10] "I arrived here on February 28, 2013, to serve a 30-month sentence for violating the Intelligence Identities Protection Act of 1982," Kiriakou wrote from his prison cell. "At least that's what the government wants people to believe. In truth, this is my punishment for blowing the whistle on the CIA's illegal torture program and for telling the public that torture was official US government policy."[11]

In the wake of these revelations, John Brennan had to withdraw from consideration for Obama's CIA director in 2008. Having served as a senior official at the CIA under the Bush administration, his connection to waterboarding was at the time deemed too controversial. Five years later, claiming he had been misled into believing that waterboarding was a valuable interrogation technique, Brennan sailed through the nomination process for the same position. Once confirmed as CIA director, he felt emboldened to defend the agency's past practices after the release of the Senate Intelligence Committee's scathing indictment.[12] After first denying to Andrea Mitchell of NBC News that the CIA had hacked Senate computers (it had), he subsequently refused to disclose to senators the names of those who had authorized CIA spying on Congress (the most obvious candidate being himself).[13] The White House remained silent.

Waterboarding, which until recently was generally agreed to be a form of torture, had somehow become a partisan issue. Senator McCain had reminded his colleagues in 2007 that it was once a war crime. "The Japanese were tried and convicted and hung for war crimes committed against American P.O.W.s," he said. "Among those charges for which they were convicted was waterboarding."[14] On the left, the late journalist and author Christopher Hitchens underwent waterboarding in 2008 and declared, "If waterboarding does not constitute torture, then there is no such thing as torture."[15] Yet by 2013, John Kiriakou sat in jail while one of the waterboarding policy's staunchest supporters, John Brennan, was appointed to head the CIA. The power of the bipartisan security state had been consolidated.

In the months following 9/11, Congress acted decisively to help the executive branch meet the terrorist challenge head-on. The 2001 Patriot Act lowered the barriers to legal surveillance by allowing the secret Foreign Intelligence Surveillance Court to review requests to suspend privacy rights. FISC vastly broadened the powers of the NSA through the "special needs" doctrine, which secretly creates exceptions to the application of the Fourth Amendment to combat terrorism.[16] The Surveillance Court hears arguments only from the Justice Department, not opposing views, and Chief Justice Roberts has unilateral power to select its members.

To underscore the seriousness of the terror threat, President Bush secretly authorized the National Security Agency to eavesdrop illegally on Americans and foreign nationals inside the United States if this surveillance seemed likely to provide information on potential terrorist activity. In 2002, a classified executive order allowed the NSA to monitor the international emails and phone calls of people inside the United States without a warrant when at least one party was believed to be a member of al-Qaeda or an affiliate, and at least one end of the communications was overseas.[17] Conducting warrantless surveillance was a sea change in NSA behavior; traditionally, the FBI conducted domestic eavesdropping after obtaining a warrant. The NSA had concerned itself primarily with foreign intelligence gathering, except for spying on foreign embassies and missions on U.S. soil. For those atypical efforts, it followed the guidelines of the Foreign Intelligence Surveillance Act and obtained a court order from the Foreign Intelligence Surveillance Court (more on this later).[18] President Bush's executive order upended that tradition.

It would take nearly four years for the warrantless surveillance program to come to light via the *New York Times*, and those who were deemed to have helped expose it would pay dearly for their actions. The administration felt so strongly that releasing information about the warrantless wiretap program could compromise the war on terror that in December 2005 it summoned the senior leadership of the *New York Times* to meet with President Bush, his lawyer Harriet Miers, national security advisor Stephen Hadley, and NSA director Michael Hayden. According to Bill Keller, the *Times'* executive editor, President Bush himself asked the newspaper not to publish. "The basic message," Keller told *New York Magazine*, "was, 'You'll have blood on your hands.'"[19] He said that after the hourlong meeting, he and *Times* publisher Arthur Sulzberger Jr. agreed they had heard nothing that changed their minds. The *Times* had already delayed publication for a year (during which President Bush was reelected) and had done further reporting in response to earlier White House requests. It had also edited out some information especially damaging to the administration. Eleven days after the meeting, the *Times* published its story.

The *Times'* decision-making process was attentive to the tradeoffs that exist between the public's right to know and legitimate security concerns. But for one of the reporters who landed the story, James Risen, and those suspected of leaking the information to him (Risen has never revealed his sources), what followed was massive retaliation.

Risen's 2006 book *State of War*, rushed to press after the publicity storm following his bombshell article, only heightened the government's interest in punishing him and forcing him to reveal his sources. He was subpoenaed three times: twice to appear before grand juries, and once to testify in the actual trial (he fought the first grand jury subpoena legally, the second was quashed by a judge).[20] His own description of his book's contribution to public understanding, delivered in a June 2011 affidavit, explains why the national security establishment would want Risen silenced:

> *State of War* included explosive revelations about a series of illegal or potentially illegal actions taken by President Bush, including the domestic wiretapping program. It also disclosed how President Bush secretly pressured the CIA to use torture on detainees in secret prisons around the world; how the White House and CIA leadership ignored information before the 2003 invasion of Iraq that showed that Iraq did not have weapons of mass destruction; documented how, in the aftermath of the invasion, the Bush Administration punished CIA professionals who warned that the war in Iraq was going badly; showed how the Bush Administration turned a blind eye to Saudi involvement in terrorism; and revealed that the CIA's intelligence operations on weapons of mass destruction in Iraq, Iran and other countries were completely dysfunctional, and even reckless.[21]

In the affidavit, Risen does not mince words as to why he is being pursued. "I believe that this investigation started as part of an effort by the Bush Administration to punish me and silence me, following the publication of the NSA wiretapping story. I was told by a reliable source that Vice President Dick Cheney pressured the Justice Department to personally target me because he was unhappy with my reporting and wanted to see me in jail. After he left office in 2009, Cheney publicly admitted that the fact that I won a Pulitzer Prize for the NSA story 'always aggravated me.'" According to Risen, the efforts to target him continued under the Obama administration, "which has been aggressively investigating whistleblowers and reporters in a way that will have a chilling effect on the freedom of the press in the United States."[22] He told documentary filmmaker Robert Greenwald that the "basic issue is whether or not you can have a democracy without aggressive investigative reporting. And I don't believe you can."[23]

Even after the real source for the domestic spying article, Justice Department lawyer Thomas Tamm, admitted to being the warrantless wiretapping leak, the administration continued to press Risen to reveal his sources. Tamm was not charged. As attorney general Holder put it in testimony before Congress on May 4, 2011, "Sometimes there has to be a balancing that is done between what national security interests are and what might be gained by prosecuting a particular individual."[24]

Former CIA officer Jeffrey Sterling was Risen's source for another bombshell in *State of War*, the revelation of a mismanaged secret operation to disrupt Iran's nuclear program—Operation Merlin—in which a Russian scientist gave Iran flawed nuclear components. Sterling was convicted under the Espionage Act in January 2015.[25] But again, Risen never revealed his source.

The disclosures from Tamm and Sterling were different. The warrantless wiretapping that Tamm revealed was a constitutional violation. A botched overseas intelligence operation like the one Sterling reported did not rise to the same standard of misconduct; it was just poor policy. Former NSA director Michael Hayden made this distinction when he told Lesley Stahl of CBS News that he thought the charges against Risen should be dropped. "The government needs to be strong enough to keep me safe, but I don't want it so strong that it threatens my liberties," Hayden said. "For his part, Risen argues that what he revealed was not a government secret, as much as a program he thought was illegal."[26]

The general response to Risen's disclosures was that warrantless surveillance was an egregious violation of existing law. President Bush told the public that he had ended the program, and in 2007 he signed an emergency gap law called the Protect America Act, which would become institutionalized through the 2008 FISA amendments. The gap law broke the original warrantless surveillance program into two parts: one about metadata phone records (Risen's discovery), and one about metadata Internet collection, which remained concealed until Snowden revealed it.

We now know that on March 12, 2004, acting attorney general James Comey and the Justice Department's senior leadership threatened to resign if the warrantless surveillance of email metadata and technical records of Skype calls continued, since they believed the president had no lawful authority to harvest this information. Comey had ordered the program stopped, and the president had issued an order renewing it anyway. Comey, Jack Goldsmith of the Office of Legal Counsel, and FBI director Robert Mueller then began drafting letters of resignation, but when the president learned of their intention to resign, he reversed himself and ended the collection of Internet metadata. On July 15, the secret surveillance court allowed the NSA under director Michael Hayden to resume bulk collection of Internet metadata through a legal provision known as pen registers. Pen registers first allowed law enforcement to collect phone numbers of incoming and outgoing calls from a single telephone line but now extended to Internet communications.[27]

The 2008 amendments to the Foreign Intelligence Surveillance Act extended the NSA's reach still further. Section 702 of the law allows the NSA, without court permission, to target noncitizens reasonably assumed to be located abroad who were communicating with U.S. persons. This means the communications of Americans can in some circumstances be collected without a warrant. When that happens, it is called incidental collection, since Americans should never be directly targeted for surveillance. The NSA had long been permitted to vacuum up information on foreigners that was harvested outside the country, but inside the country, it had needed a warrant to monitor any communication that took place on a wire (as opposed to satellite or radio transmission). Section 702 removed that requirement.[28]

The rules for proper collection under section 702 are not always followed, and mistakes are made. New America's Open Technology Institute has chronicled all violations of the section since the 2008 amendments, and the most compliance violations occurred in 2014 (sixty-one) and 2015 (seventy-three), the years immediately following the Snowden heist of June 2013. They have since fallen off dramatically (four in 2016), although this may be because of the time lag between when a violation is committed and when it is revealed.[29]

This general trajectory of expanding permissible surveillance and trusting government to restrain itself is unsurprising. Since it is hard for any politician to be "against security," a laissez-faire approach has a compelling logic. Candidate Obama had criticized the Bush administration's aggressive use of the state secrets privilege, which allows the executive branch to withhold evidence in a court of law on national security grounds. From January 2001 to January 2009, the Bush administration invoked the state secrets privilege in more than one hundred cases, more than five times the number of cases invoked by all previous administrations.[30]

When the Obama Justice Department reviewed the previous administration's record, however, it basically found its predecessors' actions to have been justified. Candidate Obama pledged to declassify Bush-era directives on interrogation, ban waterboarding, and close the military prison at Guantánamo, but the political pressure against each of these moves was fierce. In the end, the new administration delivered on the first two objectives and hit a brick wall on the third. The expanding security state continued to receive increased appropriations, and the Obama administration prosecuted more cases under the Espionage Act than all previous administrations combined.[31]

The consequences of placing an entire realm of government and private-sector activity effectively beyond public scrutiny were slowly coming to light. For starters, those who criticized what they saw as excesses in the pursuit of security risked being seen as people who didn't want America safe in the first place. As a result, whistleblowers on national security processes were by definition suspicious.

The expectations regarding citizens who receive a national security letter, which is issued to protect the country from its enemies, illustrate this risk. National security letters are the modern-day equivalent of colonial America's writs of assistance. A recipient of a national security letter—essentially an FBI-issued subpoena authorizing an investigation "to protect against international terrorism or clandestine intelligence activities"—must turn over all information the government requests. Most such letters also include a nondisclosure requirement, which means that the recipient is bound by a gag rule not to talk to anyone about having received it.

While national security letters were not a new technique (the authorities under which they are issued date to the 1970s and 1980s), section 501 of the 2001 Patriot Act had expanded opportunities for their use.[32] The Electronic Frontier Foundation has chronicled the FBI's extensive use of this power and consistently sought the repeal of section 501. According to Micah Sifry of Personal Democracy Media, fifty thousand national security letters are issued each year.[33] Since the Patriot Act expanded the use of them, three recipients have successfully challenged their letters and gotten the gag order rescinded. The Calyx Institute's Nicholas Merrill and Brewster Kahle, the founder of the Internet Archive and Alexa, are two of the three.[34] Microsoft also challenged a national security letter from the FBI in 2013 and won.[35] Google, which has challenged the practice in court, revealed that it receives up to 999 national security letters a year, affecting at least a thousand Google accounts.[36] In March 2013, a federal judge, Susan Illston, ruled that national security letters impinged on free-speech rights and were therefore unconstitutional.[37] Ladar Levinson, the founder of LavaBit, an encryption tool for email allegedly used by Edward Snowden, shut down his company to fight a national security letter rather than comply with the FBI's request to turn over the accounts of LavaBit users.

The Obama administration also oversaw the harvesting and stockpiling of unprecedented amounts of surveillance data. To house these digital collections, Washington built a 1-million-square-foot data storehouse, known as the Intelligence Community Comprehensive National Cybersecurity Initiative Data Center, in Bluffdale, Utah. Once fully operational, Bluffdale will effectively serve as the NSA's cloud.[38] The $2 billion facility was to be up and running in September 2013, but unexplained chronic electrical surges wiped out hundreds of thousands of dollars of equipment and delayed its opening by a year. The amount of data that the NSA will be able to store there is classified, but engineers on the project told Siobhan Gorman of the *Wall Street Journal* that they think its capacity will be bigger than Google's largest data center.[39]

Whistleblowing When Leaks Are Intolerable

Part of the reason that the war on leaks could proceed without constraints is that national security whistleblowers did not have the law on their side. The legal taboo on national security whistleblowing crystallized decades ago, when workers with access to classified information were excluded from the 1978 Civil Service Reform Act that put in place whistleblower protection for all other government employees. The landmark 1989 Whistleblower Protection Act continued to insist that the national security realm be treated differently.

The debates over the act's revision in both 2009 and 2012 featured arguments for empowering all government employees as "stewards of accountability," to cite 2009 testimony from deputy assistant attorney general Rajesh De, who would later become the NSA's general counsel.[40] When the law was updated again in 2012, the bill that first passed the House protected all government employees, as whistleblower advocates had wanted. Yet the version that President Obama signed into law continued to treat national security workers as a separate category.[41] Explanations of this outcome differ. Some saw the protection of national security workers as legislation Congress could never pass.[42] Others saw it as a casualty of political horse trading.[43] Regardless, the separate but equal system continued, and whistleblower advocacy organizations like the Government Accountability Project supported the compromise in order to save the bill.[44]

While that bill was being debated in Congress, on October 10, 2012, the White House countered the likely national security exclusion with Presidential Policy Directive 19 (PPD-19). It promised whistleblower protection for members of the intelligence community so long as they did not disclose classified information, but it did not explicitly extend that coverage to contractors like Snowden.[45] The White House would later claim that the directive would have provided protection for Snowden, but many disagreed, including Alan Chotkin, the executive vice president and counsel of the Professional Services Council, and Angela Canterbury of the Project on Government Oversight.[46] Some pointed to the Intelligence Community Whistleblower Protection Act of 1998 as additional support for whistleblowers, but it provides no protection against retaliation.[47] According to Dan Meyer, who led the Whistleblowing and Source Protection Program at the Office of the Intelligence Community Inspector General, or IC IG, the act is a "misnomer," since it was concerned only with the rights of employees to transmit classified information to Congress.[48] President Obama's executive order provided the justification for Meyer's position in the Office of the Director of National Intelligence.

President Obama's PPD-19 thus created a potential conflict between statute and executive order, since the former explicitly excludes employees that the latter includes.[49] The national security exemption thus casts a long shadow over any system designed to encourage whistleblowing, especially after the Snowden revelations, when the intelligence community was simultaneously encouraged to identify and eradicate insider threats (those likely to leak classified information).

The classification of an organization's budget creates additional conflicts for whistleblowing. In 2010, the budget for intelligence was 250 percent larger than it had been on September 10, 2001. In FY 2007, the National Intelligence Program's appropriated budget was $43.5 billion. It reached a peak of $54.6 billion in FY 2011, subsided a bit to $50.5 billion in FY 2014, and then rose to $53.9 billion in FY 2016.[50] It appears that the ostensible end of the Iraq War did not significantly change the budgetary picture. Since intelligence budgets are classified and intelligence agencies are never audited, the precise contours of the spending are impossible to track, but it is clear that expenditures on contracts were and are a major component of this spending. Business proprietary concerns create an additional screen behind which self-interested wrongdoing can thrive.

All Leakers Are Equal, but Some Are More Equal Than Others

The hard-line stance on leaking that fueled the Bush and Obama administrations' war on leakers did not extend to high-ranking government officials. General David Petraeus's government career ended in scandal in 2012, when an affair he had been conducting with his biographer Paula Broadwell went public, forcing his resignation as CIA director. The investigation that followed showed that Petraeus had shared eight notebooks, known as "black books," of highly classified information with Broadwell as deep background for her book. The government said the black books included "the identities of covert officers, war strategy, intelligence capabilities and mechanisms, diplomatic discussions, quotes and deliberative discussions from high-level National Security Council meetings, and defendant David Howell Petraeus's discussions with the President of the United States of America." Yet Petraeus was never charged with violating the Espionage Act. Instead, in a plea deal, he was fined $100,000 and given two years' probation.[51] "Laws are letters on a page," remarked Edward Snowden. "They don't jump off a page and defend your rights." He sees an obvious double standard when "David Petraeus shared confidential conversations with the president, yet did not serve a single day in jail and is out doing speaking tours."[52]

The same applies to former CIA director Leon Panetta, who unknowingly shared classified information on the bin Laden raid with the makers of a film on the topic, *Zero Dark Thirty*. For reasons that are unclear, screenwriter-producer Mark Boal and director Kathryn Bigelow were in the audience at an awards ceremony for participants in the May 2011 operation that killed Osama bin Laden, held at CIA headquarters on June 24, 2011. Panetta's speech was top secret; Boal and Bigelow had no security clearance but were granted entry for the event. Panetta said he was unaware of their presence, which raises the question of how they happened to be there. The Department of Defense Office of the Inspector General launched an investigation in response to a letter from the chair of the House's Homeland Security Committee, Peter King (R-NY), expressing concern that the filmmakers had received "top-level access to the most classified mission in history."[53]

What the investigation showed regarding Panetta's involvement is a matter of contention. The official inspector general report, obtained by Judicial Watch through a 2012 Freedom of Information Act request, said that his speech did not contain information regarding the intelligence chain that led to bin Laden, the most controversial classified information allegedly shared at the CIA awards ceremony. The report did not incriminate Panetta. Yet an earlier draft of the report, which showed up on the Project on Government Oversight website, did implicate him. The official version of the report, released only after Panetta's retirement, had been sanitized.[54]

Senator Charles Grassley (R-IA) got involved when whistle-blowers contacted his office in December 2012, alleging that DOD acting inspector general Lynne Halbrooks was suppressing the original IG report to protect Panetta (who had since become secretary of defense) and to further her quest to become the permanent DOD inspector general (a position that requires presidential nomination and Senate confirmation).[55] Both conflicts of interest caught Grassley's attention, and his staff launched an investigation in which they found that the unscrubbed version of the report, which implicated Panetta and other senior officials in the mishandling of classified information, had been circulated internally for final review before release. It was ready to go, but then Halbrooks had gutted the report, claiming that official policy dictated that all information relating to the Central Intelligence Agency be removed from the document. According to Grassley, however, this should have happened *before* a final version was circulated, not after. Otherwise, it amounts to censorship of a report investigating allegations of high-level misconduct. Grassley called the sanitized report "a second-class piece of work that is not worth the paper it is written on." He added that the investigation should have been conducted by the CIA's inspector general, not the DOD's, since the alleged impropriety involved a CIA event.[56]

Bungling aside, the release of the uncensored report enraged Halbrooks, who launched a full-court press search for the leaker, reviewing over thirty thousand internal emails. It turned out to be Dan Meyer, the director of whistleblowing and transparency in the Office of the Inspector General at the Department of Defense (the same Dan Meyer who would later be transferred to the office of the Director of National Intelligence after Obama's PPD-19). Meyer, like others in the office, thought the original report was good to go and admitted sharing it with Congress at his supervisor, John Crane's, request. Halbrooks, who had been the leader of DOD's watchdog organization and Meyer's boss at the time, then sought to have his security clearance revoked. Grassley concluded, "In the end, Mr. Meyer bore the brunt of blame for the POGO leak. The principal targets of the investigation, Panetta, Vickers and Bash, skated. Mr. Meyer exposed their alleged misconduct and got hammered. Justice got turned upside down."[57]

Irving Charles McCullough, inspector general of the intelligence community, rescued Meyer by offering him a new job as executive director of the Intelligence Community Whistleblowing and Source Protection Program in the Office of the Director of National Intelligence (headed by James Clapper). He took a new job in a new place with his old job description, which he could not show me because it was classified.[58] Meyer's work for Clapper and McCullough protected the confidentiality of sources and aimed to prevent targeted reprisals.[59] But although he would never himself acknowledge it, the national security exclusion for whistleblower protection and the intelligence community's Insider Threat Program made his mission complicated. In March 2018, the IC's point man for whistleblower protection was terminated for reasons that remain murky; it may have been a consequence of a whistleblower retaliation settlement Meyer reached with the Pentagon in September 2016.[60] For the Project on Government Oversight, Meyer's ouster was disturbing "because whistleblower retaliation concerns are so pervasive in the US intelligence community that they even have infected the offices that are supposed to be a safe haven for those who report abuse."[61]

According to Dan Meyer, his exit from the intelligence community left four open inquiries in its wake: a Merit Systems Protection suit against director of national intelligence Dan Coats; an Equal Employment Opportunity formal investigation against Wayne A. Stone, the acting inspector general who fired Meyer; an investigation by an unidentified inspector general into the execution of the IC Whistleblowing Program in 2017 and 2018; and an ironic IC whistleblower reprisal complaint, filed in December 2017 by Dan Meyer against Wayne Stone with Meyer's former employer. As of December 2018, it had not yet been acted upon.[62]

Meyer's earlier boss, John Crane, lost his job as DOD deputy inspector general in 2013 for raising questions about the botched investigation of the *Zero Dark Thirty* leak and about the DOD inspector general's refusal to investigate alleged document destruction related to former NSA employee Thomas Drake's case. Drake was charged with violating the Espionage Act by sharing classified information on NSA programs with *Baltimore Sun* reporter Siobhan Gorman. (We will get to know Drake better in the next chapter.) Crane says he was fired for "blowing the whistle on internal whistleblowing processes." He also asserts that Halbrooks ordered him "to use the whistleblower program to suppress whistleblowing, and whistleblowers, especially with respect to Congress."[63] Crane's concerns are not unique to the Pentagon. Speaking of IG challenges more generally, Justice Department inspector general Michael Horowitz told the *New York Times* in November 2015, "The bottom line is that we're no longer independent."[64]

Crane sought action to restore his job and credibility for the whistleblower mission of the DOD IG. In an October 11, 2017, letter to Crane, retaliation and disclosure chief Karen Gorman confirmed the seriousness of the case while arguing it could not be pursued further without congressional intervention.[65] Yet the Office of Special Counsel ruled against Crane eleven months later, special council Henry Kerner stating in a September 10, 2018, letter to President Trump that the Justice IG "found no evidence that [the Defense Department] IG improperly destroyed documents related to the audit."[66]

As for the woman at the helm when the series of missteps occurred, even the appearance of interference in an IG investigation of misconduct is serious business. Halbrooks resigned her position in April 2015 to take a job in the private sector. According to her LinkedIn profile, she is currently a partner for white-collar crime defense in the Washington law firm Holland and Knight. She does not list her tenure as acting inspector general in her LinkedIn employment history. Perhaps it was unwise to let an IG position go unoccupied for so long that an acting IG was necessary. Yet Halbrooks's lengthy interim leadership of the Pentagon's watchdog was in no way unusual. A 2015 Project on Government Oversight study revealed that the average length of time an IG position stood vacant during the Obama administration was 613 days.[67]

Where national security whistleblowing is concerned, Grassley is right: no one is watching the watchdog. If the IG botches an investigation, the IG decides whether it has engaged in misconduct, and the verdict it is likely to reach is obvious. And if the IG can be silenced politically, it cannot serve as a legitimate executive branch watchdog.

When leaks are intolerable, whistleblower protection is difficult to ensure and the status of the leaker matters. Those who leaked information to journalists, such as Thomas Drake, Jeffrey Sterling, and John Kiriakou, were charged with violating the Espionage Act. Former CIA directors David Petraeus and Leon Panetta shared classified information with a lover and with movie producers, respectively, and went largely unpunished.

Upon assuming the presidency, President Obama surely learned things he had not known about the dangerous world his predecessors had to navigate, which in part accounted for the security state's bipartisan consolidation. Yet it is also true that the powerful will always err on the side of secrecy. Fortunes and empires are built by exploiting information disparities. In addition to its role in upholding national security, secrecy remains a vital component of any functioning capitalist system. Since profit can be derived from knowing just a bit more than your competitors, many a profit margin has its origins in some modicum of secrecy. The idea of proprietary information exists to protect against piracy. Yet just as secrecy can be exploited as a power resource in the national security realm, so too can it be manipulated by financial elites in ways that undermine democracy. Financial fraud, like profit margins, flourishes in the shadows.

It is certainly true that secrecy is sometimes necessary to defend the United States or to protect a market advantage. But there are enormous incentives, as well, for the powerful to insist on excessive secrecy. Those in positions of power will always have a vested short-term interest in asserting its necessity. But as the consolidation of the bipartisan security state shows, in the long run, excessive secrecy can damage both security itself and democratic values. As the late senator Daniel Patrick Moynihan put it in his book *Secrecy*, "At times, in the name of national security, secrecy has put that very security in harm's way." He concludes, "Secrecy is for losers."[68]

It may be true that "secrecy corrodes self-government, just as it strengthens self-defense."[69] Yet the trade-off between security and liberty has been present since the founding of the republic, so it alone cannot entirely explain the Obama administration's fierce pursuit of leaks and leakers. The financial and political power of the security state also fueled the president's stance. Since the most damning critiques of the security state inevitably involve breaches of confidentiality, there was little room for legitimate national security whistleblowing.

CHAPTER SIX

Surveillance

W HEN PRESIDENT TRUMAN ESTABLISHED the National Security Agency in 1952, he was seeking to address major intelligence failures in the Korean War. The NSA's original mission was the collection of signals intelligence (SIGINT), defined as intelligence gathered from secret and coded messages. Along with human intelligence (HUMINT), SIGINT is one of the two main sources of secret information.

During the Cold War, transparency and national security were considered mutually exclusive. Since the NSA's definition of signals intelligence included anything America's adversaries sought to conceal, it followed that America's own secrets must be similarly valuable to the enemy. Sharing American information freely was thus equivalent to handing over to adversaries what the NSA sought to secure. In a zero-sum global order, those who were not with the United States in the struggle to contain Soviet expansionism were against the United States, and leakers were by definition aiding and abetting America's principal enemy.

This zero-sum worldview led the NSA to abuse its powers in the 1960s and early 1970s. In Operation Shamrock, for instance, major U.S. telecommunications companies clandestinely shared information about the phone calls of U.S. citizens who were on the

NSA's watch list, which included everything from the entire women's liberation movement to Senator Frank Church.[1] In 1975, as a result of the Church Committee's examination of IC abuses, the Senate established the permanent Select Committee on Intelligence and promulgated other largely classified reforms in 1976 to rein in intelligence community overreach. Spying of any sort on Americans was prohibited without a court order. The Reagan administration added Executive Order 12333 in December 1981 to make it clear that citizens of other countries were not under the protection of the U.S. Constitution, so surveillance activities overseas that did not touch on Americans were still fair game.[2]

The lessons of the Church Committee's findings eventually faded for Congress, but not for the NSA. Shortly before 9/11, it found itself under congressional scrutiny again, not for overreaching but for being too risk averse and slow to adapt to the enormous changes in communications the Internet had wrought. It was criticized for its insularity and reluctance to enlist the private sector to help the nation meet new threats.[3] Later, the independent 9/11 Commission found that the NSA had adhered to self-imposed rules that were stricter than those set by federal law.[4] Since the U.S. intelligence community had indisputably dropped the ball with the 9/11 attacks, the pressure to reform was enormous.

The Internet revolution had profoundly changed the principal means of military communication established since the agency's founding. When the exchange of military information took place through separate channels, one could conduct signals intelligence without interfering in commercial or personal communications. The Internet allowed personal, commercial, and military communications to traverse the same digital space. The once distinct lines between military and personal or commercial became blurred. In the Internet age, the NSA would also take on information assurance (protecting America's information systems from theft or damage) and network warfare, otherwise known as cybersecurity.

The digital age thus presented a two-pronged challenge for the NSA's operations. First, electronic mail mingled military and commercial/personal communications, making surveillance of military signals in isolation more difficult. Second, globalization increased exchanges between Americans and foreigners exponentially, so monitoring the communications of foreigners often incidentally caught Americans who were protected by the U.S. Constitution.

Just as the new and more amorphous security threat necessitated commercial involvement in the nation's defense, Internet communications created new opportunities for surveillance. With norms of operation changing rapidly, defining prudent conduct in this new space was inevitably contentious. Where whistleblowers saw illegal and unconstitutional encroachments on liberty, Congress and the executive branch largely saw necessary evils.

The Trailblazer Controversy

The stories of ThinThread and the program that replaced it, Trailblazer, neither of which was fully realized, illuminate the pressure the NSA was under to stay on top of its game. In 2000, the NSA warned the incoming George W. Bush administration that the digital revolution necessitated a rethinking of the NSA's policies and authorities so as to remain consistent with the Constitution's prohibition of "illegal searches and seizures" without warrant and "probable cause."[5] ThinThread was an attempt to navigate the transition from the old world to the new within constitutional strictures. Until that time, the NSA would seize digital information only when it had a warrant and probable cause, and it focused on foreign rather than domestic communications.

The idea behind ThinThread was that you could vacuum up massive amounts of information without authorization, but then immediately encrypt it so that it could not be read. So much of the world's Internet traffic passed through U.S. servers, however, that it proved almost impossible to keep foreign and domestic communication separate. Rather than exclusively analyze foreign communications, ThinThread inevitably picked up plenty of interactions with American citizens or those on American soil. The Foreign Intelligence Surveillance Act of 1978 forbids the monitoring of domestic exchanges without a warrant, which requires a probable cause and a known suspect. ThinThread addressed this problem with privacy controls and an encryption feature that automatically rendered all American communications anonymous until a proper warrant was secured. The data the program gathered could not be accessed until a court had given analysts an encryption key to do so. In other words, the data could be harvested en masse but could actually be read only with a warrant. ThinThread was an effort to make mass surveillance constitutional while harnessing the power of the Internet to the cause of American national security.[6] The system was designed to flag suspicious patterns that necessitated warrant requests without infringing on the privacy rights of American citizens.[7]

In pilot tests, ThinThread was wildly successful, processing prodigious amounts of data. One of its advocates, NSA deputy director of operations Richard Taylor, later told the 9/11 Commission that ThinThread could have identified the hijackers prior to the attack, perhaps thereby preventing it.[8]

Bill Binney, a thirty-six-year NSA veteran, was the principal architect of ThinThread. According to Binney, it was based on a three-level encryption system that exploited the unique numbering system for IP addresses and land-line telephone numbers. Every telephone number in the world starts with a world zone number, and there are nine zones. When we dial an international phone number, we have to get to an international switch. In the United States, you dial 01 or 011 before the foreign number. Dialing 01 gets you to an operator, and dialing 011 gets you to a station if you don't need an operator. If you're in any other country in the world, you dial 00 first, then the country code and number. If you're making a domestic call, you dial 1. Thus, by looking at the prefix the NSA knows immediately who is calling from inside the United States. The same unique naming principle also applies to IP addresses. At least theoretically, it was a straightforward proposition to devise an algorithm to flag American-originated calls for immediate encryption and Fourth Amendment protection.[9]

The NSA decided to scuttle ThinThread before 9/11, in part because of privacy concerns. Michael Hayden, who became the NSA director in March 1999, flatly opposed it, ostensibly because NSA legal staff was wary of it. After 9/11, ironically, that same legal staff reversed its position and endorsed programs that paid far less attention to the very privacy concerns that had formerly been so weighty.

With the in-house effort shelved, the NSA asked private contractors to build a rival system, Trailblazer, at far greater cost. Trailblazer was a unified effort to modernize surveillance in a digital, cellular, and fiber-optic world.[10] It entirely lacked the privacy protections that were built into ThinThread. Unlike ThinThread, Trailblazer was the brainchild of contractors rather than NSA employees. Deputy NSA director William Black, who had worked at the NSA for decades, then moved to the defense contracting firm SAIC and then back to the NSA to assume the number two position, negotiated the Trailblazer contract.[11] He funneled hundreds of millions of dollars in contracts to SAIC, and the revolving door between the agency and private companies spun madly as NSA employees cashed in by taking jobs as contractors to work on Trailblazer.

The project was an unmitigated disaster: hundreds of millions of dollars over budget and years behind schedule without tangible results.[12] It was finally canceled in 2006 after billions of taxpayer dollars had been poured into it. Hayden told James Bamford, "We learned that we don't profit by trying to do moon shots, by trying to take the great leap forward, that we can do a lot better with incremental improvement, spiral development."[13] Hayden thought Trailblazer failed because it aimed too high. Binney, on the other hand, remains convinced that ThinThread could have prevented the events of September 11 and that the decision to abandon it for Trailblazer was "all about money." ThinThread cost $3.2 million. The first appropriation for Trailblazer was $3.8 *billion*. For contractors, Trailblazer meant a continued flow of spending; for the NSA after 9/11, money was no object. ThinThread meant the NSA did not need incremental money to do its job well, and it had the added virtue of keeping oversight of controversial new programs in house rather than outsourcing them to a private company.

One could argue that Trailblazer was designed to get the most bang for the buck, but Binney calls that reasoning "a fabrication so they can get money and feed. It's a feeding process."[14] Jesselyn Radack of the Government Accountability Project concurred: "Their motto became 'keep the problem going to keep the money flowing,' and so there was not an incentive to actually solve data collection problems or to improve them but rather to keep using them as funding vehicles to raise unbelievable amounts of money."[15] Former NSA senior official Thomas Drake, who once served as executive manager of all four ThinThread subsystems, agreed: "There are such vast sums of money involved, and when you have very senior officials seeking not just to sustain existing contracts but also to grow them you have to insist on the persistence of an existential challenge to the United States. It never really delivered an actual solution. It just became this funding vehicle for contractors. Follow the money," Drake said, "and you will see where the priorities were."[16]

Former NSA employee turned whistleblower Kirk Wiebe remembers that when the Trailblazer dead end was becoming apparent, a former member of the NSA leadership, Bill Sullivan, came out of retirement to get the program back on track. Wiebe reports Sullivan told him that NSA values had completely flipped in his time away from the agency. For old-timers, the top priority had been the mission of protecting the country. The second priority was loyalty to the organization. The third priority was self-interest. Now the order was reversed.[17]

Former NSA deputy director John "Chris" Inglis isn't convinced by critics' arguments that there was some sort of conspiracy or misconduct in the NSA's choice of Trailblazer over ThinThread. "In order to believe their version, you'd have to believe that the Inspector General was in on this conspiracy," Inglis said. "You'd have to believe that the technologists who can see the difference between something that will scale and has efficacy in terms of being the better solution deliberately chose to ignore it. That the Department of Justice, which has some responsibility to follow through on IG allegations, turned a blind eye. That the Congress ignored it." Where Binney, Wiebe, and Drake see self-interested action at the expense of the common good, Inglis sees a good-faith effort that simply came up short. "In the end, I do not think that Trailblazer was the right choice," he says. "The NSA was struggling at the time to figure out how to navigate a world that was increasingly networked. Trailblazer ultimately failed because it could not scale, but ThinThread wasn't the answer either."[18] One is left to wonder how events might have been different had ThinThread been proposed *after* 9/11 rather than before. According to Inglis, the NSA was "hugely conservative" prior to 9/11.

That ThinThread did not provide a view inside the United States (because all the data on Americans was immediately encrypted, leaving nothing for the analyst without a warrant to assess) was an exasperation to Vice President Cheney, who had little concern for constitutional violations when the nation's safety was at stake. President Bush's October 2001 secret executive order on NSA protocols gave Cheney what he wanted. The NSA program STELLARWIND authorized warrantless collection of metadata on U.S. phone calls, and that authority was extended to the Internet in 2002. Metadata is data about data, which sounds boring, but it actually can be the story of your life. Without knowing the content of a particular call, investigators can deduce where you are, whom you talk to, how frequently, for how long, and when, all of which can reveal a lot about who you are. A spy need no longer follow you around: your life rhythms can be digitally ascertained from afar.[19]

Bush's secret executive order essentially flipped standard NSA surveillance from targeted searches (search then seize) to dragnet searches (seize then search). The NSA may have been slow to adapt to the era of Internet communications, but Bush's secret order propelled that adaptation dramatically forward with a promise of a wide berth for experimentation.[20] And experiment the NSA did. What began as emergency measures were soon adopted as the new normal.

Insiders Sound an Alarm

The scuttling of ThinThread was the lens through which Binney, Drake, and Wiebe viewed the transformation in NSA operating procedures sparked by 9/11. Binney quit his job at the NSA to protest the STELLARWIND program, which he viewed as deliberately targeting Americans. Both he and Wiebe retired from the NSA on October 31, 2001. They had NSA approval to market the Thin-Thread concept commercially and believed that aspects of the software could be used to detect Medicare fraud. The venture never got off the ground. They could not secure any government contracts—because, they believe, they were blackballed by the NSA.[21]

In September 2002, Binney and Wiebe teamed up with Diane Roark, a former staff member on the House Permanent Select Committee on Intelligence (which oversees the NSA), and Edward Loomis, a former NSA computer scientist, to file a confidential complaint with the Pentagon's inspector general about waste and fraud in the Trailblazer program. They saw it as a feeding trough for contractors rather than as a legitimate investment of taxpayer money. Like Binney and Wiebe, Roark had resigned her position after growing increasingly frustrated by the complacency she encountered when highlighting potential abuses of power, which she had thought was part of her job description. Loomis served as a cryptologist at the NSA from 1964 to 2001 and had come to the ThinThread project as an NSA lifer. He resigned in protest in September 2001, after ThinThread was officially rejected to make room for Trailblazer. Thomas Drake, then still employed at the NSA, did not sign the complaint but was covertly involved as an unnamed DOD senior executive source in the investigation.[22]

The Pentagon inspector general issued an audit in 2004, of which a heavily redacted version was released through a Government Accountability Project (GAP) Freedom of Information Act request in 2011. Based on reading between the lines of that seriously edited document, the investigators seem to have initially found that there was some mismanagement, but they acknowledge revising their findings after commentary from senior leadership. The report also noted that many people interviewed asked that they not be identified for fear of management reprisal.[23]

Edward Loomis told the television program *Frontline* in December 2013 that the IG report was quite favorable toward Thin-Thread. It criticized the program for a lack of maintenance backup support, which Loomis says was true (the original programmers were let go) but could have been easily fixed. Most of the redactions were Trailblazer critiques.[24] John Crane, who was deputy assistant inspector general in the Pentagon at the time of the 2004 audit, concurred that the unredacted version conclusively vindicated the complainants' perspective. Crane also pointed out that it is unprecedented for an IG report to reference fear of management reprisal, since cooperating with the inspector general is every employee's personal responsibility. His complaint that the IG was obligated to investigate the allegations of fear of management retaliation but failed to do so has gone unaddressed. This failure is what destroyed Thomas Drake's career.[25]

After the report was issued, Binney and Wiebe persisted in lodging complaints from the outside through all available channels. Despite what they saw as the blackballing of their start-up venture, they continued to make their case that NSA surveillance innovations must not violate constitutional rights. Both received DOJ letters of immunity in January 2010 that gave them a modicum of personal protection from prosecution as they continued to publicly condemn NSA practices.

Thomas Drake remained at the NSA despite his grave reservations about the flipping of protocols after 9/11. His activities slowly came under suspicion after he complained to NSA director Keith Alexander in 2005 about contracting malfeasance. Drake also shared information with Congress, and when that did not stop the runaway train (no one at the time was interested in killing intelligence programs), he took his observations to the *Baltimore Sun*'s Siobhan Gorman.[26] In Drake's view, "As a result of 9/11, the government unchained itself from the Constitution fully and completely. They just completely abandoned the legal regime that had been put in place from the previous 23 years. They willfully and deliberately turned it on its head."[27] Wiebe, Drake, and Binney saw the NSA's transformation as unconstitutional and felt a duty to expose it, however possible. From the NSA's perspective, they were a threat to national security.

Their lives changed when the *New York Times* exposé of warrantless wiretapping broke in December 2005, and Gorman's stories about financial waste and bureaucratic dysfunction at the NSA, including the Trailblazer versus ThinThread controversy, first appeared in the *Baltimore Sun* on January 29, 2006, continuing for months. While the *Sun* series ran, the FBI struggled to identify the leakers and became mistakenly convinced that the *Times* story and the *Sun* articles must have come from the same source.[28] All the people who had signed the Trailblazer complaint became suspects.

Binney and Wiebe cooperated fully with the investigation, but that did not prevent the FBI from simultaneously raiding their homes on July 26, 2007. Binney stepped naked from the shower to find an FBI agent holding a gun to his head. His house was ransacked with his wife and youngest child present. Agents locked Wiebe's Welsh corgi in the bathroom and ordered his daughter and his mother-in-law, who was in her bathrobe, to stay on the couch until they had finished their search.[29] They took materials, including computer hard drives and laptops, from both homes that have yet to be returned. The next day, Binney and Wiebe were summoned to the NSA and stripped of their security clearances. Binney had obtained his in 1965, Wiebe in 1964.

A few days after the July FBI raids, Drake met with Binney and Wiebe for lunch to compare notes and discuss next steps. As summer ended, Drake was relieved of his NSA responsibilities and transferred to a position at the National Defense University. FBI agents visited his home on November 28, 2007, and seized materials. On that same day, Drake's top secret/sensitive compartmented information (TS/SCI) clearance was suspended, and the following day he was placed on paid administrative leave and recalled from his position at the university.[30] He met with federal investigators three times, convinced he could get them to see the government's crimes. Instead, it became clear that prosecutors thought he was the criminal.[31] In April 2008, federal prosecutor Steven Tyrell told Drake they had found three classified documents in his basement and two in his email archive.[32] Drake resigned from the NSA that month, before he could be fired.

Drake claims that he did not knowingly have classified materials in his home. The documents in his basement were less sensitive material he had obtained for the DOD inspector general's investigation of Trailblazer. The IG advises all complainants to keep copies of relevant documents.[33]

Drake says he "raised the gravest of concerns through all the proper channels, reporting massive contract fraud, management malfeasance and illegalities conducted by the NSA, including critical intelligence information and analysis that was never reported or shared by the NSA. Had this vital and actionable intelligence been properly analyzed and disseminated by the NSA, it could have led to the capture of the Sept. 11 hijackers and prevented the attacks."[34] The Obama administration responded on April 14, 2010, charging him with ten felony counts of unlawful retention of classified information, obstruction of justice, and making false statements under the Espionage Act. If he had been successfully prosecuted, Drake would have faced thirty-five years in prison.

Drake told *60 Minutes* in May 2011 that his prosecution was meant to send a "chilling message" to prospective whistleblowers: "Do not tell truth to power; we'll hammer you."[35] Because he felt the charges were retaliation for whistleblowing, he refused to plea-bargain when urged to do so by federal prosecutors. The administration's case collapsed later that summer when J. William Leonard, director of the Information Security Oversight Office under President George W. Bush, agreed to testify on Drake's behalf. Prosecutors dropped all ten felony charges, and Drake was sentenced on July 15, 2011, to one year's probation after pleading guilty to a misdemeanor charge, exceeding authorized use of a computer.[36] The *New York Times* editorial page concluded, "Treating potentially embarrassing information as a state secret is the antithesis of healthy government."[37]

In 2012, the Pentagon Office of the Inspector General began investigating Drake's allegations that he had been retaliated against for whistleblowing. Drake tried to obtain the documents that had been seized from his home in November 2007—the same materials that the IG had urged him to retain—as evidence of his cooperation in the Trailblazer audit, but prosecutors told him that the documents had been destroyed as a matter of routine policy.[38] A subsequent IG investigation of whether the documents had been improperly destroyed ensued. In 2014, the IG rejected Drake's charges that there had been retaliation against him but also acknowledged that he had cooperated with its office as an anonymous source in the Trailblazer audit and other contracting controversies.[39] Stripped of his security clearance and pension, former NSA analyst and decorated air force and navy veteran Thomas Drake now supports himself with a job at a Washington-area Apple store.

According to Washington whistleblower advocate and attorney Stephen Kohn, the Drake case is clear evidence that something is wrong with our national security whistleblowing processes. "If you look at someone like Drake," said Kohn, "that's a catastrophic result. Drake had to plead guilty to a crime and was driven out of his profession. The current system is designed at best to create an illusion that there is a safe channel for whistleblowing, and we don't need to do anything more. Nothing could be further from the truth. We know what works. It needs to be put into place."[40]

Senior NSA officials insist that Binney, Wiebe, and Drake overstepped the bounds of propriety in what the officials saw as a quest to remake NSA practices. Former deputy NSA director Chris Inglis communicated with Drake on routine matters several times in 2006 and 2007 and says that Drake never once expressed concerns of any kind to him.[41] According to former NSA director General Keith Alexander, Binney and Drake "were criminals in what they were doing."[42] The real leaker in the warrantless wiretapping case, Thomas Tamm, was never prosecuted. Edward Loomis, the NSA cryptographer who resigned in protest after ThinThread was canceled, does not incur the same level of wrath as Binney and Drake, perhaps because he does not view himself as a whistleblower. After FBI agents in Kevlar vests came to his home on July 26, 2007, Loomis cut off all contact with the outside world for three years.[43]

More than one very senior official expressed regret that the government had not prosecuted Drake to the full extent of the law. Doing so would have required revealing secret NSA processes, so, according to these members of the senior leadership, a decision was made that the cost of making a felony under the Espionage Act stick to Drake was too high. Large portions of Drake's misdemeanor trial, however, remain unavailable to the public.[44]

Inside the NSA

Because those accused of wrongdoing are often bound by confidentiality commitments, writing about whistleblowers is intrinsically difficult. In national security, classification further complicates getting both sides of the story. Without the help of a former Harvard classmate, Carnegie Mellon professor Kiron Skinner, this book would have been impossible to complete. In fall 2013, in the wake of the Snowden revelations, she connected me with a new NSA faculty briefing program, necessitated by the Snowden security breach. The result was a rare invitation for a day-long briefing with Carnegie Mellon faculty at the National Security Agency on January 16, 2014.

The day before our briefing was to take place, I received a logistical email from an NSA official clarifying where we were to be and when, as well as the rules governing our visit. Among other strictures, no electronic devices of any kind could enter the NSA. The email closed with the tagline *"We have never been victims of destiny. We have always been masters of our own."*

I had no idea who else would be part of our delegation until the other participants were revealed via email as I was heading out the door of my home in Middlebury, Vermont, to drive to the Albany airport on my way to Baltimore. I hastily printed out the briefing book with photos and bios on the briefing participants, but found no information whatsoever on what the day would bring—other than a 7:50 a.m. pickup at the Marriott in Fort Meade, Maryland, where most of us would be staying.

Fort Meade is a sprawling complex, with special exits off the Baltimore-Washington Parkway for NSA employees only. It took some time for my cab to navigate around it to the hotel. When I arrived, the hotel lobby was brimming with sloppily dressed middle-aged men wandering about aimlessly looking for something to do with themselves. It turned out there was also a big mathematics conference in town, giving the place a geeky ambience of esoteric but powerful knowledge. I fell asleep that night imagining I had stepped right into a spy thriller.

The next morning, when I reported to the hotel lobby, our group quickly emerged out of nowhere and assembled to board an unmarked van to go to NSA headquarters. As we approached the sprawling complex with its gleaming buildings and massive wrap-around parking lot, we hit the security checkpoint. The guard there wondered where our badges were. Our leader told him that we were on the director's list, we all showed our IDs, and we were waved through without drama. *Too bad*, I thought. I had come looking for drama and absurdity.

As instructed, we left all our electronics and baggage in the NSA van. There was no alternative at this point. I wished that I had gotten around to installing file encryption on my laptop, but it was too late.

We were ushered into Building B2. The hallways featured a history of cryptology and SIGINT told through America's wars. We passed exhibits on World War I, World War II, Korea, Vietnam, and the Cold War before turning a corner to get to the enormous Operation Iraqi Freedom and Operation Enduring Freedom exhibits. Returning to where we had entered the building, we stopped briefly at a black granite wall carved with the 171 names of fallen civilian and military cryptologists. "They served in silence," the accompanying plaque read. We passed an elevator bank, which had a wraparound stenciled banner at the top of the walls repeating the phrase "Defending Our Nation/Securing the Future." No small mission for this place. The halls had mysterious directional signs like "2B1016–2B1018," which became less mysterious after we learned that, like those at MIT, the buildings at NSA headquarters have only numbers, no names.

Our briefings took place in the NSA Central Security Service, or NSA/CSS. The secure doors to the NSA/CSS entrance were flanked on the right with inspiring quotes from Einstein ("We can't solve problems by using the same kind of thinking we used when we created them") and Galileo ("All truths are easy to understand once they are discovered; the point is to discover them").

Our host was Emily Goldman from the NSA Director's Office. A Stanford PhD in political science, she taught at the University of California, Davis, for twenty years before entering public service. In response to media coverage sparked by Snowden's revelations, she told us, her office was interested in getting the truth out. The Chatham House Rule would be the operative norm: in writing about our visit, we could attribute remarks to "an NSA official" or "a member of the NSA senior leadership" but not use real names—except for hers.

The room we were in had very imposing technology. There was a large screen on the far wall opposite the briefer and four smaller flat screens spanning the perimeter of the room for 360-degree access. Two panels in red letters next to the largest screen at the front of the room announced the security level as "unclassified."

A senior official who had worked at the NSA for twenty-seven years stood at the front of the room. She wore a turquoise jacket and spoke with an authoritative voice while slides flashed rapidly on all sides. With an intense staccato delivery, radiating an almost frightening competence, she determinedly repeated her talking points: The NSA is a law-abiding agency. It respects privacy. People confuse our capabilities, she told the group, with what we actually do. What they don't realize, she said, is that while the NSA is obsessed with security, it is equally obsessed with compliance. It answers to its "customers" and designs its "products" accordingly. Her reliance on business language made me wonder: what if I don't want to be a "customer"?

We learned that NSAW stands for NSA Washington, but there are also NSA/CSS branches in Colorado, Texas, Hawaii (Edward Snowden's point of entry), and Georgia. NSOC stands for National Security Operations Center, which monitors and oversees the missions across the five different locations. "It's important to integrate offensive and defensive approaches for optimal defense," she explained. Yet perceptions surely matter; I thought about how one person's shield can be another's offensive weapon. General Alexander is right, the briefer told us, when he says, "It's neither a choice nor a balance; it is and always must be both." In other words, we can and must have both security *and* privacy. It's not about balancing. It's not about choosing.

And who better to get that tricky matter right than the innovative NSA? "The NSA has more patents," our briefer told us, "than the rest of the entire intelligence community combined," as well as the highest number of government badge researchers. The compression techniques that made CD technology possible were first developed at the NSA. Employees swear an oath of allegiance to the Constitution before beginning their service. Emily Goldman interjected that the president had called for a national conversation on privacy and security. "This meeting is part of that agenda," she said. An agency on task, the NSA was following the president's lead—at least, that was the impression conveyed by our briefers.

I was visiting at the right moment to learn something potentially useful. After Edward Snowden had made headlines, the NSA had reoriented its public relations 180 degrees, in large part because its leaders believed the public's negative perceptions of the agency were rooted in misunderstanding. The NSA had previously been so secretive that one intelligence expert, Stanford professor Amy Zegart, had commented that there were more courses on the history of rock and roll at America's top twenty-five universities than on the history of U.S. intelligence. Academics can't teach courses on subjects for which there is no information. Public education has grown all the more important because so much of America's critical infrastructure, which the NSA is tasked to help protect, is in private hands.

I was invited there, I thought, because the NSA has had to ask the American people to trust that it is implementing its rules well, even when there is evidence of sloppiness. Yet it is impossible to verify that the NSA is telling the truth, just as it is impossible to produce evidence that it isn't.

A highly ranked NSA official reminded us, "The Fourth Amendment isn't an international treaty." Spying on foreigners is perfectly legal under the Constitution. The Fourth Amendment doesn't protect foreigners, only Americans. The trouble arises when communication between a targeted foreigner and an American gives rise to "incidental collection." Then the NSA applies its "minimization rules" and protects the identity of those U.S. citizens on whom data was incidentally collected. "We have respect for privacy and minimization rules pounded into us from day one of our employment at the agency," the senior official told us. Another emphasized that "respect for privacy is baked into our DNA."

The courts have read the Fourth Amendment as requiring reasonable precautions to protect privacy. This standard does not require that the government show probable cause before it can collect information. Definitions of reasonableness are forced to change as technology advances. "It used to be we focused on proper acquisition," the senior official continued. "Now the focus is on what we do with what we acquire, and minimization procedures become critical."

Our briefers were supremely conscious that they could give us only unclassified information. It was clear that these classification gradations were sometimes difficult to keep at all times squarely in mind. One researcher, who had been with us all day, paused during his briefing to ask his superior, "I can go U/FOUO [unclassified/ for official use only], can't I?" His caution seemed to epitomize a highly rule-based work culture. I began to grasp that if I were looking for a ripe literary opportunity with dark plot twists and shady characters, I would not find it here.

Everything the NSA does is request-based, and the agency's comparative advantage is that people do not know exactly how it does what it does. That is why the 2016 hacks, which effectively turned the NSA's own cyber weapons against it, were so devastating.[45] Most requests come in the form of "We need information on topic X," and here metadata can be extremely useful. The NSA located bin Laden by zeroing in on the families of his couriers.

Through analysis of metadata, it was able to determine with whom these people were in contact. It searched records for years past and found phone numbers that linked back to al-Qaeda.

The NSA referred to its enterprise of post-Snowden damage control as "Media Leaks." At the time of my visit, it was cooperating with the FBI to devise a damage assessment and had fifteen hundred employees working exclusively on Media Leaks full-time. Those are people who would normally have been doing something else.

Since the Snowden revelations, our briefers explained, dozens of targets have modified procedures in response to what they learned. They have taken active steps to thwart the NSA's mission, changing both service providers and processes. Our briefers confessed that the NSA doesn't talk publicly about this because it doesn't want targets to know that the NSA knows what they are doing.

In a nutshell, the NSA was and is in an enormous public relations bind defending itself against Snowden's allegations, and intelligence agencies are, almost by definition, not set up to do public relations. Every time they communicate to defend themselves, they risk compromising what they do. That reality can be used as cover, to be sure, but it does not make the challenge any less real.

In response to the damage Snowden had done, one panel told us, private-sector providers of telecommunications are also doing different things. They are moving to encryption, which protects Americans and suspicious foreigners alike. It also adds greatly to the NSA's workload, so the net effect of Snowden's breach is that the NSA will have to spend up to three times as much as it formerly did to keep America safe.

At one point, looking around the room at the faces and demeanors of the NSA employees ringing our table, I couldn't help noting how appealing a group they were. They seemed refreshingly preoccupied with disinterested service in an era dominated by commitment to money and self-promotion. None seemed to have a chip on his or her shoulder or an embattled and under-fire manner. Rather, they seemed like people who knew they had an important job to do, from which Snowden was a major distraction.

Meanwhile, the discussion at the table had turned to authorities. The Authorities Integration Group was founded in 2012 to be

sure that authorities (that is, authorizations) were being applied in
consistent fashion. Each authority comes with its own set of procedures. Our briefers attempted to explain to us how it all works, but
their description of how they navigate "a complex regulated area"
was impenetrable for the uninitiated. Part of the problem is that
the technology is so sophisticated that its appropriate regulation is
hard to render in simple terms. I couldn't begin to reproduce it
here. President Obama, after sitting through a highly technical and
jargon-filled presentation on how to deal with the Snowden leaks,
is said to have asked NSA director Alexander if he could explain it
again, "this time in English."[46] There isn't a person on the planet
who could describe how the NSA protects the privacy of Americans in a dragnet surveillance world in terms your or my grand-
mother could understand. This basically means the NSA's public
relations challenges will be never-ending.

Despite this difficulty, spending a day hearing the NSA describe what it does did help dispel some of my suspicions. Here I
am not alone. University of Chicago Law School professor Geoffrey Stone, who was one of five people appointed by President
Obama to review NSA operations after Snowden's revelations, also
started his work with a skeptical attitude. But probing what the
NSA actually does transformed his perceptions. Stone is worth
quoting at length:

> I came away from my work on the Review Group with a
> view of the NSA that I found quite surprising. Not only did
> I find that the NSA had helped to thwart numerous terror-
> ist plots against the United States and its allies in the years
> since 9/11, but I also found that it is an organization that
> operates with a high degree of integrity and a deep com-
> mitment to the rule of law. . . . This is not to say that the
> NSA should have had all of the authorities it was given. . . .
> But the responsibility for directing the NSA to carry out
> those programs rests not with the NSA, but with the Exec-
> utive Branch, the Congress, and the Foreign Intelligence
> Surveillance Court, which authorized those programs—
> sometimes without sufficient attention to the dangers they
> posed to privacy and civil liberties. The NSA did its job—it

implemented the authorities it was given. . . . It gradually became apparent to me that in the months after Edward Snowden began releasing information about the government's foreign intelligence surveillance activities, the NSA was being severely—and unfairly—demonized by its critics. Rather than being a rogue agency that was running amok in disregard of the Constitution and laws of the United States, the NSA was doing its job.[47]

Around midafternoon in our darkened conference room, someone wordlessly opened a window shade on what had turned into a gloriously sunny day. The sudden light was startling. I exclaimed aloud, "Sunlight!" A faculty colleague added, "Too much sunlight for the NSA?" Without missing a beat, an official on the other side of the table replied, "Sunlight is the best disinfectant."

Intelligence community employees are raised in a culture of reticence, where providing no information is the best means of ensuring that no advantage gets compromised. "Classified material is off-limits for a reason," explained former NSA director General Keith Alexander. "It's not because we don't trust the American people and the good guys; it's because you can't just give it to the good guys without giving it to the bad guys."[48]

Secrecy thus prevails for three reasons. First, there are concerns about somehow inadvertently providing the enemy with the missing piece of the puzzle. Second, there is fear of exposing oneself to harm by being personally associated with an intelligence operation. Intelligence employees have no one guarding them, so anonymity is a means of ensuring security for their families and friends. Finally, there is the ever-present fear of embarrassment, of inadvertently revealing something that should not be revealed, with career-ending implications.[49] Small wonder, then, that anonymity and secrecy are the coin of the realm. A corollary is that bending the truth is permissible if it throws the enemy off track.

To get a powerful sense of the importance of secrecy for national security, one need only visit the National Cryptological Museum, which is part of the Fort Meade complex. Before the bombing of Pearl Harbor, U.S. authorities were convinced they had cracked the Japanese diplomatic code, but Japan learned that the Americans had cracked it and exploited that information to ensure that the attack on Pearl Harbor was a complete surprise. When the enemy knows what you know, it can provide an enormous advantage. This worked to the Allies' favor in the battle of Midway, which was won in part through intentional U.S. disinformation. When you don't want your enemy to know what you know and don't know, complete secrecy is the best means of advancing your interests. When in doubt, information will be classified precisely for that reason. In such a world, there is no such thing as overclassification. "I think what people do is err on the side of caution," said former NSA director Alexander. "If you lose Enigma encryption without knowing it, for example, you lose the war. People think like that, and correctly so."[50]

The importance of secrecy in what the NSA does makes oversight a great challenge and makes it all too easy to confuse whistleblowers with people who wish harm to the United States. Yet even in the national security area, we need whistleblowers to keep powerful people honest and ensure that actions taken in the name of security are within the spirit and letter of the law. "The NSA deserves the respect and appreciation of the American people," Geoffrey Stone concluded. "But it should never, ever, be trusted."[51] To see why, we need look no further than the Snowden controversy.

CHAPTER SEVEN

Snowden

THE LEGAL FRAMEWORKS FOR navigating security and privacy were made obsolete by rapid technological change and the intelligence community's exponential expansion after 9/11. Laws that had been designed for a different era became ambiguous, especially with the extensive use of contractors. In this environment, a powerful and sprawling security state coupled with antiquated laws for overseeing its activities set the stage for conflict between whistleblowers and government. Edward Snowden was the perfect flashpoint. He had specifically targeted employment at the consulting firm of Booz Allen Hamilton because its national security contracts could give him direct access to classified information.[1]

The former CIA employee and NSA contractor Edward Snowden stole millions of classified government documents, and in May 2013 fled Hawaii for Hong Kong, where he carefully released a fraction of them to the journalists he had selectively chosen. Now a global media sensation, Snowden tried to make it from Hong Kong to Latin America with the help of WikiLeaks founder Julian Assange, who himself had engineered a massive release of classified information (stolen by Bradley Manning) to hand-selected journalists in 2010. Snowden wound up stranded in the transit lounge of Moscow's Sheremetyevo Airport, eventually secured political asylum, and resides in Russia to this day.

What exactly did Snowden reveal? The most obvious thing was the transformation in NSA protocols that had taken place since 9/11. But he also exposed a widening gap between American and European attitudes toward privacy rights. Since the United States controls much of the Internet's architecture, the NSA had unprecedented surveillance opportunities—and it had fully exploited them, much to the indignation of some of our European allies, who are less willing to trade privacy for security. Snowden also highlighted a conflict of interest between Silicon Valley, which wants to sell its products globally and not have them viewed as a Trojan horse for NSA snooping, and the U.S. government, whose intelligence gathering depended on exploiting unencrypted Internet communications, a comparative American advantage that no longer exists.

In siphoning off unprecedented amounts of classified information and selectively sharing it with the world, Snowden provoked a controversy that inspired two diametrically opposed interpretations. To some, his transgressions could never be justified. For others, the NSA was undermining democracy by bending the Constitution in ways of which the American people were wholly unaware. Was Snowden a leaker betraying his country? Or a whistleblower upholding democratic values? Could he be both?

Snowden pulled the curtain back on an NSA dedicated to keeping America safe by doing unprecedented things that were at the time deemed legal. But the verdict is not yet in on whether they were constitutional. With the massive security breach his secret sharing entailed, it was difficult to identify Snowden as a whistleblower as long as NSA activities did not seem to violate existing law. Yet his status changed in May 2015, when the U.S. Court of Appeals for the Second Circuit upheld a 2007 ruling that collecting millions of Americans' phone records had been an illegal misapplication of section 215 of the Patriot Act.

The Heist

Snowden started off at the CIA believing that leakers should be shot.[2] He left after his supervisor placed a negative note in his personnel file, which Snowden said was retaliation for pointing out a computer vulnerability.[3] After leaving the CIA, he took a job with Dell in Switzerland in 2009, where he began siphoning off classified information. Snowden told *Wired* magazine that his job at Dell was to sit down with the CIA's chief information officer and chief technology officer, who would give him their hardest technology problems, and it was his job to fix them.[4] He then took a job as a contractor for Booz Allen Hamilton in 2013, although it involved a significant pay cut (he said his salary went from $200,000 to $125,000), in order to have more extensive access to classified data.[5] Intelligence officials described him as a systems administrator, but Snowden told the *Guardian* he was actually hired as an "infrastructure analyst," a polite term for a hacker.[6] According to the *New York Times*, his final position as a Booz Allen contractor for the NSA in Hawaii gave him "unusually broad, unescorted access to raw SIGINT under a special 'Dual Authorities' role."[7]

This position gave him the perfect cover for stealing documents, since his job was to oversee a backup of NSA data, which requires copying documents en masse. He exploited seams in the NSA's security architecture to scrape top secret documents from the systems he was hired to manage (he was allowed to use a flash drive, something forbidden for other employees), but his biggest challenge was how to get his contraband into the right hands. He targeted Glenn Greenwald, then a journalist for the *Guardian*, whose work he admired. Having learned from the WikiLeaks saga that journalists were crucial for interpreting classified documents for the world, he needed someone he could trust to help him disseminate the right information while keeping the potentially harmful material under wraps.[8]

In a story that has since become legend, Snowden found his way to Greenwald in cloak-and-dagger fashion through documentary filmmaker Laura Poitras, who requested Greenwald's encryption key so that Snowden could send him something. Greenwald at that time had no idea how to encrypt anything, so Snowden sent him a how-to video tutorial. For Greenwald, who had no way of knowing whether his source was legitimate, it seemed like too much work to learn how to encrypt something for someone he was not sure was worth trusting. But when Snowden contacted him again with the same request a month later, he followed through with the information Snowden needed to send him materials under the radar.

What Snowden provided convinced Greenwald he was dealing with a real source and a real story, and that it was worth traveling anywhere to meet him. On May 20, 2013, Snowden quietly left his job and home in Hawaii for Hong Kong, where he claimed to be receiving medical treatment.[9] Greenwald and Poitras soon joined him there.

When he was finally able to examine Snowden's entire cache of materials, Greenwald was amazed by its meticulous organization, which must have taken months to accomplish. Each flash drive had an intricate filing system. Greenwald told *Rolling Stone*, "On the front page were, let's say, 12 files. You click on one of the files and there are 30 more files. You click on one of those files and there are six more, and finally you got the documents. And every last motherfucking document that he gave us was incredibly elegant and beautifully organized. . . . It's 1,000 percent clear that he read and very carefully processed every document that he gave us by virtue of his incredibly anal, ridiculously elaborate electronic filing system that these USB sticks contained."[10] A former NSA coworker told *Forbes* that Snowden was "a genius among geniuses" who "was in a class of his own," and for that reason was given full administrator privileges, with virtually unlimited access to NSA data.[11]

Snowden was also highly aware of the need to protect his data. NSA deputy director Rick Ledgett told CBS News that Snowden would work at his computer under a hood that covered both the screen and his head and shoulders, so that no one could see what he was doing.[12]

The thumb drive of clandestine documents that Snowden passed on to Poitras and Greenwald had a read-me-first file that said, "Many will malign me for failing to engage in national relativism, to look away from [my] society's problems toward distant, external evils for which we hold neither authority or responsibility, but citizenship carries with it a duty to first police one's own government before seeking to correct others."[13] All of this was true, to be sure, and yet there was one complicating factor. Snowden had sworn an oath not to do what he did. Compared to the WikiLeaks revelations, the Snowden files were in a league of their own. Only

6 percent of the WikiLeaks documents were classified at the "secret" level. The Snowden files were all top secret or above.[14]

What Snowden's documents revealed, taken as whole, was the complete transformation in NSA operating procedures after 9/11. Before that date, the NSA's awesome power was explicitly not to be directed at U.S. citizens. But under President George W. Bush's secret executive order of October 2001, dragnet searches were permitted under approved conditions. What began as an emergency measure following an attack on American soil quickly became standard operating procedure. One of Snowden's documents, a 2009 draft NSA inspector general report, chronicles this quiet transformation.[15]

With Snowden safely beyond the reach of federal law enforcement in Hong Kong and his materials in the hands of the three journalists he had chosen—independent documentary filmmaker Laura Poitras, Glenn Greenwald, and the *Washington Post's* Bart Gellman—bombshell stories followed in rapid succession. On June 5, the *Guardian* released a top secret decision of the Foreign Intelligence Surveillance Court that ordered Verizon Communications to provide metadata on phone conversations within the United States and between the United States and abroad.[16] The following day, both the *Guardian* and the *Washington Post* revealed the existence of the PRISM program, which strongly encourages technology companies to allow the NSA to vacuum up email and social media data in real time.[17] And a few days later, the *Guardian* broke the story of BOUNDLESS INFORMANT, an NSA system that details and maps by country the voluminous information the NSA collects.[18]

On June 14, 2013, federal prosecutors charged Snowden with violating the Espionage Act. His actions in subsequent days seemed to confirm the accusation. On June 23, he got the Chinese government to allow him to fly to Moscow and then to somewhere in Latin America, despite American protests. WikiLeaks and Julian Assange sent a thirty-one-year-old British advisor, Sarah Harrison, to Hong Kong; she accompanied Snowden to Moscow and did not leave his side for months.[19] According to Assange, this was at Snowden's request.[20]

The United States revoked Snowden's passport while he was in transit to Moscow, leaving him grounded in Russia. He spent the next few days in the transit section of Moscow's Sheremetyevo Airport, waiting for the Russians to grant his asylum request. Senior intelligence officials and some members of Congress maintained that Snowden was able to stay in Russia only through a quid pro quo agreement that compromised American national security. Their case was strengthened when Russian defense lawyer and Vladimir Putin supporter Anatoly Kucherena visited Snowden several times in his airport no-man's-land, after which Snowden was given a visa.

All three of Snowden's handpicked interpreters have stressed the caution with which Snowden shepherded the documents he had stolen so that the public interest might be served. Bart Gellman told NPR that Snowden "gave these documents, ultimately, to only three journalists. What he said he wanted was for us to use our own judgment and to make sure that his bias was kept out of it so that we could make our own judgment about what was newsworthy and important for the public to know. And he said we should also consider how to avoid harm."[21] In May 2013, before they ever met face-to-face, Snowden told Gellman, "I understand that I will be made to suffer for my actions, and that the return of this information to the public marks my end."[22]

Many administration officials insisted, however, that by revealing clandestine programs, Snowden seriously compromised U.S. intelligence operations. The documents he gave Gellman and Greenwald inspired stories about the NSA's interception of email traffic, mobile phone calls, and radio transmissions around the world. According to a running catalogue of leaks compiled by the Lawfare Institute in cooperation with the Brookings Institution, Snowden leaked at least thirty-seven times on classified intelligence tools or methods; he disclosed at least nine overseas bases for intelligence operations; on at least thirty occasions he leaked information about foreign officials and systems that the NSA has targeted; and he revealed at least nineteen Internet service providers and platforms the NSA has penetrated or attempted to penetrate.[23] None of these revelations bolstered U.S. security.

From his protected perch in Moscow, Snowden compared the NSA's powers to the British practice of issuing general warrants in colonial America. The FISA court, he told Gellman in a December 2013 interview, "is authorizing general warrants for the entire country's metadata. The last time that happened, we fought a war over it."[24] His critics wondered why he needed to steal so many files (some 1.7 million documents) if his interest was solely in blowing the whistle on NSA misconduct.

President Obama pardoned Chelsea Manning (whom we will meet later) before leaving office, but Snowden received no such treatment. The Espionage Act charges against him remain in place. In June 2018, Snowden reached his five-year anniversary of residence in Russia. He remains outspoken via Twitter, in April 2018 criticizing the "Russian government's totalitarian demand" to ban encrypted communications for Russian citizens.[25]

How Snowden Became a Whistleblower

Conducting research for this book, I was routinely struck by the polarization of views created by partisan definitions of whistleblowing. Our nonpartisan definition provides a better lens for viewing the critical issues: a whistleblower is an insider who has evidence of illegal or improper conduct and exposes it, either to the authorities or to the press. In government, misconduct is illegality or a violation of constitutional norms.

The national security community's zero tolerance for disclosure of classified information left no room for legitimate national security whistleblowing. In the broader public, suspicions lingered regarding excessive secrecy. Shared ground for a common dialogue about what is and is not whistleblowing, about which behaviors the law should reward and which it should punish, was hard to find in the Snowden case. Not surprisingly, his revelations inspired both sides of this divide to rise to defend or attack him immediately— rather than reserve judgment until more evidence was in hand.

To be a bona fide national security whistleblower, it is not enough to believe that one is exposing wrongdoing; one must actually do so. And here the matter of what Snowden actually exposed becomes contentious. According to Obama administration officials, the NSA's activities had been vetted by all three branches of government and were perfectly legal. A panel of presidential advisors had tacitly agreed that NSA activities were legal but that serious reforms were in order. The executive summary of the panel's final report

made no fewer than forty-six recommendations and urged President
Obama to rein in NSA data mining.[26] The president responded to
that advice in a speech on January 17, 2014 (the day after my NSA
briefing), agreeing that reforms were necessary but taking minimal
action. Days later, an independent executive branch board, the Privacy and Civil Liberties Oversight Board, reported that it could not
identify "a single instance involving a threat to the United States in
which the telephone records program made a concrete difference in
the outcome of a counterterrorism investigation."[27]

But on New Year's Day, 2014, the *New York Times* and *Guardian*
editorial boards had already proclaimed Snowden a whistleblower.
That description backed up Snowden's perspective, although at the
time it was premature. The evidence in hand that the NSA had operated illegally was not persuasive. But perhaps the *Times* and *Guardian*
had access to information that had not yet been made public.

Whether the laws permitting those NSA actions were constitutional is another matter entirely. Moreover, that something can be
done legally does not necessarily mean that it should be done. Although the *New York Times* and *Guardian* may have been too quick
to reach their verdict, the passage of time proved them right.

Snowden's status was ambiguous for some time. As we have
seen, leaks do not by themselves constitute whistleblowing. Actions
sanctioned by law and approved by responsible authorities cannot
be considered government misconduct. In leaking classified material to the world, Snowden broke multiple oaths of loyalty: to his
country, to his government, and to his employer. In so doing, like
Assange and Bradley (later Chelsea) Manning, he compromised intelligence sources in oppressive countries, many of whom could
have paid dearly when exposed.

Yet Snowden also unveiled a complete transformation in NSA
practices, sanctioned by all three branches of government, of which
the American people were entirely unaware. Some considered it
unconstitutional to institutionalize emergency wartime measures
as standard procedure. Breaking an oath to expose NSA practices
that the Supreme Court has deemed unconstitutional would become another matter entirely. But if the rule of law is to prevail,
constitutionality, like whistleblowing, cannot be in the eye of the
beholder. The Supreme Court has the final word. That's why the

debates over Snowden's significance proved so contentious. Both sides had compelling arguments, but the question could not be settled with the initial information at hand.

Snowden was thus a mere leaker, not a whistleblower, until the courts intervened to vindicate his actions. One of his chosen communicators, Glenn Greenwald, would counter, "If disclosing proof that top-level national security officials lied outright to Congress about domestic spying programs doesn't make one indisputably a whistle-blower, than what does?"[28] Here Greenwald was referring to director of national intelligence James Clapper's testimony under oath when Senator Ron Wyden asked him whether the NSA collected "any type of material at all on millions or hundreds of millions of Americans." Clapper replied, "No, sir . . . not wittingly." Greenwald had unlikely allies in Darrell Issa and other House Republicans, who also saw Clapper caught in a lie and demanded his resignation. Snowden has said that seeing Clapper mislead the public was his "breaking point"; he decided to leave Dell for Booz Allen three days after watching Clapper's testimony.[29] The Obama White House insisted that Clapper had not deliberately misled Congress.[30]

As long as there was no evidence that the NSA had violated constitutional norms, it was possible to contest Snowden's status as a whistleblower. But that is no longer the case. A federal judge ruled in 2007 that the NSA's collection of millions of Americans' phone records was an illegal misapplication of section 215 of the Patriot Act, and the U.S. Court of Appeals for the Second Circuit upheld that decision in May 2015. On June 2, 2015, Congress passed the USA Freedom Act, which put a stop to NSA bulk collection practices that the Patriot Act, it turned out, had never actually authorized, and adopted a new legal mechanism proposed by President Obama. Under that new regime, telephone metadata can be queried only when there is a "reasonable articulable suspicion" that the search term is associated with international terrorism. The results must be limited to two hops from the suspect rather than the original three.[31] Applying the two-hop rule, the NSA can query everyone who interacts with a suspect, and of that secondary group, everyone who interacts with a member of it. Future court decisions may provide additional evidence of the importance of

Snowden's whistleblowing, but the contribution he has already made is unlikely to be undone.

The NSA's lawyers never anticipated the 2015 court of appeals ruling. In July 2013, the director of national intelligence declassified the cover letters from the Department of Justice for materials that were sent to all members of Congress on December 14, 2009, and February 2, 2011. Before voting to reauthorize section 215 of the Patriot Act, the cover letters show, every member of Congress had access to a top secret document describing the bulk data collection programs that section 215 then permitted. That document itself has not been declassified, so it is impossible to assess it, but the cover letters make it clear that Congress was not voting in the dark.[32] Senator Wyden had requested that the details about the NSA's programs also be released to the public, but the Obama administration, deferring to the wishes of the intelligence community, kept the information classified.[33]

The court of appeals delivered its decision on May 7, just weeks before section 215 of the Patriot Act was set to expire and when Congress had legislation before it that was likely to end the government's collection of telephone metadata. To some, it seemed like an unusually political move for the judicial branch. According to former NSA general counsel Rajesh De, it is not that the NSA's lawyers got something wrong when they approved the NSA actions as consistent with the spirit and letter of section 215. Rather, it is that the court reversed years of decisions that suggested the contrary (something similar, the careful reader may recall, happened with STELLARWIND, thanks to Comey and Mueller). "Congress had reauthorized this provision twice," said De. "The Obama Administration went out of its way to raise the flag for Congress, saying you're about to vote on this law, make sure you understand what it entails. I don't know what else the executive branch could have done to ensure that Congress was fully aware of what it was voting for. And then forty-six judges had signed off on it after Congress had re-upped the provision twice." It is one thing, De told me, to render a judgment on the limits of the Patriot Act with a clean slate: "If I were the lawyer while the first petition was being presented and had to argue for the telephone metadata program that was authorized under this statute, I could very well see

myself having doubts as to whether we could win that argument."[34]
But that same authority looks very different after Congress has
twice reauthorized it and a few dozen judges have approved it.

In short, while the NSA was doing things that Edward
Snowden and some Americans disapproved of, our laws at the time
permitted them to do so. All that changed in May and June 2015,
and this change placed Snowden's actions and those of the purported NSA whistleblowers who preceded him in a new light.
While the NSA's surveillance programs had been authorized by all
three branches of government, the Second Circuit Court of Appeals sided with Snowden's judgment that the programs were unconstitutional. At the same time, Snowden also aided and abetted
unfriendly powers by disclosing classified materials. Yet it is difficult to deny that if he had not shared classified information with
the press, the sweeping changes in NSA practices would have remained unknown to the American people, and the reforms passed
by Congress would not have been thought necessary.

Did Snowden Act Alone?

Members of the intelligence community found it troubling that
Edward Snowden fled to Hong Kong and then found asylum in
Russia. That he retained a Moscow lawyer with Kremlin connec-
tions set off additional alarm bells. Why did he choose Hong
Kong, a place he had never visited, as the place to break his story?
Why is he now in Russia?

I interviewed Edward Snowden both publicly and privately in
March 2017. The Middlebury College Activities Board had invited
him to speak from Moscow via Google Hangout, and the student
organizers asked me if I would be willing to moderate. Since he
was controversial, they did not want the standard Q&A format but
instead wanted me to take a more conversational approach. They
negotiated a contract with his agent whereby I would be able to interview him for fifteen minutes privately as part of the sound check
for the event, and then continue with a public interview followed
by audience questions.

In both the private interview and the public one, Snowden was
relaxed and forthcoming, despite acknowledging (when I asked

him directly) that our conversation was no doubt being monitored. "We are not safe and secure here," he said. "Google stores a copy of our conversation, and Google participates in the PRISM program. There is a warrant out for my arrest, so yeah, they are getting a copy through PRISM."[35]

Because it generates the appearance that he has been compromised and is cooperating with the Russians, Snowden is uncomfortable with his new home, which he says he did not choose. During our private sound check before the public interview, he asked if the student organizers introducing him could avoid mentioning his Moscow location. They obliged.

According to one of Snowden's attorneys, Jesselyn Radack, the involvement of Russia and China in Snowden's flight path is simple to understand: "There are only two countries on the planet that really have the muscle to stand up to the US—China and Russia."[36] NSA whistleblower Bill Binney gave a more precise reason: "A lot of places have extradition treaties with the United States. China and Russia are two that don't."[37] One could argue that Snowden was exploiting a legal loophole in choosing Hong Kong, which has a 1996 extradition treaty with the United States that predates its absorption by mainland China. China and the United States have no such treaty. That legal ambiguity could conceivably have provided him with some protection. It could also explain why China would permit Snowden to leave Hong Kong for Moscow, since turning him over to the United States would have been tantamount to public acknowledgment of Hong Kong's sovereignty in certain matters.

According to Glenn Greenwald, Snowden chose Hong Kong "to ensure his physical safety from US interference as he worked with me and Laura on the documents; Hong Kong, he felt, provided the best mix of physical security and political strength."[38] Binney concluded, "Snowden probably wanted to go someplace where they weren't going to extradite him while he figured the asylum piece out."[39] Snowden himself says he chose Hong Kong because "they have a spirited commitment to free speech and the right of political dissent," and because he believed the city could and would resist pressure from the U.S. government.[40]

Many commentators have focused on how Snowden wound up in Russia, which is easy to understand if you take Snowden's explanation at face value; he said he never intended to stay there. He was waiting to catch a flight to Havana when he learned the State Department had revoked his passport, leaving him trapped in the transit lounge. Thus it was the State Department, he says, that put him in Russia.[41]

What was his desired final destination? Since Ecuador granted asylum to Julian Assange, it seems a likely possibility. In 2014, Snowden acknowledged that getting asylum in Ecuador "would have been great."[42] On June 24, the day after Snowden got stranded in Moscow, Julian Assange told reporters that WikiLeaks had paid for Snowden's accommodations in Hong Kong and for his flight out.[43]

The journalist Edward Epstein repeatedly questioned where Snowden was between May 21, when he landed in Hong Kong, and June 1, when he was thought to have checked into Hong Kong's Mira Hotel. Snowden all along maintained that he had been camped out in the Mira throughout, so fearful for his safety that he emerged from the hotel "maybe a total of three times" for those first eleven days.[44]

Since many people in the intelligence community had focused on it, I asked Snowden about the missing eleven days. He responded, "This is a question I am glad you asked. . . . I want them to scrutinize my every claim, but then I want them to turn around and scrutinize the government." He warned me to be skeptical of tribal identity, as members of the intelligence community want to believe that such a large security breach had to be the work of a spy. "I think it is fair to say that the senior leadership of the NSA probably hate me a little bit."[45]

There was no concrete evidence to corroborate Snowden's claims at the time of our conversation, but the requisite documents magically surfaced five days later, when the missing receipts proving he had been at the Mira throughout were featured in a March 21 *Intercept* piece by Glenn Greenwald. The *New Yorker*'s Jane Mayer, the *Washington Post*'s Bart Gellman, and the *New York Times*' Scott Shane all tweeted Greenwald's article.[46]

So where was Snowden during that second ambiguous period, from June 11 to 23? We now know that his Hong Kong lawyer connected him with clients who were refugees from Sri Lanka and the Philippines, and that they sheltered Snowden undetected for thirteen days in a Hong Kong slum, where the authorities were unlikely to look, while a workable escape plan took shape.[47]

It is still not clear where Snowden thought he was going when he left Hong Kong. In Laura Poitras's documentary film *Citizenfour*, Assange enters the picture as Snowden's expeditor. In the film, he appears to be the person who orchestrated Snowden's flight from Hong Kong and tried to negotiate a private plane to get him out of Moscow. According to Snowden, what you see in *Citizenfour* is him trying to figure out his next move. "I didn't actually think I would make it that far. It seemed hard to believe, given the spying capacity of both the CIA and NSA, that I could succeed with getting from Hawaii to Hong Kong, let alone somewhere else from there."[48]

But why go there? General Alexander found Snowden's flight to Hong Kong highly suspicious, since Snowden had no prior connection to the place. If his aim was to get asylum in Latin America, why wouldn't he head there directly? "Somebody had to lead him in that direction," Alexander said to me. "Snowden claims to be a brilliant person, and it seems to me likely that someone led him fairly well by playing to his ego." Alexander feels it is clear what Putin was getting from Snowden by giving him a safe haven. "Just look at what Putin has done to other people," he said. "They're not going to let him sit in Russia for free. There has to be something in it for Russia."[49]

The insinuation that Snowden is a spy infuriates Jesselyn Radack. "I'm sorry if Keith Alexander and Diane Feinstein and Mike Rogers and even John Kerry are going to continue to try to perpetuate the myth that Snowden has to be a spy for either the Chinese or the Russians," she said. "I think they need to check with our own FBI here, which has determined that Snowden had no help from a foreign country."[50] On January 19, 2014, a senior FBI official told David Sanger and Eric Schmitt of the *New York Times*, "It was still the Bureau's conclusion that Snowden was acting alone." Intelligence officials quoted in the same piece had "no doubt" Snowden's stolen materials were in the hands of Chinese and Russian intelligence.[51] Yet if that were indisputably the case, why was there never a determination that Snowden was "an agent of a foreign power," a legal designation that is required before the government can gather intelligence on an American citizen abroad?[52] The NSA's new director, Admiral Mike Rogers, said Snowden is "probably not" a foreign agent.[53] Speaking in June 2016 as a private citizen after his retirement from the NSA, former deputy director Chris Inglis, who oversaw the internal NSA investigation of the Snowden security breach, said that he did not think Snowden was acting as a foreign agent at the time of his flight from Hawaii, nor was his intended destination either Russia or China. Rather, he thought Snowden had undertaken his action on the fly and didn't think it through.[54]

Taking Snowden at his word that he fled Hawaii as an independent actor, might it still not have been possible for the Russian and the Chinese to extract his data while he was staying in their respective countries? After interviewing Snowden in Moscow for fourteen hours in December 2013, Gellman is convinced that Snowden disabled his computers before going to Russia so that there was no possible way to extract data from him. In other words, Snowden threw out the keys. Gellman says he believes it, because Snowden led seminars for the Defense Intelligence Agency on data protection, so he would know how to keep his materials out of Russian hands, at least for a while, if that was his objective (anything that is encrypted can be decrypted if the code breaker is willing to invest the requisite time and money).[55] Snowden has said he destroyed the materials so that they would not wind up in the wrong hands before he left Hong Kong.

I tested this potential explanation on General Alexander, who pointed out that while he did a lot of self-education working with programs like TrueCrypt and anonymizers like Tor, Snowden was an IT specialist, not a cryptology expert. Alexander reasoned, "The Russians have really well-trained people. If they wanted to get something out of him, they could. They're not going to let him stay in Russia for free."[56]

The number of documents Snowden actually extracted is also still a matter of contention. The 1.7 million figure was frequently cited in the media, but Snowden himself claims he touched 1.7 million documents but took far fewer.[57] Snowden has acknowledged that he took both military documents, which he never intended to allow to be published or to get into the hands of U.S. enemies, and those that disclosed the massive surveillance capabilities of the NSA, which he did want published. But why did he take both types of documents if his intent was not to harm the United States or trade that information for protection? Was it simply that he had no choice but to vacuum up all that he could, knowing he would sort it out later and take the necessary precautions? Alexander still didn't understand why Snowden took so many documents if his motives were as stated. "There's a lot more to the story that leads me to be very suspicious about his intent. There's a lot that we don't know. I'm being very honest . . . there are too many things that do not add up."[58]

Snowden himself says he has "not disclosed any information to anyone other than responsible journalists" and also responds with a rhetorical question: why would a Russian spy get stuck for weeks in the transit zone of Moscow's Sheremetyevo International Airport?[59] He also pointed out that if he had negotiated any sort of quid pro quo with China, he would have flown to Beijing and stayed there, not to Hong Kong. "Hong Kong has an extradition treaty with the United States," Snowden reminded me. "Beijing does not."[60]

While being harbored by the refugees and pondering his next move, Snowden conducted two parallel negotiations through his Hong Kong lawyers, one with the government of Hong Kong and another with WikiLeaks. With respect to the former, Snowden asked his lawyers to feel out the position of the Hong Kong authorities on the U.S. extradition request. Word came back through a third party that Snowden should feel free to leave. Snowden was left to judge whether that message was reliable or trustworthy. He clearly decided to take the chance and had a lawyer accompanying him just in case the message from the government was disinformation. WikiLeaks filled in his remaining needs from there.[61]

Whom should we believe? Snowden's insistence that he acted independently and the evidence that exists to back that up seem to me persuasive, although the fact remains that we won't absolutely know for sure until years from now.

The NSA's Existential Challenges

Regardless of how one interprets them constitutionally, the Snowden revelations were a nightmare for the NSA. Culturally, the NSA was at an enormous disadvantage in defending itself. Having a public relations strategy was not something the NSA had ever had to think about. "It was definitely like a tidal wave," said Rajesh De. "It was unpleasant on so many levels. We were still very worried about the harm the disclosures had caused, so there was all this operational worry. Different things came out and often were wrong and sometimes a little bit right. Everybody was mad at us, all the time, everybody. I felt like I didn't have a friend in the world. Congress was mad. Even the people who supported what the agency does and didn't feel like it had done anything wrong were mad because they had been placed in a defensive posture. The White House was mad because [the revelations] had messed up the agenda of everything else going on. Everywhere you turned, it was somebody yelling at you for something. We were not prepared to deal with this, and that's frustrating because no one even had a game plan. It was long hours and very tough."[62]

While the rules governing any NSA program are highly complicated, there are basically three sources of authority for legal surveillance. The first is the now-retired section 215 of the Patriot Act, which formerly authorized the collection of telephone and Internet metadata. The NSA's metadata program is complex, and General Alexander himself conceded that no one person at the NSA understands all of its dimensions. In 2011, the FISA court slammed the NSA for improper filtering. In response, the NSA shut down the nascent Internet metadata program that deployed "pen registers" because it was too unwieldy and cumbersome to harvest metadata in bulk from U.S. domestic communications while adequately protecting privacy.[63] The telephone metadata program, however, proceeded full throttle. At a debate with Professor David Cole at Johns Hopkins University, former NSA and CIA director Michael Hayden emphasized the usefulness of metadata. "We kill people based on metadata," he said.[64]

Since the volume of data is overwhelming and it is hard to add staff in the post–Cold War political climate, the NSA has outsourced much of the analytical work to contractors.[65] Snowden was but one of a vast army of private contractors with top secret security clearances. A private company, United States Investigation Services (which also cleared Aaron Alexis, charged with killing twelve people at Washington Navy Yard in 2013), conducted the background checks for Snowden's top secret clearance.[66] The Justice Department sued United States Investigation Services under the False Claims Act for fraud. Its thirst for a positive bottom line led it to rubber stamp security clearances and vacuum up payment without actually investigating each case.[67] The company agreed to settle for at least $30 million in 2015.[68]

The second source of authority is section 702 of the Foreign Intelligence Surveillance Act of 2008, which established the Foreign Intelligence Surveillance Court and empowered it to waive the privacy rights of Americans under certain conditions. Section 702 authorized the PRISM program of legal intercept, as well as upstream collection. Both programs target foreigners who are in contact with Americans. PRISM does downstream collection: it obtains material directly from the servers of nine U.S.-based Internet companies: Microsoft, Yahoo, Google, Facebook, AOL, PalTalk, Skype, YouTube, and Apple. The NSA requests materials from companies for security reasons, and the providers have largely complied.[69] With upstream surveillance, the NSA collects materials by wiretapping the undersea fiber-optic cables that carry about 80 percent of global Internet traffic. The raw data can be queried only with FISC authorization.[70]

Section 702 had to be renewed by December 31, 2017, although Trump administration officials were insisting, just weeks short of the deadline, that warrantless surveillance would continue even if the law expired (it was renewed).[71] Such an ambitious surveillance program has had its fair share of compliance violations.[72]

Senior NSA officials, including General Alexander, repeatedly insisted that Edward Snowden did not have access to raw data (intercepted content that has not yet been reviewed and minimized), which requires FISC authorization to peruse, and that only a very limited circle of people could tap into that data with the requisite permission. There is no evidence to suggest otherwise. Yet Snowden did walk away with a large cache of documents confirming that the amount of incidental collection under section 702 of the FISA Amendments is staggering. In July 2014, thanks to a *Washington Post* four-month investigative study, we learned that Snowden did have access to FISA data that had already been reviewed and minimized to protect the privacy rights of Americans whose communications were incidentally collected. The *Post* found that nine of every ten account holders whose communications were intercepted were caught in a net the NSA had cast for somebody else. It also found that this method of tracking communications "led directly to the 2011 capture in Abbottabad of Muhammad Tahir Shahzad, a Pakistan-based bomb builder, and Umar Patek, a suspect in a 2002 terrorist bombing on the Indonesian island of Bali." There may have been other successes, but at the request of CIA officials, the *Post* withheld examples that officials said would compromise ongoing operations.[73]

Why is surveillance of telephone records a potential violation of the Fourth Amendment, while metadata analysis of social media and email isn't? Part of the answer is the technological differences in the communication media. When you make a phone call, you are communicating directly with another human being. When you use email or social media, you are also addressing others, but you have voluntarily uploaded your communication to the cloud. And once it is in the cloud, rather than on a computer in your home, you have effectively traded away some privacy rights for efficiency and consumer convenience.[74] For businesses, the move to the cloud widely expands the data available for harvesting and presents unprecedented opportunities for growth and innovation. From the government's perspective, the cloud is a gold mine for preempting terrorism. Because government and business have a shared interest in social and economic stability, the chances are very good that companies will deliver what government requests, unless they believe their cooperation will hurt profitability.

The third and perhaps most wide-ranging basket of authorities is Executive Order 12333, issued by Ronald Reagan in 1981. Promulgated after the Church Committee reforms had reined in domestic surveillance, 12333 underscored that foreigners were still fair game. It authorizes the MUSCULAR program, a joint effort of the NSA and its British counterpart, the Government Communications Headquarters (GCHQ), which siphons off data from fiber-optic cables as it crosses the U.S. junctions of global voice and data networks outside the United States.[75] MUSCULAR goes through the back door without permission, intercepting data around the world, without the knowledge of companies or section 702 authorization.[76]

In addition to the NSA-GCHQ partnership, the Five Eyes intelligence-sharing alliance of five Anglophone countries (Australia, Canada, New Zealand, the United Kingdom, and the United States) allows allies to trade intelligence that might be illegal for them to collect themselves but that falls into a legal gray area when it comes from a friend.

The vulnerable point for vacuuming data through upstream collection is at the switches in fiber-optic networks, and the overwhelming majority of phone and Internet communication passes through switches on American or English territory, regardless of where it originates. As one of the top secret slides exfiltrated by Snowden reveals, "a target's phone call, e-mail, or chat will take the cheapest path, not the physically most direct path. You can't always predict the path," but "your target's communications could easily be flowing into and through the United States."[77]

"PRISM is an end-of-day kind of transfer of data. The upstream collection program takes everything on all the lines, both telephone and Internet communications," Bill Binney explained to me. "Eighty percent of international communications travel through US switches, so this is a significant resource. But when you take in everything, you can't understand it all. That's why they issued the White House Big Data Initiative in early 2012. They solicited private industry to come up with algorithms that will go through those massive amounts of data to figure out what's important for people to look at. That's a direct admission that they can't handle all the data they're taking in. That's why they built Bluffdale, to handle all this new stuff they're collecting. And that's why they need these algorithms, because they don't have enough people to do the analysis, they couldn't hire enough NSA employees to do it."[78]

Despite the media focus on the PRISM program, Binney says, upstream collection is the larger and more all-encompassing surveillance effort.[79] One of Michael Hayden's greatest concerns about the Risen story exposing the Bush administration's warrantless wiretapping was the disclosure of America's enormous comparative advantage.[80] After the story broke, the Bush administration did everything it could to rebrand its new tactics as the Terrorist Surveillance Program in order to emphasize warrantless surveillance's importance for the war on terror.

The White House vouched for the legality of NSA programs, and bipartisan congressional watchdogs backed them up. For James Risen and Eric Lichtblau of the *New York Times*, the revelations showed the NSA had become "the virtual landlord of the digital assets of Americans and foreigners alike," but they saw nothing to suggest that NSA eavesdroppers have violated the law by targeting ordinary Americans.[81] And no one to date has filed a lawsuit challenging the constitutionality of the PRISM program, in no small part because "there is nothing in the story that does not reflect exactly what someone who understands the law of this area would have predicted."[82]

Snowden also shed light on the evolving relationship between the government and Silicon Valley. The nine technology companies that shared materials under the PRISM program usually complied with government requests for information. Did they have to do so? After the public outcry at their involvement, they certainly had to present it that way. The tech giants of Silicon Valley were compelled to cooperate with U.S. government requests for data, but their collaborative relationship turned confrontational in 2014, when Google and Yahoo complained that the NSA had intercepted some of their data (by tapping fiber-optic cables on British territory) without asking first.[83] NSA general counsel Rajesh De disputed the notion that Google, Yahoo, and others were not fully aware of NSA data collection.[84]

Both sides in this controversy were probably correct, but they were focusing on different programs. De was referencing warrant-based interceptions under the PRISM program; Silicon Valley was protesting upstream surveillance overseas under Executive Order 12333. "Overseas, if you're targeting terrorist communications and you want to collect it, you're authorized to collect it," explained General Alexander. "You don't have to go to the company to get it. If one of our sensors sees the suspect's name go by, they grab it. That's the essence of it. We say 'we aren't targeting Google, we're targeting the terrorists.' Google may respond, 'well, we'll teach you. We'll encrypt it.' My comment on that is, 'okay, you'll teach us. But many people will die.'"[85]

Absent other alternatives, the taboo on national security whistleblowing in the United States made future sensational leaks more likely. The burden of proof is currently on the whistleblower to persuade his or her superiors that the costs of the identified misconduct outweigh the security benefits. Since those whom whistleblowers have to persuade are generally supporters of the criticized policy, the risks of blowing the whistle without protection are too high for any prudent individual. Under those circumstances, leaking to journalists, who have clear First Amendment protection, will remain the chosen option.

Thanks to Snowden, Americans now know that the NSA's standard operating procedure was radically transformed after 9/11, and the questions his revelations raised led to further breakthroughs in understanding. We know that in our hyper-connected digital world, NSA activities can unwittingly violate other nations' privacy laws.[86] We know that the legal interpretation of section 215 of the Patriot Act is classified, so that the laws that enable surveillance are effectively secret. We know that the Privacy and Civil Liberties Board, a group authorized by Congress in 2007 to ensure privacy safeguards, did not get a full-time chairman until May 2013, and as of June 2013 had met with President Obama exactly once. We know that nine of ten Internet users whose communications were vacuumed up by the NSA were not targeted foreigners.[87] We know America's ownership of the Internet's architecture, which gives the NSA unprecedented surveillance advantages, also generates enormous resentment. In short, Snowden's leaks may have been a crime that the administration had to prosecute, but he started a debate the country desperately needed to have.[88] But he also ended an era of cybersecurity dominance for the NSA.

Could Snowden Have Stayed Home?

Could Snowden have "stayed home and faced the music," as many of his critics in the intelligence community think he should have done? Like many seasoned intelligence veterans, former NSA director General Alexander believed there is more to Edward Snowden than meets the eye, in part because he was certain Snowden's disclosures did enormous damage to American national security. "I do think there's more there," he told me in reference to Snowden's moves. "I just don't know what it is. I don't think we'll ever know all of it. But if I were to pick the people who were the best at information gathering, honestly—it's the Russians. Just look at what they did in Crimea."

"Yeah, that was interesting how we were caught flat-footed," I said. "And there was some kind of real intelligence failure, it seems, on the part of the United States, as far as understanding what was happening there. Do you think there's any possible linkage between that and—"

General Alexander bristled at the words "intelligence failure." Our slowness in detecting Russian activities in Crimea, in his view, was a direct consequence of Snowden's revelations. "I wouldn't call them intelligence failures," he interrupted.

> I would say that Russia and others benefited from the leaks. So your ability to see what other nations and terrorists are doing has been damaged. That's not a failure. That's a problem with our entire system caused by Snowden. . . . If you give everybody 'here's how we'll detect you getting a bomb on board an airplane,' and you show that to all the bad guys, they will study it and say, 'look here, these two routes aren't covered.' And they'll shift their focus to those. In this case, I think it's the same thing. We gave them all the information about what we do and that's going to cost us. Remember Putin's KGB background. He knows the importance of secrecy and privacy and how to keep an operation really quiet so that others can't find it out. So I would say that what these leaks have done is made our ability to track the movements of other nations more difficult.[89]

Rajesh De believed Snowden had plenty of options for protest that he did not exercise. He could have gone to the leadership and the NSA inspector general. If that failed, he could have tried the Pentagon or intelligence community inspector general. If he exhausted those internal options and still got no satisfaction, he could have turned to Congress.[90] As President Obama put it in an August 2013 press conference, "There were other avenues available for somebody whose conscience was stirred and thought that they needed to question government actions."[91]

Yet the likelihood that the inspector general would condemn a policy that the NSA leadership had deemed vital, De admitted, is minimal.[92] The inspector general's function is not to mediate policy differences. Since these particular policies had all been reviewed by NSA lawyers and in some instances directly authorized by Congress, the inspector general would have been unlikely to find them problematic. The Department of Defense Authorization Act of 1987 states that any person who believes he or she has been subject to a prohibited reprisal may submit a complaint to the inspector general, who is required to investigate unless he or she determines that the complaint is frivolous.[93] Unless the misconduct exposed is illegal, charges are likely to be dismissed. "If you read the inspector general act, it says 'no one who goes to the IG will be retaliated against,'" explained whistleblower protection lawyer Stephen Kohn. "But there's no law to protect complainants. To put it bluntly, they left their employees barefoot and frightened. It's as simple as that."[94]

Former NSA deputy director Chris Inglis shared De's sense that Snowden did not exhaust the possibilities for lodging an internal complaint, and to his mind this precludes considering Snowden a whistleblower. "If you're a whistleblower, you have insider privilege, which comes with insider responsibility to take the extra care and time to get it right," said Inglis.[95] Snowden told the European Parliament that he complained internally to at least ten NSA officials before taking the course that he did.[96] But as the NSA public affairs department was quick to emphasize, he has offered no evidence to support this claim.[97] His one documented attempt to contact the NSA leadership followed his participation in intelligence oversight training designed to teach NSA employees how to protect and defend the U.S. Constitution while shielding the nation.[98]

In an effort to show that Snowden had made no real effort to file an internal complaint, the NSA released an email he sent to the NSA general counsel on April 5, 2013. In it, Snowden refers to training he has received and asks whether "executive orders have the same precedence as law." The general counsel's office wrote back three days later to say, "Executive Orders (E.O.s) have the 'force and effect of law.' That said, you are correct that E.O.'s cannot override a statute."[99] Snowden was thought to be asking about the hierarchy of laws governing NSA programs.

But there is an alternative explanation. Perhaps Snowden wanted to know if he had any chance of whistleblower protection. National security employees were explicitly excluded under the 2012 Whistleblower Protection Enhancement Act but given partial and ambiguous protection under Presidential Policy Directive 19. The NSA general counsel's reply that executive order cannot trump statute would have told him he had no such chance.

I had the opportunity to float this alternative explanation with Snowden. When he approached the NSA general counsel in April 2013 before his flight, was he trying to determine whether the more whistleblower-friendly executive order might supersede the distinctly unfriendly statute, which defined national security whistleblowing as a contradiction in terms? It was clear that he had thought a lot about how the existing legal apparatus might or might not protect him. He replied, perhaps unsurprisingly, that he had not been aware that any sort of whistleblower protection existed for members of the intelligence community. "I wish I would have been clever enough to have framed my emailed question with that in mind," he admitted with a smile, but he had not.[100]

So Snowden was not parsing his status before the law in the way I had imagined, but he obviously knew that staying in the country would land him in jail and keep the information his documents contained from ever being revealed. Given the sensitivity of the materials, it is hard to argue with Snowden's conclusion that he had to leave the country to get his message to the public, even though Dan Meyer believes he could have reported it through the DOD's intelligence oversight process and received whistleblower protection. "He should have come to me," Meyer said.[101] Speaking at Georgetown University Law Center in February 2014, NSA inspector general Dr. George Ellard also insisted, "Snowden could have come to me."[102] Ellard's credibility, however, was rather diminished in 2016, when he was fired from his job for retaliating against whistleblowers.[103]

To ascertain his likely reception, Snowden needed to look no further than the treatment of those who had challenged the transformation in intelligence practices before him. He would not have had much luck appealing to a Congress that had explicitly excluded national security and intelligence workers from the 2012 Whistleblower Protection Enhancement Act. As a contractor rather than a federal employee, his status was doubly precarious.[104]

None of the officials who maintained that Snowden had options articulated a compelling case for how Snowden would have survived the whistleblower process and sparked reform through the proposed channels. Avenues for complaining from within did exist, but the absence of prior successes would have given any thoughtful person pause. Jesselyn Radack laughed at the idea that Snowden could have stayed home and "faced the music." She called it a "fantasy" that Snowden could have received a fair trial. The 1917 Espionage Act, which was designed to prosecute spies, is now being used to prosecute those who leak classified information. Where classified information is involved, court proceedings must take place in secret, placing the defendant at a profound disadvantage and making it impossible for anyone to independently assess whether the trial was fair.[105] "When there is no public attention," GAP's executive president Louis Clark said, "everyone gets rolled by the national security state."[106]

The volume and intensity of the reaction against Snowden, both at home and abroad, show the extent to which Americans were unaware of what their government was doing behind the closed doors of classification, just as Europeans were unaware of their own governments' roles in collaborating with the United States. He became a lightning rod for partisan conflict. In September 2016, the House Intelligence Committee completed a review of the Snowden disclosures and announced that the federal government "will eventually spend billions" of dollars "to attempt to mitigate the damage Snowden caused." Without defining the term, the executive summary proclaimed that "Snowden was not a whistleblower" and also declared him "a serial exaggerator and fabricator."[107]

The truth is more complicated. Had Snowden not shared classified information with the press, the sweeping, perhaps unconstitutional changes in NSA practices following 9/11 would have remained unknown to the American people. Despite the unavoidable breach of confidentiality and the great damage his revelations may have caused, the conversation he initiated provided a public service. While his place in history has yet to be fully determined, Snowden could one day be seen as America's first traitor-patriot.

Small wonder, then, that surviving members of the 1975 Church Committee wrote an open letter in March 2014 calling for the convening of a twenty-first-century Church Commission.[108] For those original members, the sense of déjà vu was palpable, but they stressed that the Internet had intervened to raise the stakes as well as the scope of potential surveillance. "The scale of domestic communications surveillance that the NSA engages in today," they wrote, "dwarfs the programs revealed by the Church Committee." Daniel Ellsberg saw things similarly in January 2014: "Lack of NSA oversight is a crisis not only of personal privacy; it is a crisis of democracy."[109]

CHAPTER EIGHT

Malevolence

EDWARD SNOWDEN SAW HIMSELF as a whistleblower in the public interest, but his commitment to eluding prosecution while getting his message out made him look more and more like a spy. He said he was sacrificing himself while doing everything in his power not to be sacrificed. And perhaps most problematic, he wound up relying on Julian Assange and WikiLeaks to secure his political asylum in Russia, which created a whole new set of problems. At the time of Snowden's fateful choice, Assange seemed to be something very different from what he would later turn out to be.

The Problematic Evolution of WikiLeaks

The digital revolution transformed the possibilities for harvesting and leaking information as well as the playing field for whistleblowers. Boss Tweed's whistleblower William Copeland had to copy incriminating information by hand and Daniel Ellsberg used a Xerox machine, but Bradley Manning sucked everything he needed onto one Lady Gaga CD. The very ease of copying, in turn, made it possible to cast a broader net, vacuuming up anything of apparent interest and waiting until later to assess what one had. There was no longer any need to have specific wrongdoing in mind and gather evidence relevant to that concern. "I would come in with music on a CD-RW ... erase the music, then write a compressed split file," Manning told a former hacker, Adrian Lamo, who would later turn Manning over to authorities—after he had shared Manning's classified materials with WikiLeaks. "No one suspected a thing.... [I] listened and lip-synced to Lady Gaga's 'Telephone' while exfiltrating possibly the largest data spillage in American history."[1]

In its original incarnation, WikiLeaks was something wholly new: a site designed for whistleblowing targeted at corruption anywhere in the world. The optimistic values that animated the original WikiLeaks, expressed on its 2006 beta site (the test version of the site before its official launch), trumpeted a potential sea change: "We believe that it is not only the people of one country that keep their government honest, but also the people of other countries who are watching that government. ... We propose that every authoritarian government, every oppressive institution, and even every corrupt corporation, be subject to the pressure, not merely of international diplomacy or freedom of information laws, not even of quadrennial elections, but of something far stronger: the individual consciences of the people within them."[2] WikiLeaks was founded as an idea, and in the words of civil rights activist Medgar Evers, "You can kill a man but you can't kill an idea." The objective was to exploit the power of the Internet as a weapon of the weak and make anonymous whistleblowing easier to do.

In practice, WikiLeaks quickly focused almost exclusively on the United States. It made its first splash in 2010 with a series of high-profile leaks dealing with the United States. In April, Assange and his website posted a thirty-eight-minute video titled *Collateral Murder*, whose footage captured U.S. soldiers in an Apache helicopter killing seventeen Iraqi civilians and two Reuters journalists in 2007. Three months later, in conjunction with the *New York Times*, Germany's *Der Spiegel*, and Britain's the *Guardian*, Wikileaks released seventy thousand classified U.S. military documents on the war in Afghanistan, the largest leak in the history of the United States since 1972, when Daniel Ellsberg released the Pentagon Papers. In October, four hundred thousand U.S. military documents relating to the war in Iraq were shared with selectively chosen media organizations that carefully perused, collated, and occasionally redacted the information they had in hand before making it available to the public.

With the simultaneous release of classified diplomatic cables and war logs to the *New York Times*, the *Guardian*, and *Der Spiegel*, former Internet hacker turned activist Julian Assange became an overnight sensation. Some Republicans, including House Homeland Security committee chairman Peter King, wanted WikiLeaks prosecuted as a terrorist organization.[3] King's plea was unsuccessful, but it turned out that WikiLeaks did not have to be officially declared a terrorist organization to be treated as one. Businesses that processed payments from WikiLeaks were free to take matters into their own hands and deny service—and they did.

Assange is not an American citizen, so he could not be charged with violating the Espionage Act. With the Internet as his principal weapon, he demonstrated the possibilities of leaking that knows no boundaries or borders. A highly controversial personality, Assange was charged with sexual assault in Sweden. When his efforts to battle extradition failed in the British courts, he took up residence in London's Ecuadorian embassy in June 2012. Ecuador granted him political asylum that August, and he has been holed up there ever since, unable to leave because he could be arrested as soon as he walks out the door.

According to Ethan Zuckerman, a fellow at Harvard's Berkman Center for Internet & Society, WikiLeaks has moved through three phases since its founding in 2006. During its first phase, it operated on a standard "wiki" model. The website was created with the purpose of publishing sensitive information from any source or country. It offered whistleblowers worldwide the ability to anonymously post evidence of corruption or dishonesty on the Internet, in any language. The original idea was that the relevant user community would then collaborate—wiki-style—to interpret and provide the appropriate context for the revelations. The documents released in this first phase were more or less a straight data dump to the Web. WikiLeaks did very little redacting. A 2008 secret report by the U.S. Army, ironically leaked to WikiLeaks, declared WikiLeaks an enemy of the state and proposed ways to undermine the organization by passing on fraudulent documents.[4]

In phase 2, with the posting of the *Collateral Murder* video in April 2010, the standard operating procedures changed. This video was a political package, meant to shock the viewer and illuminate a particular political point of view rather than merely to inform. *Collateral Murder* is a work of antiwar propaganda, and by releasing it, WikiLeaks abandoned straightforward transparency. The edited final version didn't call attention to an Iraqi who was toting a rocket-propelled grenade, a fact that would transform the viewer's interpretation of American actions.[5] There was very little if any wiki in the WikiLeaks of this period. What prompted the change? WikiLeaks' founders had at first thought that simply disclosing controversial information would inspire political action. But they apparently found that the issues were complex, and providing the unspun evidence alone was insufficient. It needed to be given a narrative frame to trigger a reaction.[6]

In the third phase, members of WikiLeaks worked in close cooperation with a select group of mainstream media organizations to analyze, redact, and release cables rather than simply uploading them en masse to the Web or editing the materials themselves to present a particular political point of view. "The media consortium," writes Professor Alasdair Roberts, "provided several essential services for WikiLeaks. It gave technical assistance in organizing data, and provided the expertise needed to decode and interpret records. It opened a channel for communication with government officials which Assange himself was unable to establish. The consortium also had access to skilled legal advisors, and by becoming complicit themselves in the release of documents, helped to shield WikiLeaks against criminal prosecution. Finally, of course, these media outlets had the capacity to command public attention to the disclosures. They were trusted by readers and had a finesse in packaging information which WikiLeaks itself clearly lacked."[7] WikiLeaks thus served as midwife for more traditional news coverage, even though the source was a collection of documents controlled by the website's founder. This blurring of the line between WikiLeaks and the press ensured First Amendment protection in the United States. But in choosing this path, WikiLeaks had traveled a great distance from its original mission.[8]

Chelsea (née Bradley) Manning: Leaker, Not Whistleblower

Private Bradley Manning contacted the former hacker Adrian Lamo in May 2010 via instant messenger and email, claiming to be the original leaker of the WikiLeaks *Collateral Murder* footage. Lamo had gained notoriety in 2004 by hacking into the internal network of the *New York Times* and adding himself to the database of op-ed contributors. In a manner that would enrage many of his fellow hacktivists, Lamo gained Manning's confidence and soon had him discussing personal issues—all recorded for posterity via chat logs and email records. "If you had unprecedented access to classified networks 14 hours a day 7 days a week for 8+ months, what would you do?"[9] Manning asked in one of these chats. He told Lamo he had been demoted and was likely to get an early discharge from the army. And then he disclosed that he had just leaked over a quarter million classified embassy cables.

That revelation led Lamo to contact army investigators and turn over the chat logs. He had been a financial contributor to WikiLeaks and claims that he agonized over the decision but believed he had no choice. He thought that Manning, who said he had been using his top secret/SCI clearance to rummage through classified military networks for more than a year, had become a threat to national security. "I wouldn't have done this if lives weren't in danger," Lamo told Wired.com. "He was in a war zone and basically trying to vacuum up as much classified information as he could, and just throwing it up into the air."[10]

Both Assange and Manning had what might be called a big-tent approach to wrongdoing. Manning did not focus on gathering evidence of particular incidents of misconduct. His charges of wrongdoing were unspecific, and he seemed to view any confidential U.S. communication as direct proof of malice. His trial was supposed to be a public proceeding, but it was shrouded in secrecy, thwarting reporters' efforts to cover it properly.[11] Some materials were leaked, though, and from those we learned that Manning claims he first tried to approach the *Washington Post* and the *New York Times*. He spoke with someone at the *Washington Post* for five minutes or so, and it went nowhere. He called the *New York Times*

using the public editor number on the website and left a message
with his Skype and email address, but no one returned his call. He
thought about dropping by *Politico*'s political commentary office,
whose address he knew, but was put off by bad weather. He then
decided to turn to WikiLeaks, an organization he had been following for some time.[12]

WikiLeaks succeeded in getting media attention where Manning on his own had failed. Before placing Manning's trove of data
online, the *New York Times* carefully reviewed every document and
consulted with the Obama administration over what should be
withheld because of legitimate security concerns. According to then
New York Times executive editor Bill Keller, the administration had
three categories of concerns. First, it wanted to protect the sources
in repressive countries who had cooperated with American diplo-
mats. The *Times* complied with these requests and was grateful
when the administration caught things the *Times* had overlooked.
The second category involved sensitive American programs, usually
related to intelligence. The *Times* carefully considered each of these
requests, weighing whether the issue was a legitimate security concern. The third category involved candid cables about foreign officials and heads of state that the State Department feared would
strain diplomatic relations. Most of these requests were denied.[13]

The great care that was taken was ultimately for naught, however, because classified materials somehow made their way to the
public domain. How these documents got into unauthorized hands
is a matter of finger pointing on both sides. Assange claimed that
the mainstream media organizations were careless with the pass-
words; others blamed internal rifts within WikiLeaks. Assange's response was to publish the cables in their unredacted entirety.[14]

What wrongdoing or misconduct did the vast collection of classified documents reveal? Some argued that Manning's enormous
stash collectively exposed the high level of secrecy in American foreign policy as well as the vast national security state that the over-
classification of information enables.[15] But excessive secrecy seems
to fall short of obvious wrongdoing, although we might want to see
less of both. Opacity can mask corruption, but it clearly does not in
and of itself constitute misconduct. Rather, the picture of American
diplomacy revealed by the illicit documents is one of competence.

The cables are well written, engaging, and even witty. Foreign dictators are exposed as corrupt hypocrites, but the Americans assessing their activities are not. As Alec Ross, senior advisor for innovation to Secretary of State Hillary Clinton, told *TechPresident*, "It wasn't whistleblowing because whistleblowing reveals acts of official government wrongdoing. What the cables revealed was right doing. Twenty-eight months later, the State Department looks good and [Julian] Assange and WikiLeaks looks silly. Their view that there should not be secret information of any sort is beyond naive."[16] If Manning blew the whistle, then, it wasn't on the United States. Manning was a leaker but no whistleblower.

At a more granular level, the cables did demonstrate Washington's propensity to put a brighter face on its ventures than was warranted. They showed, for instance, that the casualty toll in Iraq from 2004 to 2009 was higher than what the Bush administration had shared with the public at the time. The United States turned a blind eye to some human rights abuses committed by the Iraqi police and army. The Obama administration worked closely with Republicans to protect Bush administration officials from criminal investigation in Spain for possible involvement in the torture of detainees. Americans were secretly involved in the conflict in Yemen.[17] In short, the cables provided evidence of clandestine activity, but they did not give clear evidence that some inarguable line had been crossed. Yemen was lying to its own people, but does that reveal the dishonesty of the U.S. government or the duplicity of Yemen's government? If the leaked documents revealed wrongdoing on the part of the United States, as Assange and Manning insisted they did, it was a debatable sort of wrongdoing.

It's also clear that the American people didn't buy the WikiLeaks argument that complete transparency bolsters democracy. The more the site disclosed, the more public opinion hardened against it. In August 2010, when the story first broke, 42 percent of respondents to an ABC News poll said that WikiLeaks' releases served the public interest. By December 2010 only 29 percent still felt that way. That month, a CNN poll showed that nearly 80 percent of Americans disapproved of WikiLeaks' release of diplomatic documents and military cables. Seventy-five percent of respondents to a CBS News poll agreed with the statement "There are some things the public does not have a right to know if it might affect national security."[18]

Nonetheless, both Assange and Manning clearly saw themselves as whistleblowers in the public interest, revealing wrongdoing of epic proportions. Manning repeatedly described his activities as whistleblowing. Assange even published a guide for whistleblowers.[19]

But intensity of belief does not validate that belief. While all those who reveal national security information are leakers by definition, not all national security leakers are whistleblowers. The harm done in making sensitive documents public must be weighed against the crimes revealed. When the damage is easy to identify but the crimes are not, the leaking cannot constitute whistleblowing, whatever the purported whistleblowers claim. Whistleblowing cannot be in the eyes of the beholder.

We need not decide whether WikiLeaks was justified in releasing confidential information, or whether Assange unfairly singled out the United States for scrutiny, to see that WikiLeaks exploited the Internet as a weapon of the weak. Its operative assumption was that transparency in a world of great power disparities is a prerequisite for both government and corporate accountability. Assange appears to believe that chipping away at secrecy through indiscriminate document dumps advances democracy. Writing from the Ecuadorian embassy in London, he told readers of the *New York Times* that "the advance of information technology epitomized by Google heralds the death of privacy for most people and shifts the world toward authoritarianism."[20] For Assange, such a world demands radical transparency.

Yet in national security and intelligence, there is an ethical complication: the matter of compromised sources. Careless redacting can kill people. The Pentagon's press secretary, Geoff Morrell, claimed in 2010 that the leaked documents continue to put at risk the lives of U.S. troops, their coalition partners, and those Iraqis and Afghans working with the United States by providing enemies such as the Taliban and al-Qaeda information on "how we operate, cultivate sources, and react in combat situations, even the capability of our equipment."[21] Members of Congress had similar views of the damage done.[22] Yet in a November 30, 2010, briefing, secretary of defense Gates described the impact of the WikiLeaks revelations in less dramatic terms: "Is this embarrassing? Yes. Is it awkward? Yes. Consequences for US foreign policy? I think fairly modest."[23]

There was also unusual collateral damage to public perceptions of the U.S. government. The State Department had warned its employees not to access any of the WikiLeaks documents, even from the *New York Times'* website, on unclassified computers at the State Department. Doing so would introduce classified information into a nonclassified environment, a security breach and a breach of work protocol. What employees did on their home computers was another matter entirely. That distinction somehow morphed into a general impression that the State Department would not hire anyone who had ever been on the WikiLeaks website or had read WikiLeaks documents on the *New York Times* website. State Department spokesman P. J. Crowley had to repeatedly correct that misimpression, which probably originated with Peter Van Buren, a former Foreign Service officer who claimed he was fired from the State Department for linking to a WikiLeaks document on his blog, and who cautioned readers about the State Department's crackdown on whistleblowers.[24]

From the State Department's point of view, once classified materials leave a classified network, the information has been irretrievably compromised. Any foreign intelligence service should be able to get its hands on the information, even if mainstream media organizations subsequently handled the materials with the utmost care. The State Department's perspective was ultimately vindicated in the case of WikiLeaks, as everything eventually wound up in the public domain. Despite being readily accessible, the WikiLeaks documents (and some of the Snowden documents) will remain classified for the foreseeable future. Were the State Department or NSA to declassify them, it would be tantamount to admitting that the materials never posed a national security risk, thereby bolstering the leaker in any legal proceedings he or she might be involved in.[25]

The speed with which the government and business disempowered WikiLeaks exposes as myth the idea of the Internet as a weapon of the weak. After the State Department cables were released in November 2010, Amazon Web Services, which rents out server space for storing digital information, quickly stopped hosting WikiLeaks' material, apparently after a call from Senator Joseph Lieberman.[26] That same day—December 1—Tableau Software, a small company that assisted WikiLeaks with its online graphics, stopped working for WikiLeaks. On December 2, the company that managed WikiLeaks' domain name, DNS.net, suspended its service, making WikiLeaks.org no longer operational. On December 3, PayPal announced that it would no longer process donations to WikiLeaks. On December 6, MasterCard severed its ties, and on December 7, so did VisaEurope. On December 20, Apple removed an app from its online store that allowed users to access the State Department cables on an iPhone or iPad. Assange called all of these moves "economic censorship." Businesses called it protecting their reputations and thus their bottom lines. When the hacker group Anonymous tried to retaliate by launching denial-of-service attacks on the offenders, it looked like a mosquito storming an elephant.[27] Government did not have to order any of this to happen. Businesses simply followed their own self-interest, which in this instance aligned with the government's.[28] In response to this corporate shunning, Daniel Ellsberg launched the Freedom of the Press Foundation in 2012 to enable donations to WikiLeaks. Edward Snowden would later join its board of directors.[29]

The crackdown on WikiLeaks demonstrated the power of business and government elites to neutralize and marginalize an entity they find unacceptable. The powerful stood firmly behind giving national security institutions the benefit of the doubt whenever controversy arose. The WikiLeaks controversy also illustrated the limits of self-defined whistleblowing. WikiLeaks was originally designed for whistleblowing targeted anywhere in the world, making it something wholly new. In theory, it was an anti-secrecy organization devoted to exposing uncomfortable truths regardless of national origin. In practice, it focused almost exclusively on the United States. With a consolidated bipartisan security state in which critical functions have been privatized, the balance of power was and is on the side of corporate and government interests.

Assange's Russia Connection

With their controversial institution deprived of Western financial and political support, Julian Assange and WikiLeaks sought new allies. Putin defended Assange repeatedly, and Russia issued him a visa in 2011. He found an eager partner in the Kremlin's main global propaganda outlet, RT, which hired him that April to host a new TV show. *World Tomorrow*, otherwise known as *The Julian Assange Show*, debuted on April 17, 2012, the five-hundredth day of the financial boycott of WikiLeaks, and it ran for twelve episodes, the last airing on July 3, 2012. Being on Russia's payroll no doubt helped accelerate the extradition charges that led Assange to take refuge in London's Ecuadorian embassy on June 19, 2012.[30]

RT's editor in chief visited Assange there in August 2013 to discuss renewing his broadcast contract. Russian media subsequently celebrated RT as "the only Russian media company" to partner with WikiLeaks, which had enabled it to access "new leaks of secret information." RT's sympathetic coverage of Assange gave him a strategic platform for denouncing the United States as well as a valuable ally in his battle to avoid extradition to Sweden to face charges of sexual misconduct.[31]

RT's coverage of WikiLeaks intensified in the run-up to the November 2016 U.S. elections. Here Russia found another useful partner in presidential candidate Donald Trump, whose calls to "lock her up" (referring to his opponent, Hillary Clinton) dovetailed with Russia's long-standing strategic interest in dividing the U.S. and Europe. On August 6, 2016, RT ran an English-language video called *Julian Assange Special: Do WikiLeaks Have the E-mail That'll Put Clinton in Prison?* as well as an exclusive interview with Assange titled *Clinton and ISIS Funded by the Same Money.* RT's most popular video on Clinton, which had more than 9 million views, was titled *How 100% of the Clintons' "Charity" Went to . . . Themselves.* Its most popular English-language video about Donald Trump, with 2.2 million views, featured Julian Assange and was titled *Trump Will Not Be Permitted to Win.*[32]

A declassified January 2017 intelligence report concluded "with high confidence" that Russian military intelligence (the General Staff Main Intelligence Directorate, or GRU) used the Guccifer 2.0 persona and DCLeaks.com to relay materials to WikiLeaks. The report also cited Russia's use of Internet trolls as well as RT as "part of its influence efforts to denigrate Secretary Clinton," with the net effect of amplifying stories on scandals (real or otherwise) related to Clinton. Putin's GRU, in short, partnered with or used WikiLeaks to maximize the impact of compromising information.[33]

Such a potent weapon for undermining Clinton's candidacy did not go unnoticed by the Trump family. On September 20, 2016, WikiLeaks tweeted at Donald Trump Jr. about an anti-Trump website it had hacked that was about to launch. WikiLeaks also provided the password for the private site and asked Donald Jr. to comment. He responded the next morning to thank WikiLeaks, saying he didn't know who was behind the attack on his father but "would ask around."[34]

Thus began a beautiful friendship. At no point during their Twitter correspondence did Trump Jr. ever question WikiLeaks' motivations or sources, even after it had published hacked documents from the Democratic Party and the Clinton campaign. On October 3, 2016, when WikiLeaks asked Trump to attack Hillary Clinton for criticizing Julian Assange, Trump Jr. tweeted back less than two hours later: "Already did that earlier today. It's amazing what she can get away with." Just two days prior, informal Trump advisor Roger Stone had tweeted, "Wednesday@HillaryClinton is done. #WikiLeaks." One possible translation of this tweet? On Wednesday, WikiLeaks will destroy Hillary Clinton's presidential quest. And on October 12, when Stone told NBC he had back-channel communication with WikiLeaks, WikiLeaks sent a private message to Donald Jr. recommending that Trump publicize the Clinton documents from WikiLeaks. Just fifteen minutes after that private message was dispatched, candidate Trump tweeted about those documents. He repeatedly praised WikiLeaks throughout the campaign.[35]

While WikiLeaks contacted Donald Trump Jr. far more times than he responded, what is remarkable here is Trump Jr.'s complete lack of understanding that it might not be wise for the son of a presidential candidate to be communicating publicly during the campaign with an organization actively allied with Russia seeking to undermine the opposing candidate.[36]

Regardless of its reasons for acting as it did, WikiLeaks' choices benefited Russia at the expense of the West. This does not necessarily mean there was active collusion, but Moscow knew it had a sympathetic ally in WikiLeaks, which it could count on to release damaging stolen documents.[37]

From the time Donald Trump announced his candidacy for president through his election in November 2016, moreover, WikiLeaks did not publish a single document critical of the Putin government.[38] During the same period, however, it published thirty thousand hacked emails from the Democratic National Committee and a slow drip of hacked emails from Clinton campaign chair John Podesta. Assange's 2016 book, *The WikiLeaks Files: The World According to US Empire*, also does not analyze a single leaked Russian document, focusing instead on "aggressive NATO expansion" and the U.S. government's 2011 "WikiLeaks fatwa."[39] The few remaining independent Russian journalists have spoken critically and on the record to the *New York Times* about Assange's pro-Putin spin, which directly endangers their lives.[40]

I asked Edward Snowden to comment on the reasons for Assange's pro-Russian leanings. He replied, "I wouldn't know. I don't talk to Julian Assange." He went on to point out, correctly, that WikiLeaks has published some documents that might be considered harmful to Putin's grip on power, such as hacked documents from the Assad government in Syria and documents criticizing Turkey's ruling party. While criticism of the United States is indeed most prominent, Snowden continued, that difference might have to do with a stronger American culture of dissent. It is noteworthy that people keep leaking highly classified U.S. documents, despite the high penalties (basically a life sentence, if prosecuted). "We have a qualitatively different culture," he said. "We still have that rebellious streak that led to the founding of our country." But he acknowledged that there is strong circumstantial evidence to suggest that some of these leaks are from hacks that can be linked to Russian state actors.[41] Assange has himself acknowledged the greater focus on American corruption, arguing that it is explained by WikiLeaks' English-language bias as well as the existence of "competitors to WikiLeaks" in Russia.[42]

We now know that Alexander Nix, chief executive officer of Cambridge Analytica (where former Trump advisor Steve Bannon was a vice president), asked WikiLeaks for help in getting thirty-three thousand of Hillary Clinton's deleted emails into the public domain. Cambridge Analytica is the data-mining and analysis firm that worked for both the Trump campaign and the Trump-aligned super PAC. Assange claimed he did not need to cooperate as he was fully capable of publishing the emails without Cambridge Analytica's help. Those deleted emails have never been published, but when WikiLeaks started publishing DNC emails stolen by Russian intelligence in July 2016, it prompted FBI director James Comey to launch a formal investigation of Russian electoral interference. Comey has said it became clear early on that Putin sought to help the Trump campaign because of his hatred for Hillary Clinton.[43] Assange has publicly acknowledged that he timed the release of the emails to do maximum damage to Clinton's prospects.[44]

For reasons that are not difficult to surmise, nobody seems to have approached Assange with the former British agent Christopher Steele's controversial file suggesting that Russian intelligence had secured *kompromat* (blackmail material) on Trump. Anti-Trump Republican Paul Singer had commissioned Fusion GPS during the primary campaigns to do opposition research on Trump. After Trump's nomination, when the Fusion GPS material was no longer useful for Republicans, the Democratic National Committee negotiated its own contract with the firm. The material that had already been gathered for Republican purposes was now available to Democrats. The privatization of intelligence made this both possible and legal.

Christopher Steele sent a memo to Fusion GPS in June 2016 that was followed by fifteen more between then and November. The June memo is worth quoting at length: "Russian regime has been cultivating, supporting and assisting TRUMP for at least 5 years. Aim, endorsed by PUTIN, has been to encourage splits and divisions in the western alliance. . . . So far TRUMP has declined various sweetener real estate business deals, offered him in Russia to further the Kremlin's cultivation of him. However he and his inner circle have accepted a regular flow of intelligence from the Kremlin, including on his Democratic and other political rivals. . . . Former top Russian intelligence officer claims FSB has compromised TRUMP through his activities in Moscow sufficiently to be able to blackmail him."[45]

That memo also referenced a dossier collated by Russian intelligence services over many years with material on Hillary Clinton that, unlike the Trump file, did not include any embarrassing conduct. In other words, according to Steele's contacts, the Russian government had potential kompromat on Donald Trump, but it lacked comparable material on Hillary Clinton.

In October 2016, just eleven days before Election Day, FBI director James Comey announced he was reopening the investigation into Clinton's use of a private email server. No announcement was made of the concurrent ongoing investigation into Donald Trump's Russian connections. Trump won the election, but the Steele dossier eventually made its way into the hands of Senator John McCain, who requested a meeting with Comey to ask what was being done. That meeting, on December 8, 2016, lasted all of five minutes. The dossier had to be turned over to President Obama.[46] Both WikiLeaks and Vladimir Putin showed no interest in misdeeds committed by the new American president, a sharp contrast to their keen shared interest in denigrating all previous American presidents. As for the lame duck Obama administration, it had first thought that Russia's goal was to undermine American democracy, but many in the intelligence community concluded a week after the election that the ultimate aim had been to make Donald Trump president.[47] Foreign intervention in American elections was a red flag for any FBI director. This fact was not lost on the future whistleblower James Comey.

Snowden, unlike Assange, has repeatedly criticized Putin on Twitter, despite living in Moscow.[48] He has also never shared material with WikiLeaks. He acknowledges that he has been approached by the FSB but insists he has given it nothing.[49] Since early 2016, he has served as president of the Freedom of the Press Foundation, whose mission is to equip media to do their job when state-sponsored hackers and government surveillance threaten traditional investigative journalism. He receives no salary and donates all his speaking fees to the foundation, which is the creation of Laura Poitras and Glenn Greenwald. The foundation's biggest accomplishment to date has been to champion a Tor-based system (Tor is software that allows you to surf the Web anonymously) called Secure Drop for harvesting leaked materials and news tips. Aaron Swartz, an advocate of the free exchange of ideas and cofounder of the social media site Reddit, conceived Secure Drop.[50] It has been adopted by many outlets, including the *Guardian*, the *New York Times*, and the *Washington Post*. Secure Drop was used to upload the leaked *Access Hollywood* video in which Donald Trump brags about committing sexual assault.[51]

While there are things we cannot know about Snowden, it is fair to say that he has been brave in his public statements despite his dependence on Russia for political asylum. While President Trump has repeatedly praised WikiLeaks via Twitter, Snowden has criticized WikiLeaks for not redacting personal information, such as Social Security numbers and credit card information, in its release of Democratic Party documents in summer 2016.[52]

Assange has evolved from supporting the curation of documents so as to avoid harm to others to unflinching advocacy of radical transparency. He criticized the Panama Papers consortium, a rival leaks organization, for not making all the documents in its possession public, calling it censorship. "It is not the WikiLeaks model," Assange told the *New York Times* before the 2016 elections. "In fact, it is the anti-WikiLeaks model." Snowden responded by telling the *Times* that WikiLeaks' "hostility to even modest curation is a mistake."[53]

Patriotic Americans may feel ambivalent about Edward Snowden, but it is hard for anyone to like Julian Assange. In January 2017, he promised to turn himself over to the Americans if President Obama would pardon Chelsea (formerly Bradley) Manning, who was serving a thirty-five-year prison sentence for sharing documents with WikiLeaks. Obama did not pardon Manning, but he commuted her sentence to four months.

Rather than serving until 2045, Manning was freed on May 17, 2017, the same month that Sweden dropped all charges against Assange.[54] Assange then broke his earlier pledge to turn himself in, claiming the clemency for Manning was a bid "to make life hard for him."[55] He remained holed up in the Ecuadorian embassy, with British police poised to seize him for jumping bail and attorney general Jeff Sessions having pledged to step up efforts to arrest him.[56]

Beginning in March 2017, WikiLeaks began a weekly release of CIA hacking techniques, which prompted CIA director Mike Pompeo, who had been an admirer of Assange when Assange was subverting the Clinton campaign, to declare WikiLeaks "a nonstate hostile intelligence service often abetted by state actors like Russia."[57]

It is not difficult to see why Assange had to become a Russian puppet. There are now rival organizations that might curate what is released, and these include well-respected media outlets that currently use Snowden's Secure Drop for uploading materials. Assange has the ideal business model for an individual shunned by Western elites and beholden to the Russian government. Malevolent forces can hide behind the anonymity WikiLeaks offers, while Assange can ensure a viable revenue stream for his operation. Small wonder, then, that despite its proclaimed commitment to radical transparency, WikiLeaks survives on donations and does not disclose its donors.[58]

Conclusion
Why America Needs Whistleblowers

I am a sort of gadfly, given to the democracy by the gods,
and the democracy is a large, noble horse who is sluggish in
its motions, and requires to be stung into life.

—SOCRATES, IN PLATO'S *APOLOGY*, 30E

IF THE EXPERIENCE OF Donald Trump's presidency inspired
anything, it is a conviction that whistleblowers matter. As
I write this, the Trump team is suspected of multiple high
crimes and misdemeanors. The Trump-Russia collusion story
has three principal strands. Categorizing these strands so as to
frame the issues at hand says nothing about the probability of
wrongdoing. On that, we must wait for the investigation being conducted by special counsel Robert Mueller, and there is no point in
speculating on the outcome before the evidence is in. Yet tracing
the main lines of the inquiry illuminates the critical role that intelligence community whistleblowers are now playing in the defense of
the republic.

First, investigators must follow the evidence on multiple instances of possible collusion between the Trump family and the Putin
government. Were the prospects of a Trump Tower in Moscow, for

example, offered in exchange for the chance to have sanctions against Russia lifted? Was support pledged for Russian interests in exchange for Russian support in manipulating the American elections? Second, there is the pattern of Trump campaign operatives meeting with Russian spies, which is far from typical campaign behavior, since foreign meddling of any kind in the U.S. electoral process is illegal. Finally, and most directly relevant to the theme of whistleblowing, is the matter of digital manipulation of the political landscape using WikiLeaks and social media as an instrument of Russian influence. In all three areas, the Russians have a long history of searching for soft targets to turn to the service of their interests.

In December 2017, Donald Trump Jr. maintained that both the FBI and the Department of Justice were "tainted" with bias against his father. "There is, and there are, people at the highest levels of government that don't want to let America be America," he explained. "My father talked about a rigged system throughout the campaign. . . . And you're seeing it." Former NSA and CIA director Michael Hayden called Trump Jr.'s rationalization "an appeal to the heart of autocracy."[1]

Corruption and the Business of Surveillance

During the Cold War, the pursuit of national security at times threatened to overrun core American values, but the U.S. Constitution, upheld by the Supreme Court, ultimately reined in the excesses of the national security state and circumscribed the expansion of executive power. Even the Reagan administration—not known as soft on national security—took the Constitution seriously enough to appoint an independent counsel to investigate the Iran-Contra scandal. When America's principal enemy was another state, the lines between domestic and international security were clearly drawn and it was easier to distinguish enemies from friends. But when the major threat to American security became a collection of nonstate actors, appreciation of the valuable contribution that national security whistleblowers can make was dangerously diminished.

The attacks of 9/11, the 2001 Patriot Act, and the 2008 amendments to the Federal Intelligence Surveillance Act added more layers of lavishly funded government activity wholly hidden from the public eye. Unprecedented amounts of money poured into the NSA for contracts to wage the war on terror. The NSA, in response, expanded its outposts in Texas, Georgia, Hawaii, Colorado, and Utah as well as its campus in Fort Meade, which is now almost ten times the size of the Pentagon. The intelligence community was effectively given a blank check to do what it felt it needed to do. The number of private companies doing outsourced NSA work nearly tripled.[2] The NSA's ballooning reach necessitated changes in how its data and paperwork were stored and processed. Intelligence contractor Edward Snowden was able to exploit the seams in those new procedures to exfiltrate his cache of top secret documents.

The outsourcing of intelligence work turned surveillance into big business. The important role that Booz Allen and other private companies play in our security doubles the secrecy effect. First, the firms handle classified material; second, every contractor has to sign a confidentiality agreement to be employed. Government by contract blurs the line between public and private interests and renders legitimate the revolving door between business and government. As all aspects of national security work began to be outsourced, that door spun ever faster. In 2014, the Sunlight Foundation reported that the number of active lobbyists with prior government experience had almost quadrupled since 1998.[3] When an unprecedented percentage of taxpayer dollars fund government activity that is largely beyond public scrutiny and when there are enormous amounts of money to be made, the need for whistleblowers grows all the more compelling. Some mechanism is needed to keep powerful people honest.

Self-interested behavior in contemporary America has assumed new forms, but public awareness of the importance of whistleblowing has lagged behind. Boss Tweed skimmed money from the public till, bought votes, and rigged elections. But corruption in the second Gilded Age is not of the quid pro quo variety. It has instead become institutionalized as part of the game itself. Harvard professor Lawrence Lessig writes, "The great threat to our republic today comes not from the hidden bribery of the Gilded Age, where cash was secreted among members of Congress to buy privilege and secure wealth. The great threat today is instead in plain sight. It is the economy of influence, now transparent to all, which has normalized a process that draws our democracy away from the will of the people. . . . We have created . . . an engine of influence that seeks simply to make those most connected rich. . . . In a way that is hard to see (because so pervasive) and certainly hard to model (because so complex), lobbyists have become the center of an economy of influence that has changed the way Washington works."[4] Where men of means once bribed the government to get their way in the first Gilded Age, today, in many instances, bribes are unnecessary, because men of means *are* the government.

Donald Trump actively defines public service as a lucrative money-making device. Corruption in nineteenth-century America took three principal forms, all involving profiting from public service, with being served rather than serving. First, there were the extortionist profits prosecuted under the False Claims Act, such as the Civil War cases of contract fraud. Second, there was the greedy skimming that took place with public works in the Boss Tweed era. Finally, there were instances of kickbacks and insider trading, as the Credit Mobilier scandal illustrates. It is striking that Donald Trump insists that all three variants, once shameful when exposed, are instead perfectly acceptable business as usual.

It is not that large-scale corruption has shifted from government to corporations, as Boss Tweed biographer Kenneth Ackerman argued.[5] It is instead that government and corporate elites are no longer facing off against one another. They are now playing the same game. "There's no question that there's now more money outside the fully reported system than ever before," said Sunlight Foundation executive director Ellen Miller, who has focused on transparency for more than three decades.[6] Hollowed-out government by contract, which dissolves the distinction between public and private action, has rendered government's daily business wholly opaque and made influence peddling the accepted currency. Transparency International defines influence peddling as legalized corruption, which "skews decision-making to benefit the few at the expense of the many."[7]

The privatization of government power has institutionalized a corruption that is difficult to combat simply because it has become routine. President Trump fully exploited this changed milieu, which raises the stakes for American whistleblowing. Nobody expects the private sector to transcend self-interest for the common good. Private corporations are formed for the explicit purposes of making money; that is their obligation to their shareholders. Yet the assumption has been that this incentive somehow magically changes when private firms are hired to execute the aspirations of government.

It doesn't help that those who challenge the economy of influence find themselves excluded from its rewards. In his memoir, disgraced lobbyist Jack Abramoff, convicted of a felony because his influence peddling crossed the line into fraud and conspiracy, explained that the best way for lobbyists to influence people on Capitol Hill is to suggest that they might want to join the firm at the end of their public service career. "The moment I said [that] to them, or any of our staff said that to them, we owned them," wrote Abramoff.[8] When moving from government service to a position as a lobbyist or contractor has become a socially acceptable steppingstone to wealth, the question of who is overseeing and serving whom can have no clear answer.

As we have seen, America has erred on the side of excess before. A shared sense that things had gone awry prompted an adjustment, the Progressive movement, after the first Gilded Age. But America's second Gilded Age has different contours, in part because the privatization of government has blurred the line between public servants and private actors, altering the relationship between America's elites and its people. The first Gilded Age ended when Progressive government initiatives such as the federal income tax and inheritance tax checked the power of the private sector. In the second Gilded Age, reining in the insatiable appetites of the wealthy is no longer a straightforward proposition because the business of government has become, largely, business. "Monetizing" public service by joining the forces one used to regulate is standard procedure.

Not surprisingly, attitudes toward corruption in the first and second Gilded Ages also differ. When William Copeland exposed the Tweed organization, the public was outraged to learn what had been going on behind closed doors and stayed outraged until government responded with reforms or the courts delivered justice. Politicians and corporations were not supposed to benefit at the public's expense, and when evidence of wrongdoing was made apparent, retribution came swiftly.

Today, corporate excess is permitted as an inevitable outcome of the operation of free markets. Shamelessly self-interested behavior has become the new normal. "The Founders feared the corruption of the American republic, as did the Jacksonians," writes Stanford historian Richard White. "Gilded Age reformers decried corruption. Today, plagued by financial scandals, we seem both fearful of corruption and resigned to it. We seem uncertain about whom it hurts and what difference it ultimately makes. The Republic seems perpetually corrupted, but instead of being outraged, we are not sure it matters."9

The Consequences of the Internet Revolution for Whistleblowing

The Fourth Amendment requires government to explain to a court why it has a compelling interest in your personal information. It protects the contents of your laptop from illegal search and seizure, but once you deposit something in the cloud, you lose that protection. While there are some protections—emails, for instance, are treated like sealed letters—the Fourth Amendment largely ends where virtual reality begins. The constitutional fiction is that Americans are volunteering to share in this way, not being enticed or manipulated to do so. Cheap and powerful cloud computing has thus enhanced the power of the security state.

The NSA was able to exploit the ambiguity opened up by the Internet revolution to harvest new forms of data in the interests of security. According to NSA whistleblower Kurt Wiebe, "Writs of Assistance caused the Fourth Amendment to be written. We're back to Writs of Assistance with collecting data about everybody. And it's worse than Writs of Assistance because the King of England couldn't put a Redcoat in every house, which is what Internet surveillance does."10

Even if it makes sense to give the government a blanket right to intercept Internet communications to protect us from harm, from a technology perspective, opening a window for government surveillance also opens a window for malevolent forces. For example, it might seem that we could authorize the government to eavesdrop on conversations over Skype to allow it to hunt down terrorists before they can strike. But the technology by which the government could do this would also create wiretapping possibilities for everyone, including criminals. There is no way to have government surveillance without increasing the likelihood of parallel criminal activity. Every technology Washington might deploy in pursuit of security is also a potential instrument of abuse. The Department of Homeland Security, for example, is close to perfecting its Biometric Optical Surveillance System, which enables the "face scan." The system can be used to pursue terrorists, such as the Boston Marathon bombers, but it can also be deployed in ways that undermine civil liberties.[11] Swapping privacy for security might unintentionally make us less secure.[12]

The Internet age thus simultaneously strengthened and weakened the hand of whistleblowers. By rendering secrecy more elusive, it increased the opportunities for exposing the misconduct of the powerful. Yet it also provided new tools with which malevolent forces bent on dividing the West could manipulate the emotions of voters. When the information is electronic, it can be shared around the world, making it next to impossible to eradicate what had once been selectively distributed.

Media organizations can also exploit legal differences among countries. With the Snowden documents in its possession and ready to be analyzed, for example, the *Guardian* used its New York office and the American Constitution's First Amendment to elude Britain's Official Secrets Act, which punishes the press for leaking classified information. Readers in the UK were able to read stories online that could never have been published in the British print version. But as the cases of WikiLeaks and Edward Snowden make clear, under the existing balance of business-government power, massive data dumps create only a temporary illusion of transparency. While technology facilitates whistleblowing and the free exchange of information, it also enhances the tools by which the powerful can retaliate and protect their interests.

While it is certainly true there has been no major terrorist attack on American soil since 9/11, that does not prove that more secrecy always means better security. Indeed, there is evidence that controversial surveillance programs have not delivered. When the Privacy and Civil Liberties Oversight Board, an independent bipartisan committee in the executive branch established after 9/11, examined the NSA's metadata program, for example, it found no evidence of significant security benefits. After reviewing seven years of the NSA amassing telephone records, the board found only one case where the program identified a previously unknown terrorist suspect. Its report concluded, "We have not identified a single instance involving a threat to the United States in which the telephone records program made a concrete difference in the outcome of a counterterrorism investigation. Moreover, we are aware of no instance in which the program directly contributed to the discovery of a previously unknown terrorist plot or the disruption of a terrorist attack."[13]

A government report declassified in April 2015 suggested that the NSA's warrantless wiretapping and bulk data program were largely ineffective in thwarting terrorism.[14] The NSA itself admits that section 215 of the Patriot Act stopped only one terrorist plot, an $8,500 fund transfer from a cab driver in San Diego to an al-Qaeda affiliate in Somalia.[15] In their 2011 exploration of the security state's contours, *Top Secret America,* Dana Priest and William Arkin reported that their military and intelligence sources could not name a single instance in which the release of information had seriously compromised security. "On the contrary," they wrote, "much harm has been done to the counter-terrorism effort itself, and to the American economy and US strategic goals, by allowing the US government to operate in the dark."[16]

Former NSA director Keith Alexander, however, continues to believe that Snowden did real damage. "The harm to our country," he told me, "cannot be denied."[17] Yet the security fallout from leaks that revealed state secrets must be weighed against the benefits of public discussion of the decisions made behind closed doors. Domestic extremists have killed more Americans than jihadists since 9/11.[18] Logic suggests that if warrantless surveillance is justified in pursuit of jihadists, it should be extended to address the threat to public order from the extreme Left and extreme Right. Few would accept such an argument, as it clearly undermines citizen rights.

The implicit assumption is that elites can make the tough calls, but how can the public possibly know whether they are making the right decisions if the information is classified? Americans are asked to trust their elites to act in the interests of the nation rather than themselves, yet there are few mechanisms in place to ensure that elites remain worthy of that trust. Inspectors general within national security agencies are supposed to be independent watchdogs who protect whistleblower rights, but when statutes explicitly exclude those agencies from whistleblower protection, they cannot always function with the independence that a genuine watchdog organization requires. Our current regime provides an illusion of oversight, but reality is another matter.

In normal times, the intelligence community will always favor greater secrecy. Director of national intelligence James Clapper's prohibition of all media contact for the intelligence community in April 2014 was the logical culmination of a process that had long been under way. Yet normal times came to an end with Donald Trump's election. The Trump team, during the campaign, in the transition, and when in office, routinely flouted existing norms of conduct, process, and confidentiality. Leaks were the currency of the realm, with the commander in chief tweeting approval or rage depending upon how they affected him personally. Michael Wolff's instant best seller *Fire and the Fury: Inside the Trump White House* was a case in point. Wolff conducted interviews with the president and most of his senior staff over an eighteen-month period ending in October 2017. After the inauguration, the president encouraged Wolff to "take up something like a semi-permanent seat on a couch in the West Wing." No ground rules were placed on his access, and Wolff made no promises as to how he would report on what he had witnessed.[19]

The truth or falsehood of Wolff's account is beside the point for our purposes. What is clear from the lack of ground rules and the 24/7 access is that the Trump campaign and administration, taking cues from the president himself, were proud to be breaking all the rules and happy to share their revolution with the world. They neglected to realize that some of their actions sabotaged the rule of law and sense of fair play that were once cherished by all Americans. The intelligence community stepped in to preserve, protect, and defend the Constitution from an authoritarian president focused on building his brand rather than serving the American people.

The Intelligence Community Blows the Whistle

Upon his inauguration, Trump immediately dismissed attorney general Loretta Lynch and appointed the Obama administration's deputy attorney general, Sally Yates, as acting attorney general. Lynch had met informally with Bill Clinton at Phoenix Sky Harbor International Airport in June 2016, while the Department of Justice was investigating his wife. The meeting hopelessly compromised Lynch's integrity and forced FBI director James Comey to step in and oversee activities normally in the attorney general's purview.

It is impossible to know whether at some point Donald Trump in his own mind officially declared war on the rule of law or whether he simply never grasped the concept. In any case, the firing of Sally Yates stands out as a powerful indication of where the Trump presidency was headed. On January 27, 2017, with none of the customary vetting, the president signed a controversial executive order that banned travelers from seven Muslim-majority countries. As protests swelled nationwide, federal judges in Massachusetts and New York blocked the order.

Yates read over their arguments and found two particularly compelling. The first was that the preferential treatment the order gave to Syrian Christians was a violation of the First Amendment's establishment clause. Second, by banning entry to both visa holders and legal residents, the order seemed to raise serious problems with due process. Rather than resign to express her objections, Yates chose to speak out in defense of American constitutional democracy. "For as long as I am the Acting Attorney General," her statement read, "the Department of Justice will not present arguments in defense of the Executive Order, unless and until I become convinced that it is appropriate to do so." She was promptly fired.[20]

Writing in December 2017 as a private citizen, Yates clarified why she felt she had to challenge the president. Our shared values, she explained, define the rule of law as applying equally to everyone, with all entitled to its protection. Trump's executive order directly violated this conception, which "recognizes that our country's strength comes from honoring, not weaponizing, the diversity that springs from being a nation of Native Americans and immigrants of different races, religions and nationalities."[21]

The firing of Yates, and of FBI director James Comey a few months later, were salvos launched against the very idea of objective standards for evaluating truth and falsehood, the premise on which American constitutional democracy depends. "Our whole system falls apart when the citizens of our country lose confidence in the justice system and the Department of Justice," Yates told students and faculty at the University of Chicago in November 2017. "But almost from the very beginning [of the Trump administration] we've seen breaches of these rules and norms from the White House."[22] Yates at first thought Trump might learn on the job, but the long list of concerns she rehearsed suggests that this learning never took place. The rule of law was under siege, and the task at hand was to educate the public.

Yates was not alone in believing that we lived in exceptional times. Other prominent members of the intelligence community shared her sense that the White House was actively eroding public confidence in law enforcement. Responding to a tweet from the president denouncing those who criticize him as promoting "fake news," former CIA and NSA director Michael Hayden replied, "If this is who we are or who we are becoming, I have wasted 40 years of my life. Until now it was not possible for me to conceive of an American President capable of such an outrageous assault on truth, a free press or the first amendment."[23] Challenging the president's repeated denigration of the FBI after his firing, James Comey tweeted, "I want the American people to know this truth: The FBI is honest. The FBI is strong. And the FBI is, and always will be, independent."[24] After former national security advisor and Trump campaign advisor Michael Flynn pled guilty to lying to the FBI, Comey quoted from the Old Testament on Instagram: "But let justice roll down like waters and righteousness like an ever-flowing stream. Amos 5:24."[25] When a Trump tweet celebrated the ouster of FBI deputy director Andrew McCabe, former CIA chief John Brennan warned Trump, "When the full extent of your venality, moral turpitude, and political corruption becomes known, you will take your rightful place as a disgraced demagogue in the dustbin of history. ... You may scapegoat Andy McCabe, but will not destroy America. ... America will triumph over you."[26]

Like the president of the United States, members of the intelligence community swear an oath to preserve, protect, and defend the Constitution of the United States. Though their job in normal times is to work behind the scenes and transcend politics, when the president repeatedly impugns the integrity of our law enforcement institutions, fails to defend the electoral system, and undermines the values on which this republic was founded, the IC is left with little choice but to violate its own norms of conduct to defend the Constitution. That is why all former CIA directors back to Reagan publicly defended John Brennan when Trump revoked his security clearance in August 2018.[27]

The Mueller investigation was similarly committed to defending the rule of law and the pursuit of justice. It was ongoing because the Trump family and campaign had unprecedented ties to a foreign government that is an enemy of the United States. The Constitution specifies, "Treason against the United States, shall consist only in levying War against them, or in adhering to their Enemies, giving them Aid and Comfort." Mueller explored, among other things, whether the Trump family had given aid and comfort to Russia to advance the interests of the Trump organization.

As an obfuscation tactic, the White House in February 2018 authorized the release of a declassified GOP-drafted memo alleging misconduct by senior FBI officials in investigating Trump's campaign.[28] The Democrats then countered with their own declassified memo challenging GOP charges. Both memos were instances of partisan activity that distracted Americans from the real issues. FISA warrants can be obtained for any individual who is two hops away from a suspected enemy of the United States. For this book, I interviewed the NSA whistleblowers Edward Snowden, Thomas Drake, Bill Binney, and others. That puts me one hop away from individuals charged under the Espionage Act and therefore a candidate for surveillance. It should therefore come as no surprise to see individuals meeting with Russian operatives being carefully watched. The IC is just doing its job.

One reluctant to address the elephant in the room might respond by saying that claims regarding serious norms violations are of necessity subjective, and hence political. That verdict, however, presupposes a lack of sincerity on the part of the IC. It assumes that their patriotism is for public consumption only, a smoke screen for a more self-interested agenda. My experiences researching this book suggest that most IC members still believe passionately in American ideals (they surely aren't in it for the money) and are fighting for the republic. That is why more than eight hundred former DOJ employees signed an open letter calling on Congress to "swiftly and forcefully respond to protect the founding principles of our Republic and the rule of law" if Trump were to fire the special counsel Robert S. Mueller III or other senior Justice Department officials. Attorney General Sessions told the White House in April 2018 that the firing of Deputy Attorney General Rosenstein could lead to his own resignation.[29] If the IC were politicized and partisan, as Trump claimed, why did we not find a rival petition from former DOJ personnel standing up for Trump principles? Why do we find former CIA and FBI director William Webster, a registered Republican and Reagan appointee, arguing in the *New York Times* that Robert Mueller is just doing his job?[30]

In short, there is indeed a political judgment involved in arguing that extraordinary times demand extraordinary actions, but IC whistleblowing to defend the republic is nonpartisan. It only looks partisan from the vantage point of presumed normalcy.

Comey and Mueller earned our trust as whistleblowers when they were prepared to resign over warrantless surveillance during the Bush administration. Both proved their integrity by taking seriously their oath to preserve, protect, and defend the Constitution of the United States. The definition of whistleblowing that has been operative in this book is an impossibility absent a working conception of American constitutional democracy and the rule of law. Under both the Bush and Trump administrations, Comey's and Mueller's actions followed from these foundational values.

Understanding how whistleblowing has functioned in American history is essential for realizing the grave threat that President Trump posed to the American experiment. When President Trump asserts that the president by virtue of his office is incapable of misconduct or violation of the law, the truth is rendered a matter of perspective and whistleblowing on the president becomes an impossible proposition. Whistleblowing, after all, as we have seen, presupposes fixed notions of right and wrong, of legality and illegality, of truth and falsehood. In the absence of those clear distinctions, whistleblowing cannot exist, save as a partisan ideological weapon rather than a servant of truth.

For Donald Trump, whistleblowing is in the eye of the beholder; it is what denigrates others and elevates him. Trump's definition renders whistleblowing a valuable partisan weapon for
advancing his interests in a fake-news world where truth and falsehood are whatever Trump decrees. To say that the IC blew the
whistle on Donald Trump's abuse of power thus at first sounds like a
partisan appeal, but that is only when we allow Donald Trump to
define our reality. Illegal leaks that expose gross norms violations
that undercut the rule of law itself are neither partisan nor political.
They are patriotic. The president can't possibly be upholding his
oath to preserve, protect, and defend the Constitution when he is
tweeting that law enforcement institutions and the people who lead
them are corrupt partisans. Trump intentionally sowed confusion
among the American electorate, so that it, too, could confuse loyalty
to Donald Trump with loyalty to the country.

In his memoir, *A Higher Loyalty*, James Comey repeatedly
compares Trump to a Mafia boss. In *Making Democracy Work*, Robert D. Putnam delineates how Mafia justice fills the vacuum that is
created when the people have lost faith in their legal institutions as
enforcers of impartial justice. The Mob can rule only when the rule
of law breaks down entirely, making Cosa Nostra deals and coer-
cion the only means of successful contract enforcement. Donald
Trump's idea of governance thus mirrors the way in which a criminal corruption network advances its interests. Put another way, all
of Trump's self-serving actions reflect faithlessness to the American
legal order rather than partisanship. For those who have dedicated
their lives to public service, his abuse of power is a call to arms.

Since only Donald Trump conceives of the position as a political appointment, FBI directors serve ten-year terms. The FBI is
above politics and loyal to the Constitution rather than to a political party, as Comey points out in *A Higher Loyalty*, so the FBI director meets alone with the president only on rare occasions.
Barack Obama met with James Comey only twice before his confirmation as FBI director, once to interview him for the job and the
second time to inform him of his imminent nomination. At their
second private meeting, the president told Comey it would be their
last, since impartial justice requires an FBI director to be independent of the president.[31]

In contrast, in the short four months before Trump fired James Comey without informing him first on May 9, 2017, Trump met with his inherited FBI director without others present no fewer than four times (on January 6, 2017, to inform him of the Steele Dossier; on January 27, 2017, for a private White House dinner; on February 8, 2017, after meeting with chief of staff Priebus; and on February 14, 2017, in the Oval Office to discuss Michael Flynn). He also spoke with Comey four times by phone (January 11, 2017, after *Buzzfeed* published the Steele Dossier; on March 1, 2017; on March 30, 2017; and on April 11, 2017). Trump also sought out Comey to hug him publicly at a White House reception for the leaders of law enforcement agencies on January 22, 2017 (Comey dodged the hug but wound up instead appearing to get a public kiss).[32]

Because of Trump's disturbing and unprecedented attempts to secure Comey's loyalty to himself rather than to the Constitution, Comey leaked some of the contents of his Trump memos chronicling his interactions with the new president to the *New York Times*. Other IC leaks documenting the same behavior can be explained and understood in the same fashion. The leaking in February 2017 of some contents of Michael Flynn's December 2016 conversations with Ambassador Sergey Kislyak, which were picked up by U.S. intelligence, exposed potentially treasonous (another word for disloyalty to the Constitution) behavior on the part of Trump advisor and future national security advisor Flynn. Flynn had denied discussing the possible removal of Russian sanctions imposed by President Obama, and the leak revealed he had lied, leading to his resignation.

The contents of some of Trump advisor and future U.S. attorney general Jeff Sessions's conversations with Ambassador Kislyak during the 2016 campaign were leaked for similar reasons. Trump welcomed Russian ambassador Kislyak and Russian foreign minister Sergey Lavrov to the Oval Office the day after Comey's dismissal, barring the American press corps from covering the meeting, although the Russian state news agency was allowed to take pictures. In a surreal twist, Americans learned from Russian news sources that the president had disclosed classified information from a U.S. ally about an ISIS terrorist threat. The White House denied that Trump had divulged the information, but the president later confirmed it on his Twitter feed. The same rationale pertains to the leaking of Trump's March 20, 2018, call with Vladimir Putin, in which NSC officials, realizing that Trump never reads their briefing books, were reduced to writing "DO NOT CONGRATULATE" in capital letters on a note card to get the president to behave presidentially. Trump congratulated Putin on his victory anyway. Two days after the leak, a furious Trump fired national security advisor H. R. McMaster.[33]

Since the IC (CIA, NSA, FBI, Office of the Director of National Intelligence) assessment when Trump assumed his office was that "Russian president Vladimir Putin had ordered an extensive effort to influence the 2016 presidential election," the president's pattern of privileging the Russians in multiple contexts was a red flag.[34] It is not proof of collusion but the pattern certainly suggested something worth investigating, especially since it represented an enormous departure from the behavior of previous presidents and IC norms. "We in the intelligence world have dealt with obstinate and argumentative presidents through the years," former NSA and CIA chief Michael Hayden wrote for the *New York Times*. "But we have never served a president for whom ground truth really doesn't matter."[35]

To be sure, some IC leaks do fall into a gray area when viewed in isolation, especially those that expose a departure from norms of national security policymaking. For example, some of the leaked transcripts of Trump's early calls with foreign leaders revealed a shocking departure from the behavior of past presidents and a woeful lack of preparation for the leadership of the free world, but they do not rise to the level of whistleblowing. Yet the leak about the note card with "DO NOT CONGRATULATE" revealed more than strategic ineptitude. It pointed to Trump's loyalty to his relationship with Putin, rather than to his own White House staff, which bears an unfortunate connection to the potentially treasonous patterns revealed by other leaks. Put another way, in normal times, we might accurately evaluate individual leaks independently, but in extraordinary times, greater attention to context is of the utmost importance. We have parted with the American ordinary when the president openly defines treason as betraying him rather than the United States or the Constitution.[36]

What We Must Do

The story of whistleblowing in America illuminates three challenges that force Americans to consider who we are and what we
are committed to defend. First, there are limits to the amount of
opacity that healthy self-government can bear. Defending democracy from its enemies requires secrecy, yet democracy demands
that the people know what their government is doing. Excessive
secrecy can enable cynical elite manipulation of the American public square through the strategic deployment of information.

The ban on national security whistleblowing is an attempt to
cordon off a part of government as a place where secrecy can flour-
ish unencumbered to defend America, but that effort is not cost-
free. Yale Law School professor Bruce Ackerman has argued that
expanded presidential power (on which the growing security state
relies), rather than Congress, is the biggest threat to republican values today. "The triumphs of the presidency in the past," he writes,
"have prepared the way for a grim future. . . . If we are to understand our basic problems, let alone try to solve them, we must recognize that they are largely a product of the twentieth—not the
eighteenth—century."[37] Harvard Law School professor Yochai Benkler aptly characterized our current predicament: "The American
body politic is suffering a severe case of auto-immune disease: our
defense system is attacking other critical systems of our body."[38]

The second challenge follows from the realization that the
pursuits of security and of prosperity need not always be self-
reinforcing. Today the interests of some American technology
companies are at direct odds with national security priorities. From
Silicon Valley's perspective, Washington's quest for perfect security
challenges global businesses' ability to win customers outside the
United States. The news that tech titans had been cooperating
with NSA requests made many non-Americans think twice about
buying apps or technology made in America. In September 2014,
Apple responded by announcing that all new iPhones would have
anti-NSA encryption programmed into them as the default user
option. At the same time, the profit motive can come into conflict
with the requirements of democracy: Facebook's insatiable desire
for ad revenue allowed Russia to intervene in our elections.[39]

Looking ahead, more Silicon Valley challenges to both government security preferences and the integrity of democracy's public square are likely.

The third challenge illuminated by the paradox of contemporary American whistleblowing is the difficulty of fostering and encouraging public-interested elite behavior when everything has been privatized. Since 1945, there has been a vast expansion of the executive branch's surveillance and war-making powers, yet its regulatory powers have been undermined by privatization. We have outsourced some inherently governmental functions (systems administration, bearing arms to defend the U.S. government, some aspects of intelligence) that should be brought back in house. Doing so would also be fiscally responsible.

During a hearing of the Senate Select Intelligence Committee in January 2014, Senator Jay Rockefeller argued for rolling back the privatization of intelligence. He was especially concerned about President Obama's announcement that telephone metadata collected by the NSA would no longer be stored by the government because the private sector could be better trusted to safeguard our rights. That is a dangerous assumption, Rockefeller said, since nothing in the Constitution protects citizens from corporate invasions of privacy.[40] Now that some companies can track us more closely than any NSA employee, we may need a constitutional amendment to protect us from corporate encroachments on the rights of citizens.[41] Whistleblowers remind us that profit maximization and the public interest are often in conflict.

The spectacle of the intelligence community blowing the whistle on Trump's actions was unprecedented and yet wholly appropriate. Brookings Institution senior fellow in governance studies Ben Wittes captured Trump's long train of abuses:

- He has demanded substantive outcomes from investigations.
- He has demanded investigations of political opponents.
- He has raged against the norms that prevent these wishes from being fulfilled.
- He has attacked—publicly and by name—people who have acted honorably to defend those norms.

- He fired the redoubtable FBI director . . . for precisely the reason that James Comey was functioning as an inconvenient bulwark.
- He has harassed Comey's management team and demanded publicly their replacement.
- He has made the environment for those assistant US attorneys committed to their jobs so uncomfortable that one literally sat in my office and told me that he was going to resign because "I don't want to stand up in court anymore and say, I'm [his name] and I represent the United States."
- He has appointed an attorney general he specifically intended to protect him and go after his opponents.

Wittes rightly concluded that "this is banana-republic-type stuff."[42] Public servants have a moral obligation to call out such misconduct.

In *Just and Unjust Wars*, Michael Walzer argues that in cases of supreme emergency, when the very existence of the state is at stake, it might be possible to fight unjustly for a just cause. He cites the carpet bombings of Dresden and the dropping of the atomic bombs on Japan as examples of such. Walzer warns us to beware of the community that does not take full heed of the moral implications of invoking supreme emergency. After all, Adolf Hitler declared a state of emergency and suspended the Weimar Republic's constitution through the 1933 Enabling Act, unleashing the Nazi revolution. In contrast, Walzer cites the British dishonoring of Arthur Harris under Prime Minister Winston Churchill as an example of leadership that fully acknowledged the supreme danger in using immoral means, taking symbolic steps to put the community back on track after the war was won and the threat to democracy had receded.

Who was Arthur Harris? Harris was the leader of Britain's bomber command and an advocate and administrator of terror bombing. After the war, Harris did not win a peerage, nor do the names of the fallen members of his bomber squadron appear on the plaque honoring the fallen in Westminster Abbey. Fighter pilots, yes. Bomber pilots, no. Churchill's dissociation from Harris after the war had been won, Walzer points out, was part of a national dissociation to restore the moral universe that Harris had violated. Churchill needed Harris to do dishonorable things during the war for a higher cause, but he also needed to condemn Harris thereafter to reaffirm the values that the British people had temporarily overthrown.[43]

Donald Trump is currently waging an unjust war against American ideals and institutions. The IC is waging a just war to protect American constitutional democracy from the enemy within by blowing the whistle on the president's assault on the rule of law. All IC leaks are unlawful by definition, but when their purpose is to expose the president's private war against the rule of law, which is wholly consistent with his public assault on the constitutional order, they must be seen in a different light as nonpartisan whistleblowing in defense of the republic.

For the American intelligence community at the time of this writing, we are in an emergency situation. When Donald Trump celebrates his deep connection with a sworn enemy of the United States, he is involved in an unjust war otherwise known as treasonous activity. Trump was elected president by the American people, but his actions once in office betrayed the Constitution he had pledged to defend, upending the moral universe that is the American rule of law. When James Comey shared personal documents with the public about his alarming conversations with the president, he did something unprecedented. Opinions differ as to whether he violated the law in so doing. That dispute does not need to be resolved, however, to see that Comey was not engaged in partisan behavior. He was violating FBI norms in order to expose a dangerous man. He did so to wage a just war in the service of We the People.

The IC's unprecedented behavior is indeed a disruption of the moral universe that will quickly need to be restored to normalcy after Trump's presidency if the rule of law is to be sustained and fortified. Once President Trump has been dishonored by being forced out of office, either through impeachment, resignation, or free and fair elections, both his trespasses and the unusual behavior of the IC must be condemned to reaffirm those values that Trump sought to overthrow. In a state of emergency, a whistleblowing IC is a necessary evil, but it is not one Americans would be wise to tolerate for any extended period of time.

Once the Trump era is behind us, the intelligence community can be encouraged to make a symbolic break with the past by doing three things. First, Congress should put a stop to all warrantless surveillance of U.S. citizens. Its costs, in both financial and civil liberties terms, vastly exceed the benefits. There is no evidence to suggest that any form of warrantless surveillance stopped a single terrorist attack on American soil.[44] It is important to keep in mind that the intelligence community has emergency exceptions that can be invoked in the presence of an imminent threat, so the default position when Congress has not declared war should be to require warrants.[45]

Second, Trump's successor should pardon Edward Snowden, who broke the law to force Americans to ask important questions. If President Ronald Reagan could pardon Mark Felt for violating FBI procedures to bring down Richard Nixon, then a Republican or Democratic president can pardon Snowden. Nothing would more starkly highlight the differences between the defenders of democracy and those who worship at the altar of dictatorship.

Third, whistleblower protection should be extended in a security-sensitive manner to cover the national security agencies. As Fletcher School professor Michael Glennon writes in his book *National Security and Double Government*, "An unrestrained security apparatus has throughout history been one of the principal reasons that free governments have failed."[46] President Trump believed the security agencies should serve him rather than the Constitution. Enhanced whistleblower protection underscores that this is not the case. It would also have the virtue of broad political appeal. Both parties support whistleblowing, and no congressperson wants to appear to oppose it. Whistleblower protection could be a bipartisan wedge in a currently dysfunctional system from which many other democracy-bolstering benefits might follow.

Some may object that the risks to homeland security are too high to permit the employees of the intelligence communities to be treated as regular government employees, but these risks cannot be assessed in a vacuum. They must be weighed against the enormous damage to American democracy that results from acquiescing in the status quo. We must also consider the collateral damage to security when whistleblowers have no options but to leak to the press.

It's tempting to turn a blind eye to the paradox of whistleblowing in America and pursue security no matter the costs. There is a sentiment among many Americans today, consistently reinforced by the media, to accept police abuses if their purported aim was to keep the public safe. But to acquiesce in the paradox—to applaud the values of whistleblowers while letting their lives be ruined—is a terrible mistake. It would amount to sacrificing what we have been endeavoring to defend.

To embrace security's imperatives without questioning them is to give up on what makes the United States a moral enterprise as well as a political and economic superpower. While they may exasperate and provoke, whistleblowers are the bellows that keep the fires of justice and the Constitution burning brightly. They take realities that the powerful view as natural or inescapable and show that they are intolerable. In so doing, whistleblowers encourage all of us to think for ourselves. What could be more American than that?

Notes

Introduction

1. Kohn, "The Whistle-Blowers of 1777."
2. *Journals of the Continental Congress, 1774–1789*, 14:627.
3. "Definition: Whistleblower Protection Act," *SearchCompliance*, last modified November 2012, http://searchcompliance.techtarget.com/definition /Whistleblower-Protection-Act.
4. U.S. Merit Systems Protection Board, "Questions and Answers about Whistleblower Appeals."
5. Arendt, "On Civil Disobedience," 74.
6. Ibid., 96, 83, 76.
7. Author interview with Angela Canterbury, February 6, 2014; Worth, "Whistleblowing in Europe."
8. Wu, "What Ever Happened to Google Books?"; Michel et al., "Quantitative Analysis of Culture."
9. U.S. Securities and Exchange Commission, "Whistleblower Program: 2017 Annual Report."
10. Author interview with Stephen Kohn, February 13, 2015.
11. Sheryl Sandberg, "The 1992 presidential race was once summed up in a pointed phrase . . .," Facebook, December 3, 2017, https://www.facebook .com/sheryl/posts/10159569315265177.
12. There are laws that would appear to provide whistleblower protection to the intelligence community (e.g., The Intelligence Community Whistleblower Protection Act of 1998 and the IC whistleblower protections that were amended to the National Security Act), but they do not provide real statutory protection from retaliation. See Dan Meyer's 2006 testimony on the former: *National Security Whistleblowers in the Post–September 11th Era.*
13. Fulbright, "The Higher Patriotism."

14. Eisenhower, "Address at the Columbia University National Bicentennial Dinner."
15. Thomas Jefferson, letter to James Madison, January 30, 1787.
16. PricewaterhouseCoopers, "Economic Crime."
17. U.S. Merit Systems Protection Board, *Whistleblowing and the Federal Employee*; U.S. Merit Systems Protection Board, *Blowing the Whistle in the Federal Government*; U.S. Merit Systems Protection Board, *Whistleblowing in the Federal Government*; U.S. Merit Systems Protection Board, *Blowing the Whistle: Barriers*.
18. Author interview with John Palguta, February 12, 2015.
19. While sampling frames varied from year to year, making rigorous statistical analysis difficult, some general patterns emerge when scholars have attempted to correct for those sampling differences (none have yet extended the corrections to the latest 2010 study).
20. Reporting changes in 2010 make only a very rough estimate possible, but the trend clearly holds.
21. Author interview with Stephen Kohn, February 13, 2015.
22. U.S. Merit Systems Protection Board, *Blowing the Whistle: Barriers*.
23. Holden, "Whistleblower Woes," 35.
24. Ethics Resource Center, *National Business Ethics Survey*, 27.
25. Miceli, Near, and Dworkin, *Whistleblowing in Organizations*, 21.
26. U.S. Occupational Safety and Health Administration, "Whistleblower Investigation Data."
27. Earle and Madek, "Mirage of Whistleblower Protection."
28. See http://www.whistleblowers.gov/.
29. For a lucid tour of this kaleidoscopic world, see Kohn, *Whistleblower's Handbook*. The complexity has not stopped would-be whistleblowers from seeking assistance. Executive director of the National Whistleblowers Center Stephen M. Kohn told Alina Tugend of the *New York Times* in September 2013, for example, that he had seen a 30 percent increase over the previous eighteen months in the number of potential whistleblowers requesting referral to a lawyer. See Tugend, "Opting to Blow the Whistle."

Chapter One. Truths

1. Allen et al., "Slavery and Justice," 9; Waxman, "America's First Anti-slavery Statute."
2. A Multinational Enterprise.
3. Waxman, "America's First Anti-slavery Statute."
4. A Multinational Enterprise.
5. Enslaving an African.
6. Hopkins, "Manifest of the Brig *Sally*."
7. Nicholas Brown & Co., letter to Esek Hopkins, September 10, 1764.

8. "Voyage of the Slave Ship *Sally*: On the African Coast."

9. Hopkins, "Sales Record for the Brig *Sally*."

10. "Voyage of the Slave Ship *Sally*: The Middle Passage."

11. Brown, letter to Nicholas Brown & Co., July 17, 1765.

12. Millock, letter to Nicholas Brown & Co., November 25, 1765.

13. Allen et al., "Slavery and Justice," 22; Lemons, "Rhode Island and the Slave Trade," 95–98.

14. Madison, Debates in the Federal Convention of 1787, Wednesday, July 18.

15. Ibid., Thursday, August 30.

16. Washington, letter to Gouverneur Morris, October 13, 1798.

17. Allen, *Our Declaration*, 278–82, 281, 34.

18. Teachout, *Corruption in America*, 38.

19. Wood, *Idea of America*, 323.

20. Wood, *Radicalism of the American Revolution*, 99–110.

21. Wood, *Idea of America*, 66, 68–71; Nicholas Parrillo has argued that far from reducing corruption, the lack of salaries increased it, because people like customs officers and tax collectors made their incomes from the people whose activities they were supposed to regulate. See Parrillo, *Against the Profit Motive*.

22. Wood, *Idea of America*, 156–58.

23. Ibid., 32–33.

24. Wood, *Americanization of Benjamin Franklin*, 96.

25. Snyder, "NSA's 'General Warrants,'" 4–5.

26. Cuddihy, "A Man's House," 64–69.

27. Snyder, "NSA's 'General Warrants,'" 3–4.

28. Adams, letter to H. Niles, January 14, 1818, in *Works of John Adams*, 10:276.

29. Payton v. New York, 445 U.S. 573 (1980).

30. Greenwald, *No Place to Hide*, 3.

31. Bailyn, *Ideological Origins*, 89–90.

32. Ibid., 86–95.

33. Shugerman et al., "Brief of *Amici Curiae*."

34. Hopkins, *Letter Book*, 7–9.

35. Fowler, *Rebels under Sail*, 54–58, 108, 65. See also Daughan, *If by Sea*, 52–54.

36. Hopkins, *Correspondence*, 12–13.

37. Fowler, *Rebels under Sail*, 72–73, 96. For the letter issuing Hopkins's orders both general and specific, see Hopkins, *Letter Book*, 15–17.

38. Jefferson, "Outline of Argument."

39. Hopkins, *Letter Book*, 20–21; Fowler, *Rebels under Sail*, 98–99.

40. Daughan, *If by Sea*, 62.

41. Hopkins, *Letter Book*, 22–25.

42. Daughan, *If by* Sea, 60–61.

43. Explanatory notes on Jefferson, "Outline of Argument."
44. Adams, autobiography, in *Works of John Adams*, 3:65.
45. Jefferson, "Outline of Argument."
46. Explanatory notes on Jefferson, "Outline of Argument."
47. Adams, autobiography, in *Works of John Adams*, 3:67.
48. Hopkins, *Correspondence*, 59–60nn27, 28, and 30.
49. Adams, autobiography, in *Works of John Adams*, 3:67.
50. Hopkins, *Letter Book*, 30, 32.
51. Coyle, McGuire, and O'Reilly, *American-Irish Historical Society*, 222.
52. Lorenz, *John Paul Jones*, 106–7.
53. Jarvis, letter to John Paul Jones, May 21, 1777.
54. Coyle, McGuire, and O'Reilly, *Journal of the American-Irish Historical Society*, 219.
55. Adams, *Adams Papers*, 5:113–14n3.
56. Coyle, McGuire, and O'Reilly, *Journal of the American-Irish Historical Society*, 226–32.
57. *Journals of the Continental Congress, 1774–1789*, 7:204.
58. Ibid., 7:77–82.
59. Adams, *Adams Papers*, 5:196–98.
60. Franklin, *Papers of Benjamin Franklin*, 25; 247–48; Crawford, *Naval Documents*, 10:1068.
61. Hopkins, *Correspondence*, 24.
62. *Journals of the Continental Congress, 1774–1789*, 10:13.
63. Ibid., 14:627.
64. U.S. Department of the Treasury, "1600–1799."
65. Chafee, "Freedom and Fear," 411–12, 422.
66. Dry, *Civil Peace*, 65–68.
67. Jefferson, First Inaugural Address.
68. Wood, *Radicalism of the American Revolution*, 336.
69. Hopkins, *Letter Book*, 36.
70. Field, *Esek Hopkins*, 246–47, 249.
71. Mulvaney, "Providence Schools Sued."

Chapter Two. Corruption

1. For the sawdust-filled shells, see Jacob Howard, speaking on S. 467, on February 14, 1863, Cong. Globe, 37th Cong., 3rd Sess., 955.
2. Andrews, *Vanderbilt Legend*, 77–84.
3. Ibid., 82. See also 37th Cong., 3rd Sess., Senate Report 75; Cong. Globe, 37th Cong., 1st Sess., 1:584–86, 609–11.
4. *St. Louis Republican* in "Shoddy-Army Contracts."
5. "Shoddy-Army Contracts."
6. Soodalter, "The Union's 'Shoddy Aristocracy.'"

7. U.S. Department of Justice, Office of Public Affairs, "Justice Department Celebrates."

8. Haron, Dordeski, and Lahman, "Bad Mules."

9. Greenbaum, "Civil War's War on Fraud."

10. Katz, "Hall Carbine Affair," 109–10.

11. Helmer Jr., "False Claims Act," 5; statement of Senator Wilson, Cong. Globe, 37th Cong., 3rd Sess., 956,

12. Ting, "Whistleblowing," 249.

13. Johnston, "Putting an End," 1170.

14. U.S. v. Griswold, 24 F. 361 (D. Or. 1885); Mitchell, Senate Report No. 834.

15. Sylvia, *False Claims Act*, 48.

16. U.S. ex rel. Marcus v. Hess, 317 U.S. 537 (1943).

17. Sylvia, *False Claims Act*, 49.

18. Ibid., 55; Bernstein Liebhard LLP, "History of False Claims Act."

19. Foer, *World without Mind*, 111–15.

20. Eleanor Roosevelt Papers Project, "Tammany Hall."

21. Lynch, *"Boss" Tweed*, 66, 50.

22. RealClearPolitics, "Ten Most Corrupt Politicians"; Ackerman, *Boss Tweed*, 2, 20.

23. Lynch, *"Boss" Tweed*, xv.

24. Ackerman, *Boss Tweed*, 20.

25. Kolbert, "Fellowship of the Ring."

26. Lynch, *"Boss" Tweed*, 297, 300–301.

27. Hirsch, "More Light on Boss Tweed," 276–78.

28. Ackerman, *Boss Tweed*, 57–58.

29. Argersinger, "New Perspectives on Election Fraud," 686–87.

30. Ibid., 672. John F. Reynolds's case study of the Jersey City scandal also demonstrates the connection between changing electoral law and the possibilities for manipulation and fraud. See Reynolds, "Symbiotic Relationship."

31. Magee to Tweed, September 16, 1868, quoted in Hirsch, "More Light on Boss Tweed," 271.

32. Werner, *Tammany Hall*, 130, 134.

33. Ackerman, *Boss Tweed*, 128; Lynch, *"Boss" Tweed*, 361.

34. Hirsch, "More Light on Boss Tweed," 272.

35. Ackerman, *Boss Tweed*, 72, 114–23.

36. Adler and Hill, *Doomed by Cartoon*, 126.

37. Ellis, *Epic of New York City*, 347–48; Adler and Hill, *Doomed by Cartoon*, 127–29.

38. Ackerman, *Boss Tweed*, 187–88.

39. Adler and Hill, *Doomed by Cartoon*, 191.

40. "A. Oakey Hall Is Dead."

41. "Number Three."

42. "Tweed's Election."

43. Bartlett, "William M. Tweed," 668.
44. Adler and Hill, *Doomed by Cartoon*, 10, 126, 129.
45. Bartlett, "William M. Tweed," 647–88 (images 651–92).
46. Shear, "Tweed, William M(agear) 'Boss,'" 1205–6; Burrows and Wallace, *Gotham*, 1008–11.
47. Ackerman, *Boss Tweed*, 274, 286–87.
48. Tweed interview, *New York Herald*, October 26, 1877, quoted in Ackerman, *Boss Tweed*, 341.
49. "William Marcy Tweed," *New York Tribune*, April 13, 1878, quoted in Ackerman, *Boss Tweed*, 345.
50. Hirsch, "Samuel J. Tilden," 800–802.
51. Kolbert, "Fellowship of the Ring."
52. Williams, *Great and Shining Road*, 76.
53. Ibid., 80–81.
54. PBS LearningMedia, "American Experience."
55. Adams, *Chapters of Erie*, chapter 4.
56. Martin, *Behind the Scenes in Washington*, 258.
57. McDonald and Hughes, *Separating Fools*, 54.
58. U.S. Senate Historical Office, *Election, Expulsion and Censure Cases*, 189–95; Schultz, *Presidential Scandals*, 146–47.
59. "Obituary: Hon. Oakes Ames"; "Obituary: Hon. James Brooks."
60. McComb City Railroad Depot Museum, "Henry Simpson McComb"; Crawford, *Credit Mobilier*, 95–97.
61. McComb, "Correspondence."
62. Renehan, *Transcontinental Railroad*, 50.
63. Poland, "Report of the Select Committee."
64. Mitchell, "Buying 'Friends.'"
65. Schwarz, "Republic of Leaks," 16–18.
66. "Credit Mobilier Suit."
67. "Monster Corruption Fund."
68. Editorial.
69. Lippmann, *Drift and Mastery*, 19.
70. White, "Information, Markets, and Corruption," 19, 41.

Chapter Three. Treason

1. "Roosevelt in the *Kansas City Star*," October 1, 1917, 8, in Hart, *Theodore Roosevelt Cyclopedia*.
2. Tucker, *Marx-Engels Reader*, 488.
3. Pipes, *Communism*, 94–95.
4. See, in particular, Communist International, "On the Combination of Legal and Illegal Work."
5. Schenck v. United States, 249 U.S. 47 (1919).
6. Anthony, "Debs, Eugene V."

7. "Debs Arrested."

8. Debs, "Speech Delivered at Nimisilla Park."

9. "Debs Arrested."

10. "Find Debs Guilty of Disloyal Acts."

11. "Debs out on Bail."

12. Quoted in Zinn, "Eugene V. Debs," 16.

13. "Debs Loses Appeal."

14. "The Debs Decision."

15. "Debs' Sentence Confirmed by Supreme Court."

16. "Plan a Demonstration to Free Eugene V. Debs."

17. Constantine, "Eugene V. Debs," 31, 33.

18. Quoted in Kennan, *Russia and the West under Lenin and Stalin*, 196.

19. Quoted in Tucker, *Soviet Political Mind*, 233.

20. Robinson, "Routinization of Crisis Government," 161.

21. Hornblum, *Invisible Harry Gold*.

22. Haynes, Klehr, and Vassiliev, *Spies*, 1–14, 135–42, 541–48. It is worth noting here that the latest evidence suggests that Ethel Rosenberg should not have received the death penalty. She was "guilty of being Julius' wife." See "Figure in Rosenberg Case."

23. Klehr, Haynes, and Firsov, *Secret World*, document 1, pp. 22–24.

24. Klehr, Haynes, and Anderson, *Soviet World*, document 46, p. 159, document 42, pp. 149, 151.

25. Tanenhaus, "Gus Hall."

26. Brown, *Rise and Fall of Communism*, 96.

27. Isserman and Healey, *California Red*, 172–74; U.S. Federal Bureau of Investigation, "SOLO."

28. Klehr, Haynes, and Firsov, *Secret World*, 148.

29. Burr, "SOLO File."

30. Quoted in Schoenfeld, *Necessary Secrets*, 158.

31. Nader, Petkas, and Blackwell, *Whistle Blowing*, 26.

32. McCarthy's congressional career ended with his being censured by the U.S. Senate by a vote of 67–22. He died of hepatitis brought on by alcoholism at the age of forty-eight. Eleanor Roosevelt Papers Project, "Joseph R. McCarthy."

33. Halberstam, *The Fifties*, 253.

34. Weiner, "Hoover Planned Mass Jailing."

35. "Hoover Sees FBI as Reds' Top Foe."

36. "US Reds Go Underground."

37. U.S. House of Representatives Committee on Un-American Activities, *100 Things You Should Know about Communism*, item 62, 15.

38. Ibid., item 1, 95.

39. *Hearings regarding the Communist Infiltration of the Motion Picture Industry*, testimony of Ronald Reagan.

40. Ibid., testimony of Walter E. Disney.

41. Gallup, *Gallup Poll*, 1:689.
42. Trumbo, "Hollywood Blacklisted My Father"; Devall and Osburn, "Blacklisted Writer."
43. Gallup, *Gallup Poll*, 1:640, 2:873–74.
44. Ibid., 1:751–52, 2:853.
45. Weisberg, "Cold War without End," 157–58.
46. McNamara and VanDeMark, *In Retrospect*, 256.
47. Ibid., 280–81.
48. U.S. National Archives, "Pentagon Papers."
49. Ellsberg, *Secrets*, 142.
50. Ibid., 203–4.
51. Ibid., 289, 263.
52. Elliott, *RAND in Southeast Asia*, 439–40.
53. Ellsberg, "Daniel Ellsberg Explains"; author interview with Mary Ellsberg, February 5, 2018.
54. Elliott, *RAND in Southeast Asia*, 457–58.
55. Ellsberg, *Secrets*, 347–49, 357.
56. Wells, *Wild Man*, 390–91.
57. While McGovern would later claim he suggested Ellsberg take the materials to the *New York Times*, Ellsberg says this is a "McGovern lie." Personal communication from Daniel Ellsberg, April 2, 2019.
58. Elliott, *RAND in Southeast Asia*, 466.
59. Ibid., 467.
60. Hersh, *Price of Power*, 384.
61. Sifry, *WikiLeaks*, 29.
62. "Text of Study on Ellsberg."
63. "Ehrlichman Scored on Ellsberg Charge"; Hersh, "President and the Plumbers."
64. Hersh, "CIA Study."
65. Arnold, "Pentagon Papers Charges Are Dismissed."
66. "Byrne Disagrees with Ehrlichman."
67. Ellsberg, *Secrets*, 183; Martin, "Anthony J. Russo"; Cooper and Roberts, "After 40 Years, the Complete Pentagon Papers."
68. Griswold, "Secrets Not Worth Keeping."
69. Cooper and Roberts, "After 40 Years, the Complete Pentagon Papers"; "The Complete Pentagon Papers."
70. Arendt, "Lying in Politics."
71. Ellsberg, *Doomsday Machine*, 1, 3, 7, 8–9.
72. Personal communication from Daniel Ellsberg, April 2, 2019.
73. Ibid.
74. Allison, "Is Nuclear War Inevitable?"
75. See, for example, http://www.nti.org/; and Shultz et al., "World Free of Nuclear Weapons."
76. Woodward, *Secret Man*, 106.

77. Felt and O'Connor, *G-Man's Life*, 202, 193.
78. Dobbs, "Watergate and the Two Lives."
79. Woodward, *Secret Man*, 61, 65.
80. Dobbs, "Watergate and the Two Lives."
81. Woodward, *Secret Man*, 70; Felt and O'Connor, *G-Man's Life*, 217.
82. O'Connor, "I'm the Guy They Called Deep Throat."
83. Dobbs, "Watergate and the Two Lives."
84. Reagan, "Statement on Granting Pardons to Felt and Miller."
85. "Watergate Story."
86. Woodward, *Secret Man*.
87. Pew Research Center, "How Americans View Government."
88. Bamford, *Shadow Factory*, 109–10, 116, 162, 277.
89. U.S. Foreign Intelligence Surveillance Court, "About the Foreign Intelligence Surveillance Court."
90. Wood, *Idea of America*, 331–32.

Chapter Four. Business

1. Van Riper, "America's Richest Counties 2014."
2. Drutman and Furnas, "Revolving Door Lobbyists."
3. Teachout, *Corruption in America*, 246.
4. Eisenhower, "Farewell Address to the Nation."
5. Ledbetter, "What Ike Got Right."
6. Roberts, "New Light on Eisenhower Speech."
7. Newton, "Ike's Speech."
8. Quoted in Lepore, "The Force." The Lockheed Corporation became Lockheed Martin in 1995.
9. U.S. Air Force, "C-5 Galaxy."
10. Hoover and Fowler, "Studies in Ethics, Safety, and Liability."
11. Rice, *The C5-A Scandal*, 106; Fitzgerald, *High Priests of Waste*, 106.
12. Fitzgerald, *High Priests of Waste*, 99.
13. Rice, *The C5-A Scandal*, 146–62.
14. Nader, Petkas, and Blackwell, *Whistle Blowing*, 44–45.
15. Carlson, "A. Ernest Fitzgerald."
16. Nader, Petkas, and Blackwell, *Whistle Blowing*, 44.
17. *The Dismissal of A. Ernest Fitzgerald by the Department of Defense*.
18. Rice, *C5-A Scandal*, 29–43, 146–62.
19. Institute of Government and Public Affairs, "Douglas Award Honorees"; Wikibooks, "Ernest Fitzgerald and the Lockheed C-5A"; Keerdoj, "The Whistle Blower."
20. Carlson, "A. Ernest Fitzgerald."
21. Fitzgerald, *The Pentagonists*, 3.
22. Ibid., appendix A, 315–16.
23. Nixon v. Fitzgerald, 457 U.S. 731 (1982).

24. Institute of Government and Public Affairs, "Douglas Award Honorees."
25. Nader, Petkas, and Blackwell, *Whistle Blowing*, 7, 15.
26. Ingraham, "Civil Service Reform Act," 18; U.S. Merit Systems Protection Board, "About MSPB."
27. Carlson, "A. Ernest Fitzgerald."
28. Wimsatt, "The Struggles of Being Ernest," 12–19.
29. Wikibooks, "Ernest Fitzgerald and the Lockheed C-5A"; Carlson, "A. Ernest Fitzgerald."
30. Fitzgerald, *High Priests of Waste*, xiii.
31. Carlson, "A. Ernest Fitzgerald."
32. Bernstein Liebhard LLP, "History of False Claims Act."
33. Macey, "Getting the Word Out," 1903–4.
34. Dyck, Morse, and Zingales, "Who Blows the Whistle?" 2214–15; Boumil et al., "Whistleblowing in the Pharmaceutical Industry," 18. The single biggest target for fraud under the False Claims Act in the twenty-first century has been the new generation of anti-psychotic drugs. Once a niche product, they are now Big Pharma's biggest moneymaker, largely because they are now prescribed for much broader uses than the most serious mental illnesses. Every major company selling anti-psychotic drugs—Bristol-Myers Squibb, Eli Lilly, Pfizer, AstraZeneca, and Johnson & Johnson—is either currently under investigation for possible health-care fraud or has already settled with the government for hundreds of millions of dollars.
35. Priest and Arkin, *Top Secret America*, 4–7.
36. *Joint Investigation into September 11th*, statement of Cofer Black (former chief of CIA Counterterrorism Center).
37. Priest and Arkin, *Top Secret America*, 52, 158.
38. Priest and Arkin, "National Security Inc."
39. U.S. Office of the Director of National Intelligence, "Members of the IC." In addition to the Office of the Director of National Intelligence, who oversees the intelligence community, there are sixteen members: Air Force Intelligence, Army Intelligence, Central Intelligence Agency, Coast Guard Intelligence, Defense Intelligence Agency, Department of Energy, Department of Homeland Security, Department of State, Department of the Treasury, Drug Enforcement Agency, Federal Bureau of Investigation, Marine Corps Intelligence, National Geospatial Intelligence Agency, National Reconnaissance Office, National Security Agency, and Navy Intelligence.
40. U.S. Office of the Director of National Intelligence, "U.S. Intelligence Community Budget"; U.S. Congressional Budget Office, "Table E-4: Discretionary Outlays since 1968," 150.
41. Harris, "How Private Firms Have Cashed In."
42. Ronald Sanders, "Result of the Fiscal Year 2007 U.S. Intelligence Community Inventory of Core Contractor Personnel."
43. Priest and Arkin, *Top Secret America*, 188.

44. Gorman, "CIA Bans Interrogation by Outside Contractors."
45. Priest and Arkin, *Top Secret America*, 184.
46. Hennigan, "Small Military Contractors Flourished."
47. Lepore, "The Force," 3.
48. Hartung, *Prophets of War*, 29.
49. Weiner, "Lockheed and Future of Warfare."
50. Hartung, *Prophets of War*, 1; Lipton, "Billions Later."
51. Lipton, "Billions Later," 2.
52. "Troubled Waters of 'Deepwater.'"
53. Hsu and Merle, "Coast Guard's Purchasing."
54. O'Rourke, "Coast Guard Deepwater Program," 5. While this may sound crazy to a landlubber, the technique is not uncommon. See Brown, Potoski, and Van Slyke, *Complex Contracting*, 175.
55. Lipton, "Billions Later," 2.
56. "Troubled Waters of 'Deepwater.'"
57. Lipton, "Billions Later," 2.
58. imispgh, "Original."
59. Witte, "On YouTube, Charges of Security Flaws."
60. U.S. Department of Homeland Security, Office of Inspector General, "Maritime Patrol Modernization Project."
61. DeKort, "Deepwater Whistleblower."
62. Ibid.
63. Lapin, "After Deepwater."
64. "'Deepwater' Whistleblower Settlement."
65. U.S. ex rel. DeKort v. Integrated Coast Guard Systems, 475 Fed. Appx. 521 (5th Cir. July 16, 2012); U.S. ex rel. DeKort v. Integrated Coast Guard Systems, 2010 WL 4363379 (N.D. Tex. Oct. 27, 2010).
66. Goodman and González, "Part 2: Robert Greenwald."
67. Lapin, "After Deepwater."
68. Darby, "Exposing the Truth."
69. "In a Soldier's Words."
70. Joseph Darby as told to Hylton, "Prisoner of Conscience," 3.
71. Sharrock, "Am I a Torturer?" 2.
72. Darby as told to Hylton, "Prisoner of Conscience," 3.
73. Sharrock, "Am I a Torturer?" 2.
74. Darby, "Exposing the Truth," 3.
75. Darby as told to Hylton, "Prisoner of Conscience," 5.
76. Darby, "Exposing the Truth," 3.
77. Sharrock, "Am I a Torturer?" 2.
78. Darby, "Exposing the Truth," 4.
79. Weiner, "Suit over Abu Ghraib."
80. Tucker, "Web of Truth," 1.
81. Ibid.
82. Ibid.

83. Ibid., 3; Eckholm, "Army Contract Official."
84. Greenhouse, Kohn, and Kohn, "Fired Army Whistleblower."
85. Tucker, "Web of Truth," 4; Verlöy, "Documents Reveal Concern."
86. Tucker, "Web of Truth."
87. Ibid.
88. *Transparency and Accountability in Military and Security Contracting Act of 2007*, statement of Bunnatine H. Greenhouse (former chief contracting officer, U.S. Army Corps of Engineers).
89. National Whistleblower Center, "Army Contracting Chief Removed."
90. Ibid.
91. Tucker, "Web of Truth," 4; *Oversight Hearing on Waste, Fraud, and Abuse in U.S. Government Contracting in Iraq*, statement of Bunnatine H. Greenhouse (former chief contracting officer, U.S. Army Corps of Engineers).
92. National Whistleblower Center, "Army Contracting Chief Removed"; Tucker, "Web of Truth"; Eckholm, "Army Contract Official."
93. Tucker, "Web of Truth," 5; U.S. Senate Democratic Policy Committee Hearings, Greenhouse statement; Davidson, "Whistleblower 'Bunny' Greenhouse."
94. Tucker, "Web of Truth," 4.
95. Eckholm, "Army Contract Official."
96. Tucker, "Web of Truth."
97. Meyers, "Did Pentagon Bend Rules for Halliburton?"
98. Tucker, "Web of Truth."
99. Eckholm, "Army Contract Official."
100. National Whistleblower Center, "Army Contracting Chief."
101. Lautenberg, Waxman, and Dorgan to Rumsfeld; Miller, "Democrats Demand Probe of Demotion."
102. *Protecting the Public From Waste, Fraud and Abuse*, statement of Bunnatine H. Greenhouse (former chief contracting officer, U.S. Army Corps of Engineers).
103. Author interview with Dan Meyer, November 20, 2015.
104. Davidson, "Whistleblower 'Bunny' Greenhouse."
105. *Protecting the Public From Waste, Fraud and Abuse*, Greenhouse statement.

Chapter Five. Secrecy

1. Thrush, "Bush's '4th Term.' "
2. Eisler and Page, "NSA Veterans Speak Out"; Finn and Horwitz, "U.S. Charges Snowden with Espionage"; Shane, "Ex-Contractor Charged."
3. Downie, "Obama's War on Leaks"; Downie, "Obama Administration and the Press"; Calderone, "Obama Administration."
4. Sifry, *WikiLeaks*, 107, 110.
5. Stirland, "Obama: 'Most Transparent Administration.' "

6. Jones, "Sympathy for the Whistleblower?"; Holzer, "SEC Delays Plans."

7. Lizza, "State of Deception."

8. Caldwell, "ACLU Says ATF Blocks Book."

9. Landay, "U.S. Intelligence Chief."

10. Downie, "Why We Don't Need Another Law."

11. Kiriakou, "Letter from Loretto."

12. McGreal, "Brennan Rejects CIA Torture Claims."

13. Council on Foreign Relations, *CIA Director Brennan Denies Hacking Allegations*; Apuzzo and Mazzetti, "Investigators Seek No Penalty."

14. Begala, "Yes, *National Review.*"

15. Hitchens, "Believe Me, It's Torture."

16. Lichtblau, "In Secret, Court Vastly Broadens Powers."

17. Nakashima, "Legal Memos Released."

18. Risen and Lichtblau, "Bush Secretly Lifted."

19. Hagan, "United States vs. Bill Keller."

20. Mayer, "James Risen's Subpoena."

21. Risen, "Affidavit," 5.

22. Ibid., 12, 16.

23. Goodman and González, "Part 2: Robert Greenwald."

24. *Oversight of the U.S. Department of Justice.*

25. Apuzzo, "C.I.A. Officer Found Guilty."

26. Stahl, "War on Leaks."

27. Gellman, "U.S. Surveillance Architecture."

28. Edgar, "Matinee Idols"; Greene, "Unintentional Noncompliance."

29. Greene, "History of Compliance Violations."

30. Priest and Arkin, *Top Secret America*, 275–77.

31. Author interview with Rajesh De, June 25, 2015.

32. *National Security Letters*, statement of John S. Pistole (deputy director, FBI). The most common authority under which national security letters are issued is the Electronic Communications Privacy Act of 1986.

33. Author interview with Micah Sifry, October 25, 2013.

34. Bustillos, "What It's Like."

35. Wilhelm, "Microsoft Challenged."

36. Gullo, "Google Fights."

37. Zetter, "Federal Judge."

38. Bamford, "NSA Building Spy Center."

39. Gorman, "Meltdown Hobbles NSA Data Center."

40. *Protecting the Public From Waste, Fraud and Abuse*, statement of Rajesh De (deputy assistant attorney general, Office of Legal Policy). On the importance of including national security employees, see *S. 372: The Whistleblower Protection Enhancement Act of 2009*, testimony of Danielle Brian (executive director, Project on Government Oversight), 17 (transcript of testimony) and 48 (prepared statement).

41. See Whistleblower Protection Enhancement Act of 2012, section 105, "Exclusion of Agencies by the President."
42. Author interview with Dan Meyer, November 20, 2015.
43. Author interview with Tom Devine, November 20, 2015.
44. Author interview with Louis Clark and Bea Edwards, December 12, 2013.
45. Oswald, "Closer Look"; Davidson, "Obama's 'Misleading' Comment"; Clark, "Intel Contractors' Whistleblower Rights."
46. Clark, "Intel Contractors' Whistleblower Rights."
47. Perry, "Intelligence Whistleblower Protections," summary.
48. Clark, "Intel Contractors' Whistleblower Rights."
49. A 2000 opinion from the Justice Department Office of Legal Counsel found executive orders and presidential policy directives were equivalent in their force and impact. Moss, "Legal Effectiveness."
50. These figures were compiled from press releases by the U.S. Office of the Director of National Intelligence, found on the ODNI website under "What We Do: IC Budget," https://www.dni.gov/index.php/what-we-do/ic-budget. They also appear here: http://icontherecord.tumblr.com/ic-budget.
51. Chappell, "Petraeus Sentenced."
52. Author interview with Edward Snowden, March 16, 2017.
53. Ives, "Congressionally Requested Action." This is the unscrubbed version.
54. Thomas, "Release of Department of Defense Information," This is the scrubbed version.
55. Because of statute, Halbrooks drifted between acting IG and principal deputy acting as IG from December 25, 2011, to September 24, 2013, but she was the head of the agency the whole time. Email to author from John Crane, July 23, 2015.
56. Grassley, "Grassley Releases Report"; Grassley to Rymer.
57. Grassley, "Grassley Releases Report."
58. Author interview with Dan Meyer, March 25, 2015.
59. Meyer, "Whistleblower Protection Reinforced at DoD"; email to author from Dan Meyer, October 4, 2018.
60. Taylor, "Whistleblower in *Zero Dark Thirty*."
61. Peterson, "Key Intel Whistleblower Official Fired."
62. Email to author from Dan Meyer, October 4, 2018.
63. Author interview with John Crane, June 25, 2015.
64. Lichtblau, "Tighter Lid on Records."
65. Gorman to Crane.
66. Clark, "Pentagon IG Staff Cleared."
67. Brian and Smallberg, "Watchdogs Needed."
68. Moynihan, *Secrecy*, 60, 227.
69. Excerpts from Gellman, "Revealing a Reporter's Relationship with Secrecy."

Chapter Six. Surveillance

1. Burr, "National Security Agency Tracking."
2. Executive Order 12333 (*Federal Register*, December 8, 1981) would later authorize some of the NSA programs that Edward Snowden and others would argue were unconstitutional. For EO 12333 as amended by 13284 (2003), 13355 (2004), and 13470 (2008), see U.S. Office of the Director of National Intelligence, "IC Legal Reference Book."
3. Author interview with Kirk Wiebe, February 6, 2014.
4. Risen and Lichtblau, "Bush Lets U.S. Spy."
5. National Security Agency, "Transition 2001," 32, available from Richelson, "National Security Agency Declassified."
6. Author interview with Thomas Drake, February 6, 2014; author interview with Bill Binney, May 28, 2014.
7. Gorman, "NSA Rejected System"; Bamford, *Shadow Factory*, 46.
8. Gorman, "NSA Rejected System."
9. Author interview with Bill Binney, May 28, 2014.
10. Bamford, *Shadow Factory*, 329, 331.
11. Gorman, "Second-Ranking NSA Official."
12. Sieff, "NSA's New Boss."
13. Bamford, *Shadow Factory*, 330.
14. Author interview with Bill Binney, May 28, 2014.
15. Author interview with Jesselyn Radack, February 6, 2014.
16. Author interview with Thomas Drake, February 6, 2014.
17. Author interview with Kirk Wiebe, February 6, 2014.
18. Author interview with Chris Inglis, March 23, 2015.
19. Author interview with Edward Snowden, March 16, 2017.
20. U.S. National Security Agency, Office of the Inspector General, "ST-09-0002 Working Draft."
21. Author interviews with Kirk Wiebe, February 6, 2014, Thomas Drake, February 6, 2014, and Bill Binney, May 28, 2014.
22. Government Accountability Project, "Bio: Binney and Wiebe."
23. U.S. Deputy Inspector General for Intelligence, "Requirements for TRAILBLAZER and THINTHREAD."
24. *United States of Secrets.*
25. Author interview with John Crane, June 25, 2015.
26. Author interview with Siobhan Gorman, February 5, 2014; Taylor, "Rejection of NSA Whistleblower's Claim."
27. Author interview with Thomas Drake, February 6, 2014.
28. Mayer, "Secret Sharer."
29. Ibid.
30. U.S. Department of Defense, Inspector General, "Whistleblower Reprisal Investigation."
31. Nakashima, "Former NSA Executive Drake."
32. Mayer, "Secret Sharer."

33. Ibid.
34. Drake, "Why Are We Subverting the Constitution?"
35. "Espionage Act."
36. See publicly available trial documents, Federation of American Scientists, "USA v. Thomas A. Drake." Because the case dealt with a national security issue, the proceedings have apparently been heavily redacted.
37. "Why Is That a Secret?"; see also "NSA Whistleblower."
38. Taylor, "Rejection of NSA Whistleblower's Claim."
39. U.S. Department of Defense, Inspector General, "Whistleblower Reprisal Investigation."
40. Author interview with Stephen M. Kohn, February 13, 2015.
41. Author interview with Chris Inglis, March 23, 2015.
42. Author interview with Keith Alexander, February 13, 2015.
43. *United States of Secrets.*
44. Phone conversation with the Maryland District Court, June 15, 2015.
45. Shane, Perlroth, and Sanger, "Security Breach."
46. Klaidman, "Obama's Defining Fight."
47. Stone, "What I Told the NSA."
48. Author interview with Keith Alexander, May 10, 2014. General Alexander stepped down as head of the NSA in March 2014, so he was speaking at the time as a private citizen, not as a representative of the U.S. government.
49. Author interview with Dan Meyer, March 25, 2015.
50. Author interview with Keith Alexander, May 10, 2014.
51. Stone, "What I Told the NSA."

Chapter Seven. Snowden

1. King, "Ex-NSA Chief."
2. Shane, "Under Snowden Screen Name."
3. Risen, "Snowden Says He Took No Secret Files"; Schmitt, "C.I.A. Warning on Snowden."
4. Bamford, "Edward Snowden."
5. Lam, "Snowden Sought Booz Allen Job."
6. Shane and Sanger, "Job Title Key."
7. Ibid.
8. Greenwald, *No Place to Hide*, 53.
9. Reitman, "Snowden and Greenwald."
10. Ibid.
11. Greenberg, "NSA Coworker Remembers."
12. "Inside the NSA."
13. Greenwald, *No Place to Hide*, 31.
14. Harding, *Snowden Files*, 146.
15. "NSA Inspector General Report."
16. "Verizon Forced to Hand over Data."

17. Gellman and Poitras, "U.S., British Intelligence Mining Data"; Marcus, "James Clapper's Answer"; Greenwald and MacAskill, "NSA Prism Program."
18. Greenwald and MacAskill, "Boundless Informant."
19. Reitman, "Snowden and Greenwald."
20. Chokshi, "Snowden and WikiLeaks Clash."
21. Gellman, "Reporter Had to Decide."
22. Gellman, "Code Name 'Verax.'"
23. "Snowden Revelations."
24. Gellman, "Edward Snowden Says Mission's Accomplished."
25. Sharkov, "Edward Snowden Slams Kremlin."
26. Clarke et al., "Liberty and Security."
27. Nakashima, "Independent Review Board."
28. Greenwald, *No Place to Hide*, 31.
29. Snowden, interview by Siebel.
30. Fung, "Darrell Issa: James Clapper Lied to Congress."
31. U.S. Department of Justice and Office of the Director of National Intelligence, Joint Statement on Declassification.
32. Turner, "DNI Clapper Declassifies and Releases."
33. Lizza, "State of Deception."
34. Author interview with Rajesh De, June 25, 2015.
35. Author interview with Edward Snowden, March 16, 2017.
36. Author interview with Jesselyn Radack, May 29, 2014.
37. Author interview with Bill Binney, May 28, 2014.
38. Greenwald, *No Place to Hide*, 49–50.
39. Author interview with Bill Binney, May 28, 2014.
40. Greenwald, "Edward Snowden."
41. Snowden, "Edward Snowden Interview."
42. Ibid.
43. Pomfret and Torode, "Behind Snowden's Hong Kong Exit."
44. Greenwald, "Edward Snowden."
45. Author interview with Edward Snowden, March 16, 2017.
46. Greenwald, "Newly Obtained Documents."
47. Author interview with Edward Snowden, March 16, 2017; Tedesco, "How Edward Snowden Escaped."
48. Author interview with Edward Snowden, March 16, 2017.
49. Author interview with Keith Alexander, May 10, 2014.
50. Author interview with Jesselyn Radack, May 29, 2014.
51. Schmitt and Sanger, "Congressional Leaders Suggest."
52. Miller, "U.S. Officials Scrambled."
53. Ackerman, "NSA Chief Michael Rogers."
54. Nakashima, "Lawmakers Say Snowden Is in Contact with Spies." The original video of the interview, which I watched on December 12, 2017, seems to have been taken down from YouTube by December 14, 2017,

when I wanted to retrieve it again to footnote it. Snowden showed the
clip at Middlebury, and it was embedded in the video of our interview, so
I knew that I had not hallucinated its earlier presence on YouTube. At the
time of this writing, it could be found here: Irari Report, *Edward
Snowden: NSA Perspective from former Deputy Director*, YouTube video,
March 30, 2016, https://www.youtube.com/watch?v=G5evenZOFUo
(key quote at 9:40). I shared this citation with Chris Inglis in an email exchange on October 9, 2018. He did not flag any errors of fact.

55. Gellman, "Reporter Talks"; Gellman, "Edward Snowden Says Mission's
    Accomplished."
56. Author interview with Keith Alexander, May 10, 2014.
57. Bamford, "Edward Snowden."
58. Author interview with Keith Alexander, February 13, 2015.
59. Snowden, "Testimony before the European Parliament."
60. Author interview with Edward Snowden, March 16, 2017.
61. Pomfret and Torode, "Behind Snowden's Hong Kong Exit."
62. Author interview with Rajesh De, June 25, 2015.
63. Gorman, "What You Need to Know on NSA Spying."
64. Quoted in Cole, " 'We Kill People Based on Metadata.' "
65. Bamford, *Shadow Factory*, 266–67.
66. Hamburger and Goldfarb, "Company Allegedly Misled Government";
    Schmitt, "C.I.A. Warning on Snowden."
67. Schneider, "Security Firm Sued"; Apuzzo, "Security Check Firm"; Nis-
    senbaum, "U.S. Accuses Security Firm."
68. U.S. Department of Justice, Office of Public Affairs, "U.S. Investigation
    Services to Settle Allegations."
69. Gellman and Poitras, "U.S., British Intelligence Mining Data."
70. Open Technology Institute, "Section 702's Excessive Scope"; Bamford,
    "They Know Much More"; "NSA Slides Explain PRISM."
71. Savage, "Warrantless Surveillance Can Continue"; Timberg, "NSA Slide
    Shows Surveillance," slide available at "NSA Slides Explain PRISM"
    (slide published July 10, 2013, titled "FAA702 Operations").
72. Greene, "History of Compliance Violations."
73. Gellman, Tate, and Soltani, "NSA-Intercepted Data."
74. Author interview with Edward Snowden, March 16, 2017; email to au-
    thor from Robyn Greene, October 22, 2018.
75. Gellman, Tate, and Soltani, "NSA-Intercepted Data"; see published NSA
    slide on FAA702 operations, "NSA Slides Explain PRISM."
76. "How NSA's MUSCULAR Program Collects Too Much Data."
77. "NSA Slides Explain PRISM."
78. Author interview with Bill Binney, May 28, 2014.
79. Ibid.
80. Bamford, *Shadow Factory*, 288.
81. Risen and Lichtblau, "How U.S. Uses Technology."

82. Chesney and Wittes, "A Tale of Two NSA Leaks."

83. Harding, *Snowden Files*, chapter 8.

84. Ackerman, "US Tech Giants."

85. Author interview with Keith Alexander, February 13, 2015.

86. Cohen, "Service of Snowden."

87. Gellman, Tate, and Soltani, "NSA-Intercepted Data."

88. "This Is Not about Snowden."

89. Author interview with Keith Alexander, May 10, 2014.

90. Author interview with Rajesh De, June 25, 2015.

91. Obama, "Remarks by the President in a Press Conference."

92. Author interview with Rajesh De, June 25, 2015.

93. Shimabukuro and Whitaker, "Whistleblower Protections under Federal Law."

94. Author interview with Stephen M. Kohn, February 13, 2015.

95. Author interview with Chris Inglis, March 23, 2015.

96. Snowden, "Testimony before the European Parliament."

97. Author meetings with senior officials at the NSA, January 16, 2014. The NSA released an email Snowden sent to the NSA's general counsel asking a legal question about a training program, but there is no evidence to date to back up Snowden's claim that he complained internally before fleeing with the stolen materials. See "Snowden Raised Concerns."

98. Author interview with Chris Inglis, March 23, 2015.

99. Sanger, "N.S.A. Releases Email."

100. Author interview with Edward Snowden, March 16, 2017. The interview with Snowden took place two weeks after I had been injured by angry protestors after engaging with Charles Murray at Middlebury College (see Stanger, "Understanding the Angry Mob at Middlebury"). Still suffering from a concussion and whiplash, I therefore interviewed Snowden wearing sunglasses and a neck brace. When we first saw each other via computer screen, Snowden burst out laughing (I did look ridiculous). After the event, his agent later commented in an email to the organizers, "Stanger is hardcore."

101. Author interview with Dan Meyer, March 25, 2015. See also Meyer and Berenbaum, "The WASP's Nest," 21n57.

102. Samuelson, "NSA Watchdog Talks Snowden."

103. Clark, "Why NSA Inspector General Lost His Job."

104. Author interview with Stephen M. Kohn, February 13, 2015.

105. Author interview with Jesselyn Radack, May 29, 2014. See also Radack, "Why Edward Snowden Wouldn't Get a Fair Trial."

106. Author interview with Louis Clark, December 12, 2013.

107. U.S. House of Representatives, Permanent Select Committee on Intelligence, "Review of the Unauthorized Disclosures of Snowden."

108. Schwarz et al., "Letter to Congress."

109. Quoted in Garrison, "Juniata Hosts Famous Leaker."

Chapter Eight. Malevolence

1. Zetter and Poulsen, "U.S. Intelligence Analyst Arrested."
2. WikiLeaks, "WikiLeaks: About."
3. McCullagh, "Congressman Wants WikiLeaks Listed"; Pillifant, "Peter King on Wikileaks."
4. Greenwald, *No Place to Hide*, 13–14.
5. Keller, "Dealing with Assange."
6. Domscheit-Berg, *Inside WikiLeaks*, 174–75.
7. Roberts, "Wikileaks," 122, 124.
8. Zittrain and Sauter, "Everything You Need to Know about Wikileaks."
9. Zetter and Poulsen, "U.S. Intelligence Analyst Arrested."
10. Ibid.
11. Carr, "Leak Case."
12. Manning, "Statement for the Providence Inquiry."
13. Keller, "Dealing with Assange."
14. Cole, "The Three Leakers."
15. Madar, *Passion of Bradley Manning*, 2–10.
16. Stirland, "Alec Ross."
17. Sifry, *WikiLeaks*, 38.
18. Roberts, "WikiLeaks," 127–28; Polls sponsored by Amy Zegart show that Americans who watch spy movies or television shows are more inclined to have favorable views of the NSA: Pincus, "Poll's Lesson for NSA."
19. Assange, "How a Whistleblower Should Leak."
20. Assange, "Banality of 'Don't Be Evil.'"
21. "Defense Department's Response."
22. Rosenbach and Stark, "Cable Guy."
23. Gates and Mullen, "DOD News Briefing."
24. Author interview with P. J. Crowley, December 11, 2013; Van Buren, "Obama's War on Whistleblowers."
25. Author interview with P. J. Crowley, December 11, 2013.
26. Sifry, *WikiLeaks*, 178.
27. Roberts, "WikiLeaks," 120–21.
28. Wu, "Why Monopolies Make Spying Easier."
29. Savage, "Snowden to Join Board."
30. Stanley, "Julian Assange Starts Talk Show"; Becker, Erlanger, and Schmitt, "How Russia Often Benefits."
31. Stanley, "Julian Assange Starts Talk Show."
32. U.S. Office of the Director of National Intelligence, "Assessing Russian Activities."
33. Ibid.
34. Ioffe, "Secret Correspondence."
35. Moyers and Harper, "Trump-Russia Story."
36. Ioffe, "Secret Correspondence."

37. Becker, Erlanger, and Schmitt, "How Russia Often Benefits."
38. Turnage, final paper for The Politics of Virtual Realities, 10.
39. Assange and WikiLeaks, *WikiLeaks Files*, introduction.
40. Becker, Erlanger, and Schmitt, "How Russia Often Benefits."
41. Author interview with Edward Snowden, March 16, 2017.
42. Maurizi, "Julian Assange."
43. Confessore, "Assange Says WikiLeaks Rejected Request"; Lapowsky, "Cambridge Analytica"; Borger and Ackerman, "Trump-Russia Collusion."
44. Savage, "Assange Timed Email Release."
45. Quoted in Harding, "How Trump Walked into Putin's Web."
46. Ibid.
47. Fandos, "Trump Links C.I.A. Reports."
48. See, for example, Edward Snowden, "#Putin has signed a repressive new law . . .," Twitter, July 7, 2016, 4:46 a.m., https://twitter.com/snowden/status/751019610258964480.
49. Rice, "Snowden's Strangely Free Life."
50. Halpern, "Nihilism of Julian Assange."
51. Greenberg, "Edward Snowden's New Job."
52. Becker, Erlanger, and Schmitt, "How Russia Often Benefits."
53. Ibid.
54. Savage, "Chelsea Manning to Be Released."
55. Hunt, "Julian Assange."
56. Adam, "Sweden Drops Assange Rape Allegation."
57. Chalfant, "CIA Head."
58. Whalen and Crawford, "How WikiLeaks Keeps Its Funding Secret"; "How does Julian Assange (Wikileaks founder) earn a living and attract people to work for him?" *Quora*, anonymous question and response, response dated January 22, 2018, https://www.quora.com/How-does-Julian-Assange-Wikileaks-founder-earn-a-living-and-attract-people-to-work-for-him.

Conclusion

1. Watkins, "Trump Jr. Suggests Conspiracy."
2. Reitman, "Snowden and Greenwald."
3. "Capitol's Spinning Door Accelerates."
4. Lessig, *Republic, Lost*, 7, 104.
5. Ackerman, "Boss Tweed."
6. Author interview with Ellen Miller, December 11, 2013.
7. Mulcahy, "Money, Politics, and Power."
8. Quoted in Leibovich, *This Town*, 163.
9. White, "Information, Markets, and Corruption," 19.
10. Author interview with Kurt Wiebe, February 6, 2014.

11. McCall, "Face Scan Arrives."

12. Adida et al., "CALEA II."

13. Privacy and Civil Liberties Oversight Board, "Report on Telephone Records Program," 234.

14. Savage, "Declassified Report Shows Doubts."

15. Cahall et al., "Do NSA's Bulk Surveillance Programs Stop Terrorists?"

16. Priest and Arkin, *Top Secret America*, xx.

17. Author interview with Keith Alexander, February 13, 2015.

18. Bergen and Sterman, "U.S. Right Wing Extremists"; Nakashima, "Domestic Extremists Have Killed More."

19. Wolff, *Fire and Fury*, excerpted in *New York Magazine*, January 8, 2018. WikiLeaks tweeted a link to a free PDF copy of *Fire and Fury* shortly after its publication, perhaps to address the accusation that the organization was a tool of Russia while sabotaging revenue for an anti-Trump manifesto. See Phillips, "WikiLeaks Shared *Fire and Fury*."

20. Lizza, "Why Yates Stood Up to Trump."

21. Yates, "Who Are We as a Country?"

22. Gillespie, "Saying No to the President."

23. Michael Hayden (@GenMhayden), "If this is who we are . . .," Twitter, November 25, 2017, 8:32 p.m., https://twitter.com/GenMhayden/status/934640869562515457.

24. James Comey (@Comey), "I want the American people to know . . .," Twitter, December 3, 2017, 2:46 p.m., https://twitter.com/comey/status/937453108401180673?wpmm=1&wpisrc=nl_daily202.

25. James Comey (@Comey), " 'But let justice roll down . . . ,' " Instagram.com, December 1, 2017, https://www.instagram.com/p/BcKtEUUg4Qa/.

26. Rossman, "Ex-CIA Chief to Trump."

27. Gazis, "Top Former Intelligence Bosses."

28. "Full Text: Nunes Memo."

29. Horwitz et al., "Sessions Told White House."

30. Webster, "I Led the F.B.I."

31. Comey, *Higher Loyalty*, 118–21.

32. Ibid., 223–27, 232–44, 247–55, 257–61, and 232 for the hug/kiss.

33. Keefe, "McMaster and Commander."

34. Comey, *Higher Loyalty*, 212.

35. Hayden, "End of Intelligence."

36. Rucker and Costa, "Bob Woodward's New Book."

37. Ackerman, *Decline and Fall of American Republic*, 4, 182.

38. Benkler, "Time to Tame NSA Behemoth."

39. McNamee, "How to Fix Facebook."

40. *Annual Open Hearing on Current and Projected National Security Threats to the United States*, video and transcript available at https://www.intelligence.senate.gov/hearings/open-hearing-current-and-projected-national-security-threats-against-united-states#.

41. Rosen, "Madison's Privacy Blind Spot."
42. Wittes, "Trump's War Deep State."
43. Walzer, *Just and Unjust Wars*, 257, 260, 323–25.
44. Savage, "Declassified Report Shows Doubts." New America's Robyn Greene reminded me that the NSA would counter by pointing out that the program has prevented attacks abroad. See https://www.dni.gov/files/icotr/Guide-to-Section-702-Value-Examples.pdf.
45. Author interview with Edward Snowden, March 16, 2017; email to author from Robyn Greene, October 15, 2018.
46. Glennon, *National Security and Double Government*, 118.

Bibliography

Abrams, Floyd, and Yochai Benkler. "Death to Whistleblowers?" *New York Times*, March 13, 2013.

Ackerman, Bruce. *The Decline and Fall of the American Republic*. Cambridge, MA: Harvard University Press, 2010.

Ackerman, Kenneth. "Boss Tweed." *Gotham Gazette*, July 4, 2005.

———. *Boss Tweed: The Corrupt Pol Who Conceived the Soul of Modern New York*. Kindle ed. Viral History Press, 2011.

Ackerman, Spencer. "NSA Chief Michael Rogers: Edward Snowden 'Probably Not' a Foreign Spy." *Guardian*, June 3, 2014.

———. "Trump-Russia Collusion Is Being Investigated by FBI, Comey Confirms." *Guardian*, March 20, 2017.

———. "US Tech Giants Knew of NSA Data Collection, Agency's Top Lawyer Insists." *Guardian*, March 19, 2014.

Adam, Karla. "Sweden Drops Assange Rape Allegation, but Britain Says WikiLeaks Founder Still Faces Arrest." *Washington Post*, May 19, 2017.

Adams, Charles Francis. *Chapters of Erie and Other Essays*. Boston: J. R. Osgood, 1871.

Adams, John. *The Adams Papers*. Vol. 5 (August 1776–March 1778). Edited by Robert J. Taylor. Cambridge, MA: Belknap Press, 1983.

———. *The Works of John Adams*. Edited by Charles Francis Adams. Boston: Little, Brown, 1856. Available electronically via Google Books and from the Online Library of Liberty.

Adida, Ben et al. "CALEA II: Risks of Wiretap Modifications to Endpoints." Center for Democracy & Technology, May 17, 2013. https://www.cdt.org/files/pdfs/CALEAII-techreport.pdf.

Adler, John, and Draper Hill. *Doomed by Cartoon: How Cartoonist Thomas Nast and the New York Times Brought Down Boss Tweed and His Ring of Thieves*. New York: Morgan James, 2008.

Alexander, Keith. Interview by author, May 10, 2014.

———. Interview by author, February 13, 2015.

———. Interview by Christopher Joye. "Interview Transcript: Former Head of the NSA and Commander of the US Cyber Command, General Keith Alexander." *Financial Review*, May 9, 2014.

Alford, Fred. "Women as Whistleblowers." *Business and Professional Ethics Journal* 22, no. 1 (Spring 2003): 67–76.

Allen, Brenda A. et al. "Slavery and Justice: Report of the Brown University Steering Committee on Slavery and Justice," October 2006. Brown University. http://brown.edu/Research/Slavery_Justice/documents/Slavery AndJustice.pdf.

Allen, Danielle. *Our Declaration: A Reading of the Declaration of Independence in Defense of Equality.* New York: Liveright, 2015.

Allison, Graham. "Is Nuclear War Inevitable?" Review of *The Doomsday Machine*, by Daniel Ellsberg. *New York Times*, December 28, 2017.

Andrews, Wayne. *The Vanderbilt Legend: The Story of the Vanderbilt Family, 1794–1940.* New York: Harcourt, Brace, 1941.

Annual Open Hearing on Current and Projected National Security Threats to the United States: Hearing before the U.S. Senate Committee on Intelligence. 113th Cong., 2nd Sess., January 29, 2014.

Anthony, Kyle. "Debs, Eugene V." *International Encyclopaedia of the First World War*, last updated October 8, 2014.

"A. Oakey Hall Is Dead." *New York Times*, October 8, 1898.

Apuzzo, Matt. "C.I.A. Officer Is Found Guilty in Leak Tied to Times Reporter." *New York Times*, January 26, 2015.

———. "Security Check Firm Said to Have Defrauded U.S." *New York Times*, January 23, 2014.

Apuzzo, Matt, and Mark Mazzetti. "Investigators Said to Seek No Penalty for C.I.A.'s Computer Search." *New York Times*, December 19, 2014.

Arendt, Hannah. "Lying in Politics: Reflections on the Pentagon Papers." *New York Review of Books*, November 18, 1971.

———. "On Civil Disobedience." In *Crises of the Republic.* New York: Harcourt Brace, 1970.

Argersinger, Peter H. "New Perspectives on Election Fraud in the Gilded Age." *Political Science Quarterly* 100, no. 4 (Winter 1985/86): 669–87.

Arlidge, John. "I'm Doing God's Work: Meet Mr. Goldman Sachs." *Sunday Times* (London), November 8, 2009.

Arnold, Martin. "Pentagon Papers Charges Are Dismissed; Judge Byrne Frees Ellsberg and Russo; Assails 'Improper Government Conduct.'" *New York Times*, May 11, 1973.

Assange, Julian. "The Banality of 'Don't Be Evil.'" *New York Times*, June 1, 2013.

———. "How a Whistleblower Should Leak Information," October 21, 2010. Available from *Mathaba* at "Julian Assange: How a Whistleblower Should

Leak Information (Full Transcript)." http://mathaba.net/news/?x=625093 .html.

Assange, Julian, and WikiLeaks. *The WikiLeaks Files: The World According to US Empire*. London: Verso Books, 2016.

Assessing the Madoff Ponzi Scheme and Regulatory Failures: Hearing before the Subcommittee on Capital Markets, Insurance, and Government Sponsored Enterprises of the Committee on Financial Services, U.S. House of Representatives. 111th Cong., 1st Sess., February 4, 2009. Statement of Harry Markopolos, chartered financial analyst and certified fraud examiner.

Awner, Jonathan L., and Denise Dickins. "Will There Be Whistleblowers?" *Regulation* 34, no. 2 (Summer 2011): 36–40.

Bailyn, Bernard. *The Ideological Origins of the American Revolution*. Cambridge, MA: Harvard University Press, 1992.

Bain, David H. *Empire Express: Building the First Transcontinental Railroad*. New York: Viking, 1999.

Bamford, James. "Edward Snowden: The Untold Story; The Most Wanted Man in the World." *Wired*, August 13, 2014.

———. "The NSA Is Building the Country's Biggest Spy Center (Watch What You Say)." *Wired*, March 15, 2012.

———. *The Shadow Factory*. New York: Anchor Books, 2008.

———. "They Know Much More Than You Think." *New York Review of Books*, August 15, 2013.

Baram, Marcus. "Madoff Whistleblower Book: Claims He Uncovered State Street Fraud, Thought about Killing Madoff." *Huffington Post*, May 25, 2011.

Barboza, David. "Executive Who Warned Enron of Troubles Is Leaving Company." *New York Times*, November 15, 2002.

Barrionuevo, Alexei. "Warning on Enron Recounted." *New York Times*, March 16, 2006.

Bartlett, Willard Root. "William M. Tweed, Impleaded with Richard B. Connolly and Abraham Oakey Hall, Plaintiff in Error, against the People of the State of New York, Defendants in Error." In *The Making of Modern Law: Trials, 1600–1926*. Gale Group, 2013. https://www.gale.com/c/making-of-modern-law-trials-1600–1926.

Baynes, Leonard M. "Just Pucker and Blow?: An Analysis of Corporate Whistleblowers, the Duty of Care, the Duty of Loyalty and the Sarbanes-Oxley Act." *St. John's Law Review* 76 (Fall 2002): 875–96.

Becker, Jo, Steven Erlanger, and Eric Schmitt. "How Russia Often Benefits When Julian Assange Reveals the West's Secrets." *New York Times*, August 31, 2016.

Begala, Paul. "Yes, *National Review*, We Did Execute Japanese for Waterboarding." *Huffington Post*, April 24, 2009.

Belson, Ken. "In a High-Profile Trial, Quick Rulings and the Leavening of Humor." *New York Times*, March 16, 2005.

———. "Prosecutors Rest in Ebbers Case; Former Auditing Chief Testifies." *New York Times,* February 24, 2005.

Benkler, Yochai. "Time to Tame the NSA Behemoth Trampling Our Rights." *Guardian,* September 13, 2013.

Bennett, Drake. "Elizabeth Warren, Champion of Consumer Financial Protection." *Bloomberg Businessweek,* July 7, 2011.

Bergen, Peter, and David Sterman. "U.S. Right Wing Extremists More Deadly Than Jihadists." *CNN,* April 15, 2014.

Bernstein, Carl, and Bob Woodward. *All The President's Men.* New York: Simon & Schuster, 2014.

Bernstein Liebhard LLP. "History of the False Claims Act—The Whistleblower Act." Accessed December 18, 2018. https://www.bernlieb. com/whistleblowers/History-Of-The-False-Claims-Act/index.html.

Bilefsky, Dan. "Ex-Leader Weds, Complicating Czech Bribe Case." *New York Times,* September 24, 2013.

Binney, Bill. Interview by author, May 28, 2014.

Bird, Kai, and Martin J. Sherwin. *American Prometheus: The Triumph and Tragedy of Robert Oppenheimer.* New York: Vintage Books, 2006.

Borger, Julian, and Spencer Ackerman. "Trump-Russia Collusion Is Being Investigated by FBI, Comey Confirms." *Guardian,* March 20, 2017.

Boumil, Sylvester James, Ashiyana Nariani, Marcia M. Boumil, and Harris A. Berman. "Whistleblowing in the Pharmaceutical Industry in the United States, England, Canada, and Australia." *Journal of Public Health Policy* 31, no. 1 (April 2010): 17–29.

Bowen, Robert, Andrew Call, and Shivaram Rajgopal. "Whistle-blowing: Target Firm Characteristics and Economic Consequences." *Accounting Review* 85, no. 4 (July 2010): 1239–71.

Brenner, Marie. "The Man Who Knew Too Much." *Vanity Fair,* May 1996.

Brian, Danielle, and Michael Smallberg, "Watchdogs Needed: Top Government Investigator Positions Left Unfilled for Years." Project on Government Oversight, June 3, 2015.

Broad, William J. "Transcripts Kept Secret for 60 Years Bolster Defense of Oppenheimer's Loyalty." *New York Times,* October 11, 2014.

Brown, Archie. *The Rise and Fall of Communism.* New York: HarperCollins, 2009.

Brown, Moses. Letter to Nicholas Brown & Co., July 17, 1765. Available from Brown University Steering Committee on Slavery & Justice: Repository of Historical Documents. http://library.brown.edu/cds/catalog/catalog.php? verb=render&id=1160786042703677.

Brown, Nicholas & Co. Letter to Esek Hopkins, September 10, 1764. Available from Brown University Steering Committee on Slavery & Justice: Repository of Historical Documents. http://library.brown.edu/cds/catalog/catalog.php?verb=render&colid=17&id=1157642129999104.

Brown, Trevor L., Matthew Potoski, and David Van Slyke. *Complex Contracting: Government Purchasing in the Wake of the U.S. Coast Guard's Deepwater Program.* Cambridge: Cambridge University Press, 2013.

Buhle, Paul, and Dave Wagner. *Radical Hollywood: The Untold Story behind America's Favorite Movies.* New York: New Press, 2002.

Burr, William. "National Security Agency Tracking of U.S. Citizens— 'Questionable Practices' from 1960s & 1970s." George Washington University: National Security Archive. Electronic Briefing Book No. 605, September 25, 2017.

———. "The SOLO File: Declassified Documents Detail 'the FBI's Most Valued Secret Agents of the Cold War.'" George Washington University: National Security Archive. Electronic Briefing Book No. 375, April 10, 2012.

Burrows, Edmund G., and Mike Wallace. *Gotham: A History of New York City until 1898.* New York: Oxford University Press, 2000.

Bush, George W. "The State of the Union Address," January 28, 2003.

Bustillos, Maria. "What It's Like to Get a National-Security Letter." *New Yorker,* June 27, 2013.

"Byrne Disagrees with Ehrlichman." *New York Times,* July 27, 1973.

Cahall, Bailey, Peter Bergen, David Sterman, and Emily Schneider. "Do NSA's Bulk Surveillance Programs Stop Terrorists?" *New America,* January 13, 2014.

Calderone, Michael. "Obama Administration Has Gone to Unprecedented Lengths to Thwart Journalists, Report Finds." *Huffington Post,* October 10, 2013.

Caldwell, Alicia A. "ACLU Says ATF Blocks Whistleblower Book on Scandal." *Associated Press,* October 7, 2013.

Callow, Alexander, Jr. "San Francisco's Blind Boss." *Pacific Historical Review* 25, no. 3 (August 1956): 261–79.

Canterbury, Angela. Interview by author, February 6, 2014.

———. "Testimony of POGO's Angela Canterbury on Transparency and Accountability." *POGO.org,* March 13, 2013. http://www.pogo.org/our-work/testimony/2013/testimony-angela-canterbury.html.

"The Capitol's Spinning Door Accelerates." *New York Times,* February 2, 2014.

Carlson, Peter. "A. Ernest Fitzgerald." *People,* December 9, 1985.

Carmichael, Mary. "Pfizer Accused of Deception on Neurontin." *Newsweek,* October 7, 2008, updated March 13, 2010.

Carr, David. "In Leak Case, State Secrecy in Plain Sight." *New York Times,* March 24, 2013.

Carter, Bill. "*60 Minutes* Set to Interview Ex-Tobacco Executive Tonight." *New York Times,* February 4, 1996.

———. "Tobacco Company Sues Former Executive over CBS Interview." *New York Times,* November 22, 1995.

Cassidy, David C. *Robert Oppenheimer and the American Century*. New York: Pi, 2004.

Center for Defense Information. *Security After 9/11: Strategic Choices and Budget Tradeoffs*. Washington, DC: Center for Defense Information, January 2003.

Chafee, Zechariah. "Freedom and Fear." *Bulletin of the American Association of University Professors* 35, no. 3 (Autumn 1949): 397–433.

Chalfant, Morgan. "CIA Head: WikiLeaks a 'Non-state Hostile Intelligence Service.'" *The Hill.com*, April 13, 2017.

Chan, Sewell. "Consumer Candidate May Avoid Senate Vote." *New York Times*, September 14, 2010.

Chappell, Bill. "Petraeus Sentenced to 2 Years' Probation, Fine for Sharing Classified Info." NPR, April 23, 2015.

"Charter 77 Foundation Awards Corruption Whistle-Blower." *Prague Daily Monitor*, May 26, 2011.

Chasteen, Mark J. "In Search of a Smoking Gun: Tortious Interference with Nondisclosure Agreements as an Obstacle to Newsgathering." *Federal Communications Law Journal* 50 (March 1998): 483–512.

Chesney, Robert, and Benjamin Wittes. "A Tale of Two NSA Leaks: One Is Unsurprising, and Damaging. The Other Is Worth Debating." *New Republic*, June 10, 2013.

Chokshi, Niraj. "Snowden and WikiLeaks Clash over How to Disclose Secrets." *New York Times*, July 29, 2016.

"Cigarette Company Considers Libel Suit." *New York Times*, November 9, 1999.

Clark, Charles S. "Intel Contractors' Whistleblower Rights Are a Work in Progress." *Government Executive*, August 20, 2013.

———. "Pentagon IG Staff Cleared of Misconduct Charges, Anti-Semitism." *Government Executive*, September 13, 2018.

———. "A Whistleblower's Case against Pentagon IG Stalls in Interagency Stalemate." *Government Executive*, October 26, 2017.

———. "Why the NSA Inspector General Lost His Job (and Wants It Back)." *Government Executive*, December 16, 2016.

Clark, Louis, and Bea Edwards. Interview by author, December 12, 2013.

Clarke, Richard, Michael Morell, Geoffrey Stone, Cass Sunstein, and Peter Swire. "Liberty and Security in a Changing World: Report and Recommendations of the President's Review Group on Intelligence and Communications Technologies," December 12, 2013. Available in "Presidential Advisory Committee's Recommendations for N.S.A." *New York Times*, December 18, 2013.

Cohan, William D. "Was This Whistle-blower Muzzled?" *New York Times*, September 21, 2013.

Cohen, Noam. "A Vision of Iceland as a Haven for Journalists." *New York Times*, February 21, 2010.

————. "A Wiki Takes Aim at Obama." *New York Times*, April 4, 2011.

Cohen, Roger. "The Service of Snowden." *New York Times*, June 27, 2013.

Cole, David. "The Three Leakers and What to Do about Them." *New York Review of Books*, February 6, 2014.

————. "We Kill People Based on Metadata." *New York Review of Books*, May 10, 2014.

Comey, James. *A Higher Loyalty*. New York: Flatiron Books, 2018.

Commission on Wartime Contracting in Iraq and Afghanistan. "Transforming Wartime Contracting: Controlling Costs, Reducing Risks." Final Report to Congress, August 2011. http://cybercemetery.unt.edu/archive/cwc/20110929213820/http://www.wartimecontracting.gov/docs/CWC_FinalReport-lowres.pdf.

Communist International, Third Congress. "Section VIII: On the Combination of Legal and Illegal Work." In *Guidelines on the Organizational Structure of Communist Parties*, 24th Session, July 12, 1921. Accessed December 18, 2018. https://www.marxists.org/history/international/comintern/3rd-congress/organisation/guidelines.htm.

"The Complete Pentagon Papers." *New York Times*, June 7, 2011.

"Conditions in Stockyards Described in the Neill-Reynolds Report." *Chicago Daily Tribune*, June 5, 1906.

Confessore, Nicholas. "Assange Says WikiLeaks Rejected Request by Data Firm Tied to Trump." *New York Times*, October 25, 2017.

Conroy, Scott. "Iraq Whistleblowers Vilified, Demoted." CBS News, August 25, 2007.

Constantine, J. Robert. "Eugene V. Debs: An American Paradox." *Monthly Labor Review* 1, no. 8 (August 1991): 30–33.

Cooper, Cynthia. *Extraordinary Circumstances: The Journey of a Corporate Whistleblower*. Hoboken, NJ: Wiley, 2007.

————. "WorldCom Whistle-blower Cynthia Cooper." Interview by Julia Homer and David Katz. *CFO Magazine*, February 1, 2008.

Cooper, Michael, and Sam Roberts. "After 40 Years, the Complete Pentagon Papers." *New York Times*, June 7, 2011.

Cornish, Audie. "Patriot Act Architect Criticizes NSA's Data Collection." NPR, August 20, 2013.

Council on Foreign Relations. *CIA Director Brennan Denies Hacking Allegations*. YouTube, March 11, 2014. https://www.youtube.com/watch?v=6apC6jNoTZo.

Coyle, John G. "The Suspension of Esek Hopkins, Commander of the Revolutionary Navy." *Journal of the American-Irish Historical Society* 21 (1922): 213.

Coyle, John G., Edward C. McGuire, and Vincent F. O'Reilly, eds. *The Journal of the American-Irish Historical Society*. Vol. 21. New York: American-Irish Historical Society, 1992.

Crane, John. Interview by author, June 25, 2015.

Crawford, Jay Boyd. *The Credit Mobilier of America: Its Origins and History.* Boston: C. W. Calkins, 1880.

Crawford, Michael J., ed. *Naval Documents of the American Revolution.* Vol. 8: 1777. Washington, DC: Naval History Division, 1980.

——. *Naval Documents of the American Revolution.* Vol. 10: 1777. Washington, DC: Naval Historical Center, 1996.

"A Credit Mobilier Suit." *New York Times,* January 15, 1878.

Crowley, P. J. Interview by author, December 11, 2013.

Cuddihy, William J. "'A Man's House Is His Castle': New Light on an Old Case." *Reviews in American History* 7, no. 1 (March 1979): 64–69.

Darby, Joseph. "Exposing the Truth of Abu Ghraib." Interview by Anderson Cooper. CBS News, December 10, 2006, last updated June 21, 2007.

Daughan, George C. *If by Sea: The Forging of the American Navy from the Revolution to the War of 1812.* New York: Basic Books, 2011.

Davidson, Joe. "Obama Issues Whistleblower Directive to Security Agencies." *Washington Post,* October 11, 2012.

——. "Obama's 'Misleading' Comment on Whistleblower Protections." *Washington Post,* August 12, 2013.

——. "Whistleblower 'Bunny' Greenhouse Wins Settlement Near $1 Million." *Washington Post,* July 26, 2011.

De, Rajesh. Interview by author, June 25, 2015.

Debs, Eugene V. "Speech Delivered at Nimisilla Park, Canton, Ohio," June 16, 1918. In *The Eugene V. Debs Reader,* edited by William A. Pelz. Chicago: Institute of Working Class History, 2000.

"Debs Arrested: Sedition Charged." *New York Times,* July 1, 1918.

"The Debs Decision." *Washington Post,* March 12, 1919.

"Debs Loses Appeal: To Serve Ten Years." *New York Times,* March 11, 1919.

"Debs Out on Bail: Pleads Not Guilty." *New York Times,* July 2, 1918.

"Debs' Sentence Confirmed by Supreme Court." *Chicago Tribune,* March 11, 1919.

"'Deepwater' Whistleblower Michael J. DeKort's Last Minute Settlement with Lockheed Martin Approved by US District Court." *Business Wire,* December 2, 2010.

"The Defense Department's Response." *New York Times,* October 22, 2010.

"Defense Industry Faces Profit Losses as Golden Decade Ends." *Huffington Post,* August 15, 2011.

DeKort, Michael. "Deepwater Whistleblower: Time to Tell All . . ." *The Project on Government Oversight (POGO) Blog,* July 20, 2009.

Devall, Cheryl, and Paige Osburn. "Blacklisted Writer Gets Credit Restored After 60 Years for Oscar-Winning Film." *Southern California Public Radio,* December 19, 2011.

Devine, Tom. Interview by author, November 20, 2015.

The Dismissal of A. Ernest Fitzgerald by the Department of Defense: Hearings before the Subcommittee on Economy in Government of the Joint Economic Committee. 91st Cong., November 17–18, 1969.

Dobbs, Michael. "Watergate and the Two Lives of Mark Felt: Roles as FBI Official, 'Deep Throat' Clashed." *Washington Post*, June 20, 2005.

Domscheit-Berg, Daniel. *Inside WikiLeaks: My Time with Julian Assange at the World's Most Dangerous Website*. New York: Random House, 2011.

———, as Daniel Schmitt (pseud.). "Wikileaks Spokesman Quits: 'The Only Option Left for Me Is an Orderly Departure.'" Interview by Marcel Rosenbach and Holger Stark. *Der Spiegel*, September 27, 2010.

Dougherty, Carter, and Jesse Hamilton. "Ex-NSA Chief Pitches Banks Costly Advice on Cyber-Attacks." *Bloomberg*, June 20, 2014.

Downie, Leonard, Jr. "In Obama's War on Leaks, Reporters Fight Back." *Washington Post*, October 4, 2013.

———. "The Obama Administration and the Press: Leak Investigations and Surveillance in Post 9/11 America." *Committee to Protect Journalists*, October 10, 2013. https://cpj.org/reports/2013/10/obama-and-the-press-us-leaks-surveillance-post-911.php.

———. "Why We Don't Need Another Law against Intelligence Leaks." *Washington Post*, December 6, 2012.

Drake, Thomas. Interview by author, February 6, 2014.

———. "Why Are We Subverting the Constitution in the Name of Security?" *Washington Post*, August 25, 2011.

Drutman, Lee, and Alexander Furnas. "How Revolving Door Lobbyists Are Taking over K Street." *Sunlight Foundation Blog*, January 22, 2014.

Dry, Murray. *Civil Peace and the Quest for Truth: The First Amendment Freedoms in Political Philosophy and American Constitutionalism*. Lanham, MD: Lexington Books, 2004.

Dyck, Alexander, Adair Morse, and Luigi Zingales. "Who Blows the Whistle on Corporate Fraud?" *Journal of Finance* 65, no. 6 (December 2010): 2213–53.

Dyson, Esther. "WikiLeaks' Flawed Answer to a Flawed World." *Project Syndicate*, December 13, 2010.

Earle, Beverly H., and Gerald A. Madek. "The Mirage of Whistleblower Protection under Sarbanes-Oxley: A Proposal for Change." *American Business Law Journal* 44, no. 1 (2007): 1–54.

Eckholm, Erik. "Army Contract Official Critical of Halliburton Pact Is Demoted." *New York Times*, August 29, 2005.

Edgar, Harold, and Benno C. Schmidt Jr. "The Espionage Statutes and Publication of Defense Information." *Columbia Law Review* 73, no. 5 (May 1973): 929–1087.

Edgar, Tim. "Matinee Idols: Ryan Lizza's Flawed Account of Surveillance Law." *Lawfare Blog*, December 13, 2013.

Editorial (untitled). *Chicago Daily Tribune*, September 23, 1884, 4.

"Ehrlichman Scored on Ellsberg Charge." *New York Times*, August 11, 1973.

Eisenhower, Dwight D. "Address at the Columbia University National Bicentennial Dinner." Speech given in New York City, May 31, 1954.

———. "Farewell Address to the Nation." Speech given in Washington, DC, January 17, 1961.

Eisler, Peter, and Susan Page. "3 NSA Veterans Speak out on Whistle-blower: We Told You So." *USA Today*, June 16, 2013.

Eleanor Roosevelt Papers Project. "Joseph R. McCarthy." In "Teaching Eleanor Roosevelt: Glossary." George Washington University, Columbian College of Arts and Sciences. https://www2.gwu.edu/~erpapers/mep/displaydoc.cfm?docid=erpn-josmcc.

———. "Tammany Hall." In "Teaching Eleanor Roosevelt: Glossary." George Washington University, Columbian College of Arts and Sciences. https://www2.gwu.edu/~erpapers/teachinger/glossary/tammany-hall.cfm.

"Elizabeth Warren." Editorial. *New York Times*, July 24, 2010.

"Elizabeth Warren Forgets." Editorial. *Wall Street Journal*, July 21, 2011.

Elliott, Mai. *RAND in Southeast Asia: A History of the Vietnam War Era*. Santa Monica: RAND Corporation, 2010.

Ellis, Edward R. *The Epic of New York City*. New York: Coward-McCann, 1966.

Ellsberg, Daniel. "Daniel Ellsberg Explains Why He Leaked the Pentagon Papers." Interview by Dave Davies. NPR, December 4, 2017. Published online January 19, 2018.

———. *The Doomsday Machine*. New York: Bloomsbury, 2017.

———. *Secrets: A Memoir of Vietnam and the Pentagon Papers*. New York: Viking, 2002.

Ellsberg, Mary. Interview by author, February 5, 2018.

Enslaving an African. Exhibit at the National Museum of African American History and Culture, Washington, DC.

"The Espionage Act: Why Tom Drake Was Indicted." *60 Minutes*, May 22, 2011.

Ethics Resource Center. *National Business Ethics Survey of the US Workforce*. Arlington, VA: Ethics Resource Center, 2014.

Evans, David. "When Drug Makers' Profits Outweigh Penalties." *Washington Post*, March 21, 2010.

Fandos, Nicholas. "Trump Links C.I.A. Reports on Russia to Democrats' Shame over Election." *New York Times*, December 11, 2016.

Farrell, Greg. "WorldCom's Whistle-blower Tells Her Story." *USA Today*, February 14, 2008.

Faulconbridge, Guy, and Maria Tsvetkova. "Putin's Russia Could Face Revolt: Whistleblower." *Reuters*, June 1, 2011.

Feder, Barnaby J. "Tobacco Company Says *60 Minutes* Avoided Data on Accuser." *New York Times*, February 6, 1996.

Federation of American Scientists. "USA v. Thomas A. Drake: Selected Case Files." Project on Government Secrecy, updated March 18, 2013. https://fas.org/sgp/jud/drake/index.html.

Feldenkirchen, Markus, Christiane Hoffmann, and René Pfister. "Germany's Choice: Will It Be America or Russia?" *Der Spiegel*, July 10, 2014.

Felt, Mark, and John O'Connor. *A G-Man's Life: The FBI, Being "Deep Throat," and the Struggle for Honor in Washington*. New York: PublicAffairs, 2006.

Field, Edward. *Esek Hopkins, Commander-in-Chief of the Continental Navy during the American Revolution, 1775–1778*. Providence: Preston & Rounds, 1898.

Fifield, Anna. "Contractors Reap $138 Bn from Iraq War." *Financial Times*, March 18, 2013.

"Figure in Rosenberg Case Admits to Soviet Spying." *New York Times*, September 11, 2008.

"Find Debs Guilty of Disloyal Acts." Editorial. *New York Times*, September 13, 1918.

Finn, Peter. "FBI Is Increasing Pressure on Suspects in Stuxnet Inquiry." *Washington Post*, January 26, 2013.

Finn, Peter, and Sari Horwitz. "U.S. Charges Snowden with Espionage." *Washington Post*, June 21, 2013.

Fitzgerald, A. Ernest. *The High Priests of Waste*. New York: Norton, 1972.

———. *The Pentagonists*. Boston: Houghton Mifflin, 1989.

Foer, Frank. *World without Mind: The Existential Threat of Big Tech*. New York: Penguin, 2017.

Foote, Sarah. "Enron's 'Whistle-blower' Speaks to MIT Sloan Students about Ethics and Corporate Responsibility." *MIT Sloan School of Management*, October 28, 2012.

Fowler, William M., Jr. *Rebels under Sail: The American Navy during the Revolution*. New York: Charles Scribner's Sons, 1976.

Framer, Andrew E. "Russian Site Smokes out Corruption." *New York Times*, March 27, 2011.

Franklin, Benjamin. *The Papers of Benjamin Franklin*. Vol. 25: October 1, 1777–February 28, 1778. Edited by William B. Wilcox. New Haven: Yale University Press, 1996.

Friedman, Lester D. *Hollywood's Image of the Jew*. New York: Frederick Ungar, 1982.

Fulbright, J. W. "The Higher Patriotism." *Progressive*, July 1966.

"Full Text: Nunes Memo on FBI Surveillance." *Politico*, February 2, 2018.

Fung, Brian. "Darrell Issa: James Clapper Lied to Congress about NSA and Should Be Fired." *Washington Post*, January 27, 2014.

Gallup, George H. *The Gallup Poll: Public Opinion, 1935–1971*. New York: Random House, 1972.

Garrison, Brendan. "Juniata Hosts Famous Leaker." *Altoona Mirror*, February 1, 2014.

Gates, Robert M., and Mike Mullen. "DOD News Briefing." Department of Defense press conference, November 3, 2010. http://www.defense.gov/transcripts/transcript.aspx?transcriptid=4728.

Gazis, Olivia. "Top Former Intelligence Bosses Sign Letter Supporting John Brennan." *CBS*, August 17, 2018.

Gellman, Barton. "Code Name 'Verax': Snowden, in Exchanges with *Post* Reporter, Made Clear He Knew Risks." *Washington Post*, June 9, 2013.

———. "Edward Snowden, After Months of NSA Revelations, Says His Mission's Accomplished." *Washington Post*, December 23, 2013.

———. "Reporter Had to Decide if Snowden Leaks Were 'the Real Thing.'" Interview by Terry Gross. NPR, September 11, 2013.

———. "Reporter Talks about What It Was Like Working with Snowden." Interview by Cyrus Farivar. *ArsTechnica*, September 12, 2013.

———. "Revealing a Reporter's Relationship with Secrecy and Sources." *Nieman Reports*, June 14, 2004.

———. "U.S. Surveillance Architecture Includes Collection of Revealing Internet, Phone Metadata." *Washington Post*, June 15, 2013.

Gellman, Barton, and Laura Poitras. "U.S., British Intelligence Mining Data from Nine U.S. Internet Companies in Broad Secret Program." *Washington Post*, June 7, 2013.

Gellman, Barton, Julie Tate, and Ashkan Soltani. "In NSA-Intercepted Data, Those Not Targeted Far Outnumber the Foreigners Who Are." *Washington Post*, July 5, 2014.

Gillespie, Becky Beaupre. "Saying No to the President." University of Chicago Law School, November 29, 2017. https://www.law.uchicago.edu/news/saying-no-president.

Glennon, Michael J. *National Security and Double Government*. New York: Oxford University Press, 2015.

Glueck, Katie. "Rand Paul Files Class-Action Suit vs. NSA." *Politico*, February 12, 2013.

Goetz, John, and Marcel Rosenbach. "Wikileaks Founder Julian Assange on the 'War Logs': 'I Enjoy Crushing Bastards.'" *Der Spiegel*, July 26, 2010.

Gold, Hadas, and Josh Gerstein. "Clapper Signs Strict New Media Directive." *Politico*, April 21, 2014.

Goldstein, Matthew. "S.E.C. Makes Largest Ever Whistle-blower Award." *New York Times*, September 22, 2014.

Goldstein, Patrick. "Why Won't Hollywood Forgive Elia Kazan?" *Los Angeles Times*, January 14, 1996.

Goodale, James C. "CBS Must Clear the Air." *New York Times*, December 6, 1995.

Goodman, Amy, and Juan González. "Part 2: Robert Greenwald on Film *War on Whistleblowers: Free Press and the National Security State*." *Democracy Now!* April 18, 2013.

Gorman, Karen. Letter to John Crane, October 11, 2017. Available from *Government Executive* in Charles S. Clark, "A Whistleblower's Case against Pentagon IG Stalls in Interagency Stalemate," October 26, 2017. https://cdn.govexec.com/media/gbc/docs/pdfs_edit/102617cc2.pdf.

Gorman, Siobhan. "CIA Bans Interrogation by Outside Contractors." *Wall Street Journal*, April 10, 2009.

————. Interview by author, February 5, 2014.

————. "Meltdown Hobbles NSA Data Center." *Wall Street Journal*, October 7, 2013.

————. "NSA Rejected System That Sifted Phone Data Legally." *Baltimore Sun*, May 18, 2006.

————. "Second-Ranking NSA Official Forced out of Job by Director." *Baltimore Sun*, May 31, 2006.

————. "What You Need to Know on New Details of NSA Spying." *Wall Street Journal*, August 20, 2013.

Government Accountability Project. "Bio: William Binney and J. Kirk Wiebe." Accessed February 3, 2014. https://www.whistleblower.org/bio-william-binney-and-j-kirk-wiebe.

————. "A Timeline of US Whistleblowers." Accessed December 18, 2018. https://www.whistleblower.org/timeline-us-whistleblowers.

————. *Whistle Where You Work #33: Whistleblowing in the Czech Republic.* Vimeo Video. Uploaded by "WhistleblowerTV," March 15, 2013.

Granick, Jennifer Stisa, and Christopher Jon Sprigman. "Jim in the News: The Criminal NSA." *New York Times*, June 27, 2013.

Grassley, Charles "Chuck." "Grassley Releases Report on Inspector General's Bungling of *Zero Dark Thirty* Investigation: Prepared Floor Statement of Senator Chuck Grassley of Iowa." Grassley.Senate.gov, December 4, 2014.

————. Letter to John T. Rymer, November 17, 2014. Available from Grassley.Senate.gov. https://www.grassley.senate.gov/sites/default/files/judiciary/upload/Zero%20Dark%20Thirty%2C%2012-02-14%2C%20final%20report%2C%20Redacted.pdf.

Greenbaum, Mark. "The Civil War's War on Fraud." *New York Times Opinionator*, March 7, 2013.

Greenberg, Andy. "Edward Snowden's New Job: Protecting Reporters from Spies." *Wired*, February 14, 2017.

————. "An NSA Coworker Remembers the Real Edward Snowden: 'A Genius among Geniuses.'" *Forbes*, December 16, 2013.

Greene, Robyn. "A History of FISA Section 702 Compliance Violations." *New America*, September 28, 2017.

————. "Unintentional Noncompliance and the Need for Section 702 Reform." *Lawfare Blog*, October 5, 2017.

Greenhouse, Bunnatine H. "Bunny," Michael Kohn, and Stephen Kohn. "Exclusive: Fired Army Whistleblower Receives $970K for Exposing Halliburton No-Bid Contract in Iraq." Interview by Amy Goodman. *Democracy Now!* July 26, 2011.

Greenwald, Glenn. "Edward Snowden: The Whistleblower behind the NSA Surveillance Revelations." *Guardian*, June 11, 2013.

————. "Newly Obtained Documents Prove: Key Claim of Snowden's Accusers Is a Fraud." *Intercept*, March 21, 2017.

————. *No Place to Hide: Edward Snowden, the NSA, and the US Surveillance State*. New York: Metropolitan Books, 2014.

Greenwald, Glenn, and Ewen MacAskill. "Boundless Informant: The NSA's Secret Tool to Track Global Surveillance Data." *Guardian*, June 11, 2013.

————. "NSA Prism Program Taps in to User Data of Apple, Google and Others." *Guardian*, June 6, 2013.

Griswold, Erwin. "Secrets Not Worth Keeping: The Courts and Classified Information." *Washington Post*, February 15, 1989.

Gullo, Karen. "Google Fights U.S. National Security Probe Data Demand." *Bloomberg*, April 4, 2013.

Gunter, Joel. "*New York Times* Considers Creating Own In-House WikiLeaks." *Journalism.co.uk*, January 26, 2011.

Hagan, Joe. "The United States of America vs. Bill Keller." *New York Magazine*, September 18, 2006.

Halberstam, David. *The Fifties*. New York: Random House, 1993.

Halpern, Sue. "The Nihilism of Julian Assange." *New York Review of Books*, July 13, 2017.

Hamburger, Tom, and Zachary A. Goldfarb. "Company Allegedly Misled Government about Security Clearance Checks." *Washington Post*, June 27, 2013.

Harding, Luke. "How Trump Walked into Putin's Web." *Guardian*, November 15, 2017.

————. *The Snowden Files: The Inside Story of the World's Most Wanted Man*. New York: Vintage Books, 2014.

Haron, David L., Mercedes Varatesh Dordeski, and Larry D. Lahman. "Bad Mules: A Primer on the Federal and Michigan False Claims Acts." *Michigan Bar Journal* 88, no. 11 (November 2009): 22–25.

Harris, Paul. "How Private Firms Have Cashed in on the Climate of Fear since 9/11." *Guardian*, September 5, 2011.

Harris, Shane. *The Watchers: The Rise of America's Surveillance State*. New York: Penguin Books, 2011.

Hart, Albert Bushnell, ed. *Theodore Roosevelt Cyclopedia*. New York: Roosevelt Memorial Association, 1941.

Hartung, William D. *Prophets of War: Lockheed-Martin and the Making of the Military-Industrial Complex*. New York: Nation Books, 2010.

Hayden, Michael. "The End of Intelligence." *New York Times*, April 28, 2018.

Haynes, John Earl, Harvey Klehr, and Alexander Vassiliev. *Spies: The Rise and Fall of the KGB in America*. New Haven: Yale University Press, 2009.

Hearings regarding the Communist Infiltration of the Motion Picture Industry, before the Committee on Un-American Activities, House of Representatives. 80th Cong. 1st Sess., October 20–30, 1947. Statements of Walter E. Disney, October 24, and Ronald Reagan, October 23.

Hellman, Lillian. *Scoundrel Time*. Boston: Little, Brown, 1976.

Helmer, James B., Jr. "False Claims Act: Incentivizing Integrity for 150 Years for Rogues, Privateers, Parasites and Patriots." *University of Cincinnati Law Review* 81, no. 4 (2013): 1261–82.

Hennigan, W. J. "Small Military Contractors Flourished After 9/11 Attacks." *Los Angeles Times*, September 9, 2011.

Henriques, Diana B. "JP Morgan Hid Doubts on Madoff, Documents Suggest." *New York Times*, February 3, 2011.

Henriques, Diana B., and Al Baker. "A Madoff Son Hangs Himself on Father's Arrest Anniversary." *New York Times*, December 11, 2010.

Henriques, Diana B., and Zachery Kouwe. "Prominent Trader Accused of Defrauding Clients." *New York Times*, December 11, 2008.

Hersh, Seymour. "CIA Study Said Ellsberg Viewed Action as Patriotic." *New York Times*, August 3, 1973.

———. "The President and the Plumbers: A Look at 2 Security Questions." *New York Times*, December 9, 1973.

———. *The Price of Power: Kissinger in the Nixon White House*. New York: Touchstone, 1984.

Higham, Scott. "Lawsuit Brings to Light Secrecy Statements Required by KBR." *Washington Post*, February 19, 2014.

Hill, Kashmir. "Lavabit's Ladar Levison: 'If You Knew What I Know about Email, You Might Not Use It.'" *Forbes*, August 9, 2013.

Hirsch, Mike D. "More Light on Boss Tweed." *Political Science Quarterly* 60, no. 2 (June 1945): 267–78.

———. "Samuel J. Tilden: The Story of a Lost Opportunity." *American Historical Review* 56, no. 4 (July 1951): 788–802.

Hitchens, Christopher. "Believe Me, It's Torture." *Vanity Fair*, August 2008.

Hoberman, J. "A Snitch in Time." *Village Voice*, March 16, 1999.

Hodge, Nathan. "Panel's War-Waste Records Sealed as Work Ends." *Wall Street Journal*, September 30, 2011.

Holden, Constance. "Whistleblower Woes." *Science*, January 5, 1996, 35.

Holzer, Jessica. "SEC Delays Plans for Whistleblower Office." *Wall Street Journal*, December 3, 2010.

Hoover, Kurt, and Wallace T. Fowler. "Studies in Ethics, Safety, and Liability for Engineers." Texas Space Grant Consortium. Accessed December 18, 2018. http://www.tsgc.utexas.edu/archive/general/ethics/galaxy.html.

"Hoover Sees FBI as Reds' Top Foe." *New York Times*, May 11, 1954.

Hopkins, Esek. *The Correspondence of Esek Hopkins, Commander-in-Chief of the United States Navy*. Edited by Alverda S. Beck. Providence: Rhode Island Historical Society, 1933.

———. *The Letter Book of Esek Hopkins*. Edited by Alverda S. Beck. Providence: Rhode Island Historical Society, 1932.

———. "Manifest of the Brig *Sally*," September 11, 1764. Brown University Steering Committee on Slavery and Justice, Repository of Historical

Documents. https://library.brown.edu/cds/catalog/catalog.php?verb=ren der&colid=17&id=1157645812109141.

———. "Sales Record for the Brig *Sally* in Antigua, 8 January 1766." Brown University Steering Committee on Slavery & Justice, Repository of Historical Documents. https://library.brown.edu/cds/catalog/catalog.php ?verb=render&colid=17&id=1157644557919802.

Hornblum, Allen M. *The Invisible Harry Gold: The Man Who Gave the Soviets the Atom Bomb*. New Haven: Yale University Press, 2011.

Horwitz, Sari, Rosalind Helderman, Josh Dawsey, and Matt Zapotosky. "Sessions Told White House That Rosenstein's Firing Could Prompt His Departure, Too." *Washington Post*, April 20, 2018.

Howe, Archibald. *Colonel John Brown of Pittsfield, Massachusetts, the Brave Accuser of Benedict Arnold*. Boston: W. B. Clarke, 1908.

"How the NSA's MUSCULAR Program Collects Too Much Data from Yahoo and Google." *Washington Post*, October 30, 2013. Document excerpted from National Security Agency, *Special Source Operations Weekly*, March 14, 2013.

Hsu, Spencer S., and Renae Merle. "Coast Guard's Purchasing Raises Conflict-of-Interest Flags." *Washington Post*, March 25, 2007.

Hunt, Elle. "Julian Assange: Chelsea Manning Clemency Was Bid to Make Life Hard for Me." *Guardian*, January 24, 2017.

Hylton, Wil S. "Prisoner of Conscience." *GQ*, September 2006.

Ignatius, David. "Edward Snowden's Misplaced Idealism." *Washington Post*, June 12, 2013.

imispgh. *Original—See other copy if this version is frozen. YouTube*, August 3, 2006. http://www.youtube.com/watch?v=qd3VV8Za04g.

"In a Soldier's Words, an Account of Concerns." *New York Times*, May 22, 2004.

IndexOnCensorshipTV. *Life After WikiLeaks: Who Won the Information War? YouTube*, May 30, 2011. http://www.youtube.com/watch?v=ISNW rttaJac.

Inglis, Chris. Interview by author, March 23, 2015.

———. Irari Report. *Edward Snowden: NSA Perspective from Former Deputy Director*. Interview by Ira Winkler and Araceli Treu Gomes. *YouTube*, March 30, 2016. https://www.youtube.com/watch?v=G5evenZOFUo&t= 574s&frags=pl%2Cwn.

Ingraham, Patricia. "The Civil Service Reform Act of 1978: The Design and Legislative History." In *Legislating Bureaucratic Change: Civil Service Reform Act of 1978*, edited by Patricia Ingraham and Carolyn Ban. New York: SUNY Press, 1984.

"In NSA Programs, Democracy Works in Secret." Editorial. *Washington Post*, June 20, 2013.

"In Praise of Whistleblowers." *Economist*, January 12, 2002.

"Inside the NSA." *60 Minutes*, December 13, 2013.

Institute of Government and Public Affairs, University of Illinois. "Douglas Award Honorees: A. Ernest Fitzgerald." Accessed December 18, 2018. https://igpa.uillinois.edu/page/douglas-honorees#section-21.

International Institute for Strategic Studies. *The Military Balance, 2002–2003.* London: Oxford University Press, 2002.

Ioffe, Julia. "Net Impact." *The New Yorker,* April 4, 2011.

———. "The Secret Correspondence between Donald Trump Jr. and WikiLeaks." *Atlantic,* November 13, 2017.

Isserman, Maurice, and Dorothy Ray Healey. *California Red: A Life in the American Communist Party.* Urbana: University of Illinois Press, 1993.

Ives, James. "Congressionally Requested Action on Released Department of Defense Information to the Media—Phase 1 (Report No. DODIG-2012-XXX)." Department of Defense, Office of the Deputy Inspector General for Intelligence and Special Program Assessments. Accessed December 18, 2018. http://pogoarchives.org/m/go/ig/dod-ig-fouo-draft-report.pdf.

Jackson, Kenneth T., ed. *The Encyclopedia of New York City.* New Haven: Yale University Press, 1995.

Jarvis, Leonard. Letter to Captain John Paul Jones, May 21, 1777. In *Naval Documents of the American Revolution,* vol. 8, *1777,* edited by Michael J. Crawford. Washington, DC: Naval History Division, 1980.

Jefferson, Thomas. First Inaugural Address. Speech given in Washington, DC, March 4, 1801.

———. Letter to James Madison, January 30, 1787. National Archives, *Founders Online.* https://founders.archives.gov/documents/Jefferson/01-11-02-0095.

———. "Outline of Argument concerning Insubordination of Esek Hopkins," August 12, 1776. National Archives, *Founders Online.* http://founders.archives.gov/documents/Jefferson/01-15-02-0547. See the explanatory notes. (Original source: *The Papers of Thomas Jefferson.* Vol. 15. Edited by Julian P. Boyd. Princeton: Princeton University Press, 1958.)

———. *The Papers of Thomas Jefferson.* Vol. 15. Edited by Julian P. Boyd. Princeton: Princeton University Press, 1958.

Johnson, Carrie. "A Backlog of Cases Alleging Fraud." *Washington Post,* July 2, 2008.

Johnston, Jeremy. "Putting an End to False Claims Act Hush Money: An Agency-Approval Approach to Qui Tam Prefiling Releases." *Vanderbilt Law Review* 68, no. 4 (May 2015): 1163–89.

Joint Investigation into September 11th: Fifth Public Hearing before the Joint House/Senate Intelligence Committee. 107th Cong., 2nd Sess., September 26, 2002. Statement of Cofer Black, former chief, CIA Counterterrorism Center. http://fas.org/irp/congress/2002_hr/092602black.html.

Jones, Ashby. "Sympathy for the Whistleblower? SEC GC's Comments Pique Interest." *Wall Street Journal,* February 1, 2011.

Jones, Ashby, and Joann S. Lublin. "Critics Blow Whistle on Law." *Wall Street Journal*, November 1, 2010.

Jones, Ben. "First Pirate Party Senator Elected in the Czech Republic." *Torrent Freak*, October 22, 2012.

Journals of the Continental Congress, 1774–1789. Edited by Worthington C. Ford et al. Washington, DC: Government Printing Office, 1904–37.

Kaminski, Matthew. "The Man Vladimir Putin Fears Most." *Wall Street Journal*, March 3, 2012.

Kantor, Jodi. "Behind Consumer Agency Idea, a Tireless Advocate." *New York Times*, March 24, 2010.

Katz, Irving. "The Hall Carbine Affair: An Essay in Historiography, by R. Gordon Wasson." Book review. *Business History Review* 47, no. 1 (Spring 1973): 109–10.

Kaufmann, Tim. "Lawmakers: Agencies Aren't Committed to No Fear Law." *Federal Times* (Springfield, VA), March 15, 2004.

Kazan, Elia. *A Life*. New York: Da Capo, 1997.

Keefe, Patrick Radden. "McMaster and Commander." *New Yorker*, April 30, 2018.

Keerdoj, Eileen. "The Whistle Blower." *Newsweek*, August 30, 1976.

Keller, Bill. "A Blogger on Trial." *New York Times*, April 21, 2013.

———. "Dealing with Assange and the WikiLeaks Secrets." *New York Times*, January 26, 2011.

Kennan, George F. *Russia and the West under Lenin and Stalin*. New York: Penguin, 1960.

Kerschberg, Ben. "The Dodd-Frank Act's Robust Whistleblowing Incentives." *Forbes*, April 14, 2011.

Kesselheim, Aaron S., and Daniel H. Solomon. "Incentives for Drug Development—The Curious Case of Colchicine." *New England Journal of Medicine*, June 3, 2010, 2045–47.

Kessler, Glenn. "Edward Snowden's Claim That He Had 'No Proper Channels' for Protection as a Whistleblower." *Washington Post*, March 12, 2013.

Khatchadourian, Raffi. "A WikiLeaks Arms Race?" *New Yorker*, January 24, 2011.

King, Rachael. "Ex-NSA Chief Details Snowden's Hiring at Agency, Booz Allen." *Wall Street Journal*, February 4, 2014.

Kiriakou, John. "Letter from Loretto—A Prison Letter from a CIA Whistleblower." *OpenWatch.net*, May 30, 2013. https://openwatch.net/i/74/letter-from-loretto-a-prison-letter-from-a-cia-w.

Klaidman, Daniel. "Obama's Defining Fight: How He Will Take on the NSA's Surveillance State in 2014." *Daily Beast*, December 31, 2013.

Klehr, Harvey, John Earl Haynes, and Kyrill M. Anderson. *The Soviet World of American Communism*. New Haven: Yale University Press, 1995.

Klehr, Harvey, John Earl Haynes, and Fridrikh Igorevich Firsov. *The Secret World of American Communism*. New Haven: Yale University Press, 1995.

Knefel, John. "Six Memorable Quotes from Edward Snowden's NBC Interview," *Rolling Stone*, May 29, 2014.

———. "Task Force: Post–9/11 U.S. Policies Were Torture." *Rolling Stone*, April 16, 2013.

Kohn, Stephen M. Interview by author, February 13, 2015.

———. *The Whistleblower's Handbook: A Step by Step Guide to Doing What's Right and Protecting Yourself*. Guilford, CT: Lyon's, 2011.

———. "The Whistle-blowers of 1777." *New York Times*, June 12, 2011.

Kolbert, Elizabeth. "Fellowship of the Ring." *New Yorker*, May 6, 2002.

Konczal, Mike. "The GOP Doesn't Oppose Richard Cordray. It Opposes His Whole Agency." *Washington Post*, May 25, 2013.

Kowalczyk, Liz. "Whistle-blower Tells of 'Illegal' Tactics, Says Drug Firm Taught Deception." *Boston Globe*, March 12, 2003.

Krainova, Natalya. "Embattled Navalny Kicks off Mayoral Run." *Moscow Times*, July 2, 2013.

Kreamer, Todd Alan. "Sons of Liberty: Patriots or Terrorists?" *Early America Review*, 1, no. 2 (Fall 1996). https://www.varsitytutors.com/earlyamerica/early-america-review/volume-1/sons-liberty-patriots-terrorists.

Krugman, Paul. "The War on Warren." *New York Times*, March 20, 2011.

Kutner, Robert. "Too Big to Be Governed?" *American Prospect*, November 5, 2010.

Lam, Lana. "Snowden Sought Booz Allen Job to Gather Evidence on NSA Surveillance." *South China Morning Post*, June 25, 2013.

Landay, Jonathan S. "U.S. Intelligence Chief Bars Unauthorized Contacts with Reporters on All Intel-Related Matters." *McClatchy: D.C. Bureau*, April 21, 2014.

Lapin, Andrew. "After Deepwater." *Government Executive*, March 1, 2012.

Lapowsky, Issie. "What Did Cambridge Analytica Really Do for Trump's Campaign?" *Wired*, October 26, 2017.

Lautenberg, Frank, Henry A. Waxman, and Byron L. Dorgan. Letter to Donald H. Rumsfeld, August 29, 2005. http://www.whistleblowers.org/storage/whistleblowers/documents/rumsfeld_congress.let_2005_8_29.pdf.

Lawfare Blog. "Catalog of the Snowden Revelations," last updated December 28, 2014. http://www.lawfareblog.com/catalog-of-the-snowden-revelations/.

Leckie, Robert. *George Washington's War*. New York: Harper Collins, 1990.

Ledbetter, James. *Unwarranted Influence: Dwight D. Eisenhower and the Military-Industrial Complex*. New Haven: Yale University Press, 2011.

———. "What Ike Got Right." *New York Times*, December 13, 2010.

Leibovich, Mark. *This Town*. New York: Penguin, 2013.

Leigh, David, and Luke Harding. *WikiLeaks: Inside Julian Assange's War on Secrecy*. New York: PublicAffairs, 2011.

Lemons, J. Stanley. "Rhode Island and the Slave Trade." *Rhode Island History* 60, no. 4 (Fall 2002): 95–104. http://www.rihs.org/assetts/files/publications/2002_Fall.pdf.

Leon, Richard J. "Federal Judge's Ruling on NSA Lawsuit." *New York Times,* December 16, 2013.

Lepore, Jill. "The Force: How Much Military Is Enough?" *New Yorker,* January 28, 2013.

Lessig, Lawrence. *Republic, Lost.* New York: Twelve, 2011.

Levitz, Jennifer. "Congress Seeks to Close Whistleblower Loophole." *Wall Street Journal,* December 1, 2009.

Lewis, Michael, and David Einhorn. "The End of the Financial World as We Know It." *New York Times,* January 3, 2009.

Lewis, Neil A. "Judge Dismisses Suit by Former CIA Operative." *New York Times,* July 19, 2007.

Lewis, Paul. "Supreme Court Rules against Obama on Recess Appointments," *Guardian,* June 26, 2014.

Lichtblau, Eric. "In Secret, Court Vastly Broadens Powers of NSA." *New York Times,* July 6, 2013.

———. "Tighter Lid on Records Threatens to Weaken Government Watchdogs." *New York Times,* November 27, 2015.

Lippmann, Walter. *Drift and Mastery: An Attempt to Diagnose the Current Unrest.* New York: Mitchell Kennerley, 1914.

Lipton, Eric. "Billions Later, Plan to Remake the Coast Guard Fleet Stumbles." *New York Times,* December 9, 2006.

Lizza, Ryan. "State of Deception." *New Yorker,* December 16, 2013.

———. "Why Sally Yates Stood Up to Trump." *New Yorker,* May 29, 2017.

"'Lone Voice': Excerpts from Testimony of Executive Who Challenged Enron." *New York Times,* February 15, 2002.

Loomis, Edward. "The *Frontline* Interviews: United States of Secrets; Edward Loomis." Interview by Jim Gilmore and Mike Wiser. PBS, December 12, 2013.

Lorenz, Lincoln. *John Paul Jones: Fighter for Freedom and Glory.* Annapolis: United States Naval Institute, 1943.

Ludlow, Peter. "WikiLeaks and the Hactivist Culture." *Nation,* September 15, 2010.

Lynch, Denis Tilden. *"Boss" Tweed: The Story of a Grim Generation.* New Brunswick, NJ: Transaction, 2002.

Lynch, Michael P. "Privacy and the Threat to the Self." *New York Times,* June 22, 2013.

Macalister, Terry. "Corporate Emperors Still Rule, Says Enron Whistleblower." *Guardian,* December 9, 2003.

Macey, Jonathan. "Getting the Word out about Fraud: A Theoretical Analysis of Whistleblowing and Insider Trading." *Michigan Law Review* 105, no. 8 (June 2007): 1899–1940.

MacFarquhar, Neil, and Alexandra Odynova. "Moscow Court Rules against Navalny." *New York Times,* April 23, 2014.

Madar, Chase. *The Passion of Bradley Manning: The Story of the Suspect behind the Largest Security Breach in U.S. History*. New York: OR Books, 2012.

Madison, James. Debates in the Federal Convention of 1787, Thursday, August 30. In "The Constitutional Convention," by Gordon Lloyd. TeachingAmericanHistory.org. http://teachingamericanhistory.org/convention/debates/0830-2/.

———. Debates in the Federal Convention of 1787, Wednesday, July 18. In "The Constitutional Convention," by Gordon Lloyd. Teaching AmericanHistory.org. http://teachingamericanhistory.org/convention/debates/0718-2/.

Manning, Bradley. "Statement for the Providence Inquiry," February 28, 2013. Transcript available from Alexa O'Brien, "Transcript: US v Pfc. Manning, Pfc. Manning's Statement for the Providence Inquiry," February 28, 2013. https://alexaobrien.com/archives/985.

Marcus, Ruth. "James Clapper's 'Least Untruthful' Answer." *Washington Post*, June 13, 2013.

Markopolos, Harry. "How to Spot a Fraud." *Bloomberg Businessweek*, September 22, 2011.

———. *No One Would Listen: A True Financial Thriller*. New York: John Wiley & Sons, 2010.

Martin, Douglas. "Anthony J. Russo, 71, Pentagon Papers Figure, Dies." *New York Times*, August 8, 2008.

Martin, Edward Winslow. *Behind the Scenes in Washington*. New York: Continental, 1873.

Martin, James Kirby. *Benedict Arnold, Revolutionary Hero: An American Warrior Reconsidered*. New York: NYU Press, 1997.

Maurizi, Stefania. "Julian Assange: Donald? It's a Change, Anyway." *La Repubblica*, December 23, 2016.

Mayer, Jane. "James Risen's Subpoena." *New Yorker*, May 24, 2011.

———. "The Secret Sharer." *New Yorker*, May 23, 2011.

McCall, Ginger. "The Face Scan Arrives." *New York Times*, August 29, 2013.

McComb, Henry S. "Henry S. McComb Correspondence, Wilmington, Del., 1863–1872." Accessed December 18, 2018. http://digital.lib.uiowa.edu/cdm/compoundobject/collection/leonard/id/25331/rec/12.

McComb City Railroad Depot Museum. "Henry Simpson McComb." Accessed December 18, 2018. http://www.mcrrmuseum.com/Henry%20Simpson%20McComb.htm.

McCoy, Kevin. "He Blew a Whistle for 9 Years." *USA Today*, February 13, 2009.

McCullagh, Declan. "Congressman Wants WikiLeaks Listed as Terrorist Group." *Cnet*, November 28, 2010.

McDonald, Scott B., and Jane B. Hughes. *Separating Fools from Their Money: A History of American Financial Scandals*. New Brunswick, NJ: Transaction, 2015.

McGilligan, Patrick. "John Berry: Man of Principle." *Film Comment* 31, no. 3 (May 1995): 46–61.

McGrane, Victoria. "Dodd, Frank at Odds over Who Should Lead New Agency." *Wall Street Journal*, August 11, 2010.

McGreal, Chris. "Brennan Rejects CIA Torture Claims in Confident Display at Senate Hearing." *Guardian*, February 7, 2013.

McLaughlin, John. "NSA Intelligence-Gathering Programs Keep Us Safe." *Washington Post*, January 2, 2014.

McLeary, Paul. "NSA Chief: Snowden 'Probably Not' Foreign Agent." *Defense News*, June 3, 2014.

McNamara, Robert, and Brian VanDeMark. *In Retrospect: The Tragedy and Lessons of Vietnam.* New York: Vintage Books, 1996.

McNamee, Roger. "How to Fix Facebook—Before It Fixes Us." *Washington Monthly*, January/February/March 2018.

Meisner, Jeffrey. "Protecting Customer Data from Government Snooping." *Official Microsoft Blog*, December 4, 2013. http://blogs.technet.com/b/microsoft_blog/archive/2013/12/04/protecting-customer-data-from-government-snooping.aspx.

Meyer, Dan. Interview by author, March 25, 2015.

———. Interview by author, November 20, 2015.

———. "Whistleblower Protection Reinforced at DoD." Interview by Federal News Radio, June 4, 2015. Federal News Network.

Meyer, Dan, and David Berenbaum. "The WASP's Nest: Intelligence Community Whistleblowing and Source Protection." *Journal of National Security Law and Policy* 8, no. 1 (Winter 2014–15): 1–49.

Meyers, Lisa. "Did Pentagon Bend Rules for Halliburton?" NBC News, October 29, 2004.

Miceli, Marcia P., Janet P. Near, and Terry M. Dworkin. *Whistleblowing in Organizations.* New York: Routledge, 2008.

Michel, Jean-Baptiste, Yuan Kui Shen, Aviva Presser Aiden, Adrian Veres, Matthew K. Gray, Google Books Team, Joseph P. Pickett, et al. "Quantitative Analysis of Culture Using Millions of Digitized Books." *Science*, January 14, 2011, 176–82.

Milbank, Dana. "Madoff Private Eye Has the Action—Now All He Needs Are the Lights and the Camera." *Washington Post*, February 5, 2009.

Miller, Arthur. *Timebends: A Life.* New York: Grove, 1987.

Miller, Ellen. Interview by author, December 11, 2013.

Miller, Greg. "U.S. Officials Scrambled to Nab Snowden, Hoping He Would Take a Wrong Step. He Didn't." *Washington Post*, June 14, 2014.

Miller, T. Christian. "Democrats Demand Probe of Demotion." *Los Angeles Times*, August 30, 2005.

Millock, Alex. Letter to Nicholas Brown & Co., November 25, 1765. Brown University Library Center for Digital Scholarship. http://library.brown.

edu/cds/repository2/repoman.php?verb=render&metsid=115764357360
7635&view=tei_image&style=xml&id=1161049266207387.xml.

Mitchell, Greg. "Leaks to the *Times* Aren't Exactly New." *Editor and Publisher*, June 1, 2006.

Mitchell, John H. Senate Report No. 834. 54th Cong., 1st Sess. Published in Congressional Serial Set, U.S. Government Printing Office, January 1, 1896. Available from Google Books.

Mitchell, Robert. "Buying 'Friends in This Congress': The Smoking Gun That Triggered a Political Scandal." *Washington Post*, July 18, 2017.

Monk, Ray. *Robert Oppenheimer: A Life inside the Center*. New York: Anchor, 2014.

"A Monster Corruption Fund with Elevens of Millions of Dollars to Bribe Congress." *Chicago Daily Tribune*, February 3, 1875.

Moody, Richard E. "Unfulfilled Expectations: An Empirical Analysis of Why Sarbanes-Oxley Whistleblowers Rarely Win." *William and Mary Law Review* 49, no. 1 (2007): 65–155.

Morgenson, Gretchen. "Finance Chief at WorldCom Failed in Bid to Raise Cash." *New York Times*, July 10, 2002.

"Mortgage Reform, Continued." Editorial. *New York Times*, July 19, 2012.

Moss, Randolph D. "Legal Effectiveness of a Presidential Directive, as Compared to an Executive Order." U.S. Department of Justice, Office of Legal Counsel, January 29, 2000. Accessed December 18, 2018. https://www.justice.gov/file/19436/download.

Moyers, Bill, and Steven Harper. "The Trump-Russia Story Is Coming Together. Here's How to Make Sense of It." *BillMoyers.com*, November 21, 2017.

Moynihan, Daniel Patrick. *Secrecy: The American Experience*. New Haven: Yale University Press, 1998.

Mulcahy, Suzanne. "Money, Politics, and Power: Corruption Risks in Europe." *Transparency International*, June 6, 2012, 11.

A Multinational Enterprise. Exhibit at the National Museum of African American History and Culture, Washington, DC.

Mulvaney, Katie. "Providence Schools Sued for Alleged Discrimination." *Providence Journal*, August 20, 2015.

Murphy, Maxwell. "Meet the SEC's 6,500 Whistleblowers." *Wall Street Journal*, July 28, 2014.

Nader, Ralph, Peter J. Petkas, and Kate Blackwell, eds. *Whistle Blowing: The Report of the Conference on Professional Responsibility*. New York: Grossman, 1972.

Nakashima, Ellen. "Domestic Extremists Have Killed More Americans Than Jihadists since 9/11: How the Government Is Responding." *Washington Post*, October 15, 2015.

———. "Former NSA Executive Thomas A. Drake May Pay High Price for Media Leak." *Washington Post*, July 14, 2010.

———. "Independent Review Board Says NSA Phone Data Program Is Illegal and Should End." *Washington Post*, January 23, 2014.

———. "Lawmakers Say Snowden Is in Contact with Russian Spies but Cite No Public Evidence." *Chicago Tribune*, December 22, 2016.

———. "Legal Memos Released on Bush-Era Justification for Warrantless Wiretapping." *Washington Post*, September 6, 2014.

———. "Panel Seeks to Fine Tech Companies for Noncompliance with Wiretap Orders." *Washington Post*, April 28, 2013.

National Security Archive. "The SOLO File: Declassified Documents Detail 'the FBI's Most Valued Secret Agents of the Cold War.'" George Washington University National Security Archive, posted April 10, 2012. http://www2.gwu.edu/~nsarchiv/NSAEBB/NSAEBB375/.

National Security Letters: Hearing before the Subcommittee on Intelligence Community Management. 110th Cong., 1st Sess., March 28, 2007. Statement of John S. Pistole, deputy director, FBI.

National Security Whistleblowers in the Post–September 11th Era: Lost in a Labyrinth and Facing Subtle Retaliation; Hearing before the Subcommittee on National Security, Emerging Threats, and International Relations of the Committee on Government Reform, House of Representatives. 109th Cong., 2nd Sess., February 14, 2006. Statement of Dan Meyer, director of civilian reprisal investigations, Office of the Inspector General, Department of Defense. https://www.c-span.org/video/?191191-1/national-security-whistleblowers.

National Whistleblower Center. "Army Contracting Chief Removed After Reporting Halliburton Contract Abuse." National Whistleblower Center, August 29, 2005. https://www.whistleblowers.org/news/army-contracting-chief-removed-after-reporting-halliburton-contract-abuse/.

———. "Homepage." Accessed December 18, 2018. http://www.whistleblowers.org/.

Navalny, Alexey. "The Blog of Navalny in English." Accessed March 11, 2014. http://navalny-en.livejournal.com/.

Newton, Jim. "Ike's Speech." *New Yorker*, December 20, 2010.

Nissenbaum, Dion. "U.S. Accuses Security Background Check Firm of Fraud." *Wall Street Journal*, January 22, 2014.

Nixon v. Fitzgerald. 457 U.S. 731 (1982).

Nocera, Joe. "The Travails of Ms. Warren." *New York Times*, July 22, 2011.

"Not Quite a Whistleblower." Editorial. *New York Times*, February 15, 2002.

"NSA Inspector General Report on Email and Internet Data Collection under Stellar Wind." *Guardian*, June 27, 2013.

"NSA Slides Explain the PRISM Data-Collection Program." *Washington Post*, June 6, 2013.

"NSA Speaks out on Snowden, Spying." *60 Minutes*, December 15, 2013.

"NSA Whistleblower Thomas Drake at National Press Club." *Minnesota Public Radio*, March 15, 2013.

"Number Three." *New York Times*, December 30, 1871.

Obama, Barack. "Remarks by the President in a Press Conference." *White House.gov*, August 9, 2013. http://www.whitehouse.gov/the-press-office/2013/08/09/remarks-president-press-conference.

———. "Obama's Speech on Drone Policy." *New York Times*, May 23, 2013. https://www.nytimes.com/2013/05/24/us/politics/transcript-of-obamas-speech-on-drone-policy.html.

"Obituary: Hon. James Brooks." *New York Times*, May 1, 1873.

"Obituary: Hon. Oakes Ames." *New York Times*, May 9, 1873.

O'Brien, Alexa. "Pfc. Manning's Statement for the Providence Inquiry." *alexaobrien.com*, February 28, 2013. http://www.alexaobrien.com/secondsight/wikileaks/bradley_manning/pfc_bradley_e_manning_providence_hearing_statement.html.

O'Connell, Aaron B. "The Permanent Militarization of America." *New York Times*, November 4, 2012.

O'Connor, John. "I'm the Guy They Called Deep Throat." *Vanity Fair*, July 2005.

O'Laughlin, John Callan. "Roosevelt Stirs House to Action." *Chicago Daily Tribune*, June 5, 1906.

Open Technology Institute. "Section 702's Excessive Scope Yields Mass Surveillance: Foreign Intelligence Information, PRISM, and Upstream Collection." *New America*. Accessed December 22, 2018. https://na-production.s3.amazonaws.com/documents/Section702_Scope.pdf.

Oppel, Richard A., Jr. "Enron's Collapse: The Overview: Despite Warning, Enron Chief Urged Buying Shares." *New York Times*, January 19, 2002.

"Opposition Blogger Navalny Voices Presidential Ambitions amid Dwindling Support." *Russia Today*, April 5, 2013.

O'Rourke, Ronald. "Coast Guard Deepwater Program: Background, Oversight Issues, and Options for Congress." Congressional Research Service, updated June 22, 2007. http://www.au.af.mil/au/awc/awcgate/crs/rl33753.pdf.

Oswald, R. Scott. "A Closer Look at Presidential Policy Directive 19." *Law360.com*, August 12, 2013.

An Oversight Hearing on Waste, Fraud, and Abuse in U.S. Government Contracting in Iraq. 109th Cong. Senate Democratic Policy Committee Hearing, June 27, 2005. Statement of Bunnatine "Bunny" Greenhouse, former principal assistant responsible for contracting, U.S. Army Corps of Engineers.

Oversight of the Securities and Exchange Commission's Failure to Identify the Bernard L. Madoff Ponzi Scheme and How to Improve SEC Performance: Hearing before the Senate Committee on Banking, Housing and Urban Affairs. 111th Cong., September 10, 2009. Statement of Harry Markopolos, chartered financial analyst and certified fraud examiner.

Oversight of the U.S. Department of Justice: Hearing before the Senate Committee on the Judiciary. 112th Cong., May 4, 2011.

Packer, George. *The Unwinding*. New York: Farrar, Straus & Giroux, 2013.

Palguta, John. Interview by author, February 12, 2015.

Papandrea, Mary-Rose. "Lapdogs, Watchdogs, and Scapegoats: The Press and National Security Information." *Indiana Law Journal* 83, no. 1 (2008): 233–306.

Parker, Richard A., ed. *Free Speech on Trial: Communication Perspectives on Landmark Supreme Court Decisions*. Tuscaloosa: University of Alabama Press, 2003.

Parrillo, Nicholas R. *Against the Profit Motive: The Salary Revolution in American Government, 1780–1940*. New Haven: Yale University Press, 2013.

Payton v. New York. 445 U.S. 573 (1980).

PBS LearningMedia. "American Experience: Transcontinental Railway— Biography: Oaks Ames." PBS. Accessed March 11, 2014. https://www. pbslearningmedia.org/resource/arct14.soc.amextcroak/transcontinental-railroad-biography-oakes-ames-1804–1873.

Pellegrini, Frank. "Person of the Week: 'Enron Whistleblower' Sherron Watkins." *Time*, January 18, 2002.

"Pentagon Papers Charges Are Dismissed, Judge Byrne Frees Ellsberg and Russo; Assails 'Improper Government Conduct." *New York Times*, May 12, 1973.

Perez-Pena, Richard. "'The Insider' Is Left out of Youth Meeting." *New York Times*, June 7, 2000.

Perry, Rodney M. "Intelligence Whistleblower Protections: In Brief." Congressional Research Service, October 23, 2014. https://fas.org/sgp/crs/intel/R43765.pdf.

Petersen, Melody. "Doctor Explains Why He Blew the Whistle at Pfizer." *New York Times*, March 12, 2003.

Peterson, Andrea. "Key Intel Whistleblower Official Fired as Spy Agencies Face Oversight Crisis." Project on Government Oversight, March 21, 2018. https://www.pogo.org/analysis/2018/03/key-intel-whistleblower-official-fired-as-spy-agencies-face-oversight-crisis/.

Pew Research Center. "Few See Adequate Limits on NSA Surveillance Program, but More Approve Than Disapprove." Pew Research Center, July 26, 2013. http://www.people-press.org/2013/07/26/few-see-adequate-limits-on-nsa-surveillance-program/.

———. "How Americans View Government: Deconstructing Distrust." Pew Research Center, March 10, 1998. http://www.people-press.org/1998/03/10/how-americans-view-government/.

Phillips, Kristine. "WikiLeaks Shared the Full *Fire and Fury* Book Online. Here's Why That May Be a Problem." *Washington Post*, January 8, 2018.

Pillifant, Reid. "Peter King on Why Wikileaks Should Be Declared a Terrorist Organization." *Observer*, November 29, 2010.

Pincus, Walter. "Poll's Lesson for NSA: Show That Surveillance Programs Actually Combat Terrorism." *Washington Post*, November 10, 2013.

Pipes, Richard. *Communism: A History*. New York: Modern Library, 2001.

Pitzke, Marc. "Outrage, Applause, Indifference: U.S. Reacts to Wikileaks Iraq Documents." *Der Spiegel*, October 23, 2010.

Plame, Valerie. *Fair Game: How a Top CIA Agent Was Betrayed by Her Own Government*. New York: Simon & Schuster, 2007.

Plame Wilson, Valerie, and Joe Wilson. "How the Bush Administration Sold the War—and We Bought It: We Knew WMD Intelligence Was Flawed, but There Was a Larger Failure of Officials, Media and Public to Halt the Neocon Juggernaut." *Guardian*, February 27, 2013.

"Plan a Demonstration to Free Eugene V. Debs." *New York Times*, March 21, 1920.

Plumer, Brad. "America's Staggering Defense Budget, in Charts." *Washington Post*, January 7, 2013.

Poland, Luke Potter. *Report of the Select Committee to Investigate the Alleged Credit Mobilier Bribery, Made to the House of Representatives, February 18, 1873*. Washington, DC: Government Printing Office, 1873.

Pomfret, James, and Greg Torode. "Behind Snowden's Hong Kong Exit: Fear and Persuasion." *Reuters*, June 24, 2013.

Poulsen, Kevin. "Ex-Hacker Adrian Lamo Institutionalized, Diagnosed with Asperger's." *Wired*, May 20, 2010.

"Presidential Advisory Committee's Recommendations for N.S.A." *New York Times*, December 18, 2013.

PricewaterhouseCoopers. "Economic Crime: People, Culture and Controls: The 4th Biennial Global Economic Crime Survey." PricewaterhouseCoopers, 2007.

Priest, Dana, and William M. Arkin. "National Security Inc." *Washington Post*, July 20, 2010.

———. *Top Secret America: The Rise of the New American Security State*. New York: Little, Brown, 2011.

Privacy and Civil Liberties Oversight Board. "Report on the Telephone Records Program Conducted under Section 215 of the USA PATRIOT Act and on the Operations of the Foreign Intelligence Surveillance Court." Privacy and Civil Liberties Oversight Board, January 23, 2014.

"Proposed Rules: Office of Special Counsel, 5 CFR Part 1800." *Federal Register*, December 30, 2014, 81475; January 22, 2015, 3182.

Protecting the Public from Waste, Fraud, and Abuse: H.R. 1507, the Whistleblower Protection Enhancement Act of 2009: Hearing before the Committee on Oversight and Government Reform. 111th Cong., 1st Sess., May 14, 2009. Statements of Rajesh De, deputy assistant attorney general, Office of Legal Policy and Bunnatine H. Greenhouse, former chief contracting officer, U.S. Army Corps of Engineers.

Protess, Ben. "Wall Street Is Bracing for the Dodd-Frank Rules to Kick In." *New York Times*, December 11, 2012.

Protess, Ben, and Nathaniel Popper. "Hazy Future for Thriving S.E.C. Whistle-blower Effort." *New York Times*, April 23, 2013.

Putnam, Robert D. *Making Democracy Work: Civic Traditions in Modern Italy*. Princeton: Princeton University Press, 1994.

"Quietly Killing a Consumer Watchdog." Editorial. *New York Times*, February 10, 2013.

Radack, Jesselyn. Interview by author, February 6, 2014.

———. Interview by author, May 29, 2014.

———. "Why Edward Snowden Wouldn't Get a Fair Trial." *Wall Street Journal*, January 21, 2014.

Randall, William Sterne. *Benedict Arnold: Patriot and Traitor*. New York: Morrow, 1990.

Reagan, Ronald. "Statement on Granting Pardons to W. Mark Felt and Edward Miller." Speech given on April 15, 1981. https://www.reaganlibrary.gov/41581d.

RealClearPolitics. "The Ten Most Corrupt Politicians in U.S. History." *RealClearPolitics.com*, January 28, 2009.

Redden, Molly. "Is the 'Chilling Effect' Real?" *New Republic*, May 15, 2013.

"Reds Raided as Menace to the US, Palmer Asserts." *Chicago Tribune*, February 10, 1920.

Regier, C. C. "The Struggle for Federal Food and Drugs Legislation." *Law and Contemporary Problems* 1, no. 1 (1933): 3–15.

Reitman, Janet. "Snowden and Greenwald: The Men Who Leaked the Secrets; How Two Alienated, Angry Geeks Broke the Story of the Year." *Rolling Stone*, December 4, 2013.

Renehan, Edward. *The Transcontinental Railroad: The Gateway to the West*. New York: Chelsea House, 2007.

Reynolds, John F. "A Symbiotic Relationship: Vote Fraud and Electoral Reform in the Gilded Age." *Political Science Quarterly* 17, no. 2 (Summer 1993): 227–51.

Rice, Andrew. "Edward Snowden's Strangely Free Life—As a Robot." *New York Magazine*, June 26, 2016.

Rice, Berkeley. *The C5-A Scandal*. Boston: Houghton Mifflin, 1971.

Rich, Frank. "Is Mike Wallace Ready for His Close-up?" *New York Times*, July 17, 1999.

———. "Smoking Guns at *60 Minutes*." *New York Times*, February 3, 1996.

Richelson, Jeffrey, ed. "The National Security Agency Declassified." George Washington University: National Security Archive, updated March 11, 2005. http://www2.gwu.edu/~nsarchiv/NSAEBB/NSAEBB24/.

Riley, Michael. "WikiLeaks May Have Exploited Photo Networks to Get Data." *Bloomberg*, January 20, 2011.

Ripley, Amanda. "Cynthia Cooper: The Night Detective." *Time*, December 30, 2002.

———. "Q&A: Whistle-blower Cynthia Cooper." *Time*, February 4, 2008.

Risen, James. "Affidavit of James Risen." *U.S. v. Jeffrey Alexander Sterling*. E.D. Virginia, 2011, No. 1:10cr485 (LMB), document 115–2. http://www.fas. org/sgp/jud/sterling/062111-risen115.pdf.

———. "Privacy Group to Ask Supreme Court to Stop N.S.A.'s Phone Spying Program." *New York Times*, July 7, 2013.

———. *State of War: The Secret History of the CIA and the Bush Administration*. New York: Free Press, 2006.

———. "Snowden Says He Took No Secret Files to Russia." *New York Times*, October 17, 2013.

Risen, James, and Eric Lichtblau. "Bush Lets U.S. Spy on Callers without Courts." *New York Times*, December 16, 2005.

———. "Bush Secretly Lifted Some Limits on Spying in U.S. After 9/11, Officials Say." *New York Times*, December 15, 2005.

———. "How the U.S. Uses Technology to Mine More Data More Quickly." *New York Times*, June 8, 2013.

Risen, James, and Nick Wingfield. "Web's Reach Binds NSA and Silicon Valley Leaders." *New York Times*, June 19, 2013.

Roberts, Alasdair. "WikiLeaks: The Illusion of Transparency." *International Review of Administrative Sciences* 78, no. 1 (2012): 116–33.

Roberts, Sam. "In Archive, New Light on Evolution of Eisenhower Speech." *New York Times*, December 10, 2010.

Robinson, Donald L. "The Routinization of Crisis Government." *Yale Review* 63 (Winter 1974): 161–74.

Rogers, Patrick. "The Outsider: Douglas Durand Blew the Whistle on His Drug Firm—and Got $79 Million." *People*, May 6, 2002.

Romero, Simon. "Ten Enron Players: Where They Landed After the Fall." *New York Times*, January 29, 2006.

Roosevelt, Theodore. "The Man with the Muckrake." Speech given in Washington, DC, April 14, 1906.

Rosen, Jeffrey. "Madison's Privacy Blind Spot." *New York Times*, January 18, 2014.

Rosenbach, Marcel, and Holger Stark. "The Cable Guy: Julian Assange Becomes the U.S.'s Public Enemy No. 1." *Der Spiegel*, December 7, 2010.

Rossman, Sean. "Ex-CIA Chief John Brennan to Trump: 'America Will Triumph over You.'" *USA Today*, March 17, 2018.

Roth, Andrew. "Court Orders House Arrest, and No Internet, for Fierce Critic of Putin." *New York Times*, February 28, 2014.

Rucker, Philip, and Robert Costa. "Bob Woodward's New Book Reveals a 'Nervous Breakdown' of Trump's Presidency." *Washington Post*, September 4, 2018.

Rushe, Dominic. "I Carried a Gun in Case Madoff Came After Me." *Sunday Times* (London), March 20, 2010.

"Russia Opposition Leader Alexei Navalny under House Arrest." BBC News, February 28, 2014.

S. Res. 522, 114th Cong., 2nd Sess. (2016), designating July 30, 2016, as "National Whistleblower Appreciation Day."

S. *372: The Whistleblower Protection Enhancement Act of 2009: Hearing before the Senate Homeland Security and Governmental Affairs Committee.* 111th Cong., June 11, 2009. Statement of Danielle Brian, executive director, Project on Government Oversight.

Samuelson, Darren. "NSA Watchdog Talks Snowden." *Politico*, February 25, 2014.

Sanders, Ronald. "Result of the Fiscal Year 2007 U.S. Intelligence Community Inventory of Core Contractor Personnel." Conference call, August 27, 2008. Transcript available from Federation of American Scientists. "August 2008 Intelligence News: US Intelligence Contractor Base: A Statistical Update and Press Briefing." https://fas.org/irp/news/2008/08/odni082708.html.

Sanger, David E. "New N.S.A. Chief Calls Damage from Snowden Leaks Manageable." *New York Times*, June 29, 2014.

———. "N.S.A. Releases Email That It Says Undercuts Snowden's Whistleblower Claim." *New York Times*, May 29, 2014.

Savage, Charlie. "Assange, Avowed Foe of Clinton, Timed Email Release for Democratic Convention." *New York Times*, July 26, 2016.

———. "Chelsea Manning to Be Released Early as Obama Commutes Sentence." *New York Times*, January 17, 2017.

———. "Declassified Report Shows Doubts about Value of N.S.A.'s Warrantless Spying." *New York Times*, April 24, 2015.

———. "Snowden to Join Board of Press Freedom Foundation." *New York Times*, January 14, 2014.

———. "Warrantless Surveillance Can Continue Even if Law Expires, Officials Say." *New York Times*, December 6, 2017.

Schenck v. United States. 249 U.S. 47 (1919).

Schipler, David K. "Free to Search and Seize." *New York Times*, June 22, 2012.

Schmitt, Eric. "C.I.A. Warning on Snowden in '09 Said to Slip through the Cracks." *New York Times*, October 10, 2013.

Schmitt, Eric, and David E. Sanger. "Congressional Leaders Suggest Earlier Snowden Link to Russia." *New York Times*, January 19, 2014.

Schneider, Joe. "Security Firm Sued by U.S. over Bad Background Checks." *Bloomberg*, January 23, 2013.

Schoenfeld, Gabriel. *Necessary Secrets: National Security, Media, and the Rule of Law*. New York: Norton, 2010.

Schreck, Carl. "Russia's Erin Brockovich: Taking on Corporate Greed." *Time*, March 9, 2010.

Schultz, Jeffrey D. *Presidential Scandals*. Washington, DC: CQ, 2000.

Schwartz, John. "Enron's Many Strands: Explanations from One Former Enron Official, Silence from Another." *New York Times*, February 17, 2002.

Schwarz, Frederic D. "Republic of Leaks." *American Heritage* 49, no. 2 (April 1998): 16–18.

Schwarz, Frederick A. O., Jr., Loch Johnson, John T. Elliff, Burt Wides, Jim Dick, Frederick Baron, Joseph Dennin, et al. "Letter to Congress, the President, and the American Public," March 17, 2014. https://www.eff.org/document/church-committee-letter.

Seagrave, Sterling. "Play about Him Draws Protests of Oppenheimer." *Washington Post*, November 9, 1964.

Seelye, Katharine Q. "A New Senator, Known Nationally and Sometimes Feared." *New York Times*, November 10, 2012.

Seligman, Joel. "The SEC in a Time of Discontinuity." *Virginia Law Review* 95, no. 4 (June 2009): 667–83.

Shane, Scott. "Ex-Contractor Is Charged in Leaks on N.S.A. Surveillance." *New York Times*, June 21, 2013.

———. "Obama Steps Up Prosecution of Leaks to the News Media." *New York Times*, June 12, 2010.

———. "Under Snowden Screen Name, 2009 Post Berated Leaks." *New York Times*, June 26, 2013.

Shane, Scott, Nicole Perlroth, and David Sanger. "Security Breach and Spilled Secrets Have Shaken the N.S.A. to Its Core." *New York Times*, November 12, 2017.

Shane, Scott, and David Sanger. "Job Title Key to Inner Access Held by Snowden." *New York Times*, June 30, 2013.

Sharkov, Damien. "Edward Snowden Slams 'Totalitarian' Kremlin over Telegram App Ban." *Newsweek*, April 18, 2018.

Sharrock, Justine. "Am I a Torturer?" *Mother Jones*, April 2008.

Shear, Allen J. "Tweed, William M(agear) 'Boss.'" In *The Encyclopedia of New York City*, edited by Kenneth T. Jackson, 1205–6. New Haven: Yale University Press, 1995.

Sherter, Alain. "Why Enron Whistleblower Sherron Watkins Doesn't Trust the SEC." CBS News, January 28, 2011.

Shimabukuro, Jon, and L. Paige Whitaker. "Whistleblower Protections under Federal Law: An Overview." Congressional Research Service, September 13, 2012. https://fas.org/sgp/crs/misc/R42727.pdf.

Shirky, Clay. *Here Comes Everybody: The Power of Organizing without Organizations*. New York: Penguin, 2008.

"Shoddy-Army Contracts." *Sacramento Daily Union*, September 27, 1861.

Show Jana Krause. *Show Jana Krause 21.1.2011–2. Libor Michálek*. YouTube, June 1, 2011. http://www.youtube.com/watch?v=DQ3lUB3kZn8.

Shugerman, Jed, John Mikhail, Jack Rakove, Gautham Rao, and Simon Stern. "Brief of *Amici Curiae* by Certain Legal Historians on Behalf of Plaintiffs." D.C. and Maryland v. Donald Trump, D.M.D. No. 8:17-CV-01596-PJM, document 58–1.

Shultz, George P., William J. Perry, Henry A. Kissinger, and Sam Nunn. "A World Free of Nuclear Weapons." *Wall Street Journal*, January 4, 2007.

Sieff, Martin. "NSA's New Boss Puts Faith in Hi Tech Fixes." *SpaceWar*, August 18, 2005.

Sifry, Micah. Interview by author, October 25, 2013.

———. *WikiLeaks and the Age of Transparency*. Berkeley: Counterpoint, 2011.

Simon, David. "The 'Nigger Wake-up Call.'" *The Audacity of Despair*, June 19, 2013. http://davidsimon.com/the-nigger-wake-up-call/.

Simpson, Connor. "The Sultry Eyes of Julian Assange." *Atlantic Wire*, August 11, 2011.

Sinclair, Upton. *Autobiography*. New York: Harcourt, Brace & World, 1962.

———. *My Lifetime in Letters*. Columbia: University of Missouri Press, 1960.

"Sinclair Gives Proof of Meat Trust Frauds." *New York Times*, May 28, 1906.

Slavery and Justice. Exhibit at the John Carter Brown Library, Brown University. Available online from www.brown.edu/Facilities/John_Carter_Brown_Library.

Slavery and Justice: Slavery and the Slave Trade in Rhode Island. Exhibit at the John Carter Brown Library, Brown University.

Smith, Gerry. "Former NSA Chief Is Working for Wall Street Now." *Huffington Post*, July 9, 2014.

Snowden, Edward. "Edward Snowden Interview—The Edited Transcript." Interview by Alan Rusbridger and Ewen MacAskill. *Guardian*, July 18, 2014.

———. Interview by author, March 16, 2017.

———. "Testimony before the European Parliament," March 7, 2014. http://www.europarl.europa.eu/document/activities/cont/201403/20140307ATT80674/20140307ATT80674EN.pdf.

———. "Transcript: ARD Interview with Edward Snowden" (interview by Hubert Siebel), January 23, 2014. Available from *Free Snowden*. https://edwardsnowden.com/2014/01/27/video-ard-interview-with-edward-snowden/.

"Snowden Raised Concerns, but No Evidence He Complained, NSA Says." *Newsweek*, May 29, 2014.

"Snowden Revelations." *Lawfare Institute*. Accessed December 18, 2018. https://www.lawfareblog.com/snowden-revelations.

Snyder, David. "The NSA's 'General Warrants': How the Founding Fathers Fought an 18th Century Version of the President's Illegal Domestic Spying." Electronic Frontier Foundation, August 14, 2007. https://www.eff.org/files/filenode/att/generalwarrantsmemo.pdf.

Solomon, Deborah. "Questions for Harry Markopolos—Math Is Hard." *New York Times*, February 25, 2010.

"The Sons of Liberty Constitution." New York State Museum, last modified February 16, 2011. http://www.nysm.nysed.gov/albany/solconst.html.

Soodalter, Ron. "The Union's 'Shoddy Aristocracy.'" *New York Times Opinionator*, May 9, 2011.

Spitz, Malte. "Germans Loved Obama. Now We Don't Trust Him." *New York Times*, June 30, 2013.

Sraell, Holly. "With the Whistleblower Provision, No One Wins." *American Banker*, August 1, 2005.

Stahl, Lesley. "The War on Leaks." CBS News, October 12, 2014.

Stanger, Allison. "Understanding the Angry Mob at Middlebury That Gave Me a Concussion." *New York Times*, March 13, 2017.

Stanley, Alessandra. "Julian Assange Starts Talk Show on Russian TV." *New York Times*, April 17, 2012.

———. "Serenity of a War Strategist: *The World According to Dick Cheney* on Showtime." *New York Times*, March 14, 2013.

Stern, Philip M. *The Oppenheimer Case: Security on Trial*. New York: HarperCollins, 1969.

Stirland, Sarah Lai. "Alec Ross, Leaving State Department for Private Sector, Talks '21st-Century Statecraft.'" *TechPresident.com*. March 11, 2013.

———. "Obama: 'This Is the Most Transparent Administration in History.'" *TechPresident.com*, February 15, 2013.

Stone, Geoffrey R. "What I Told the NSA." *Huffington Post*, March 31, 2014.

———. "WikiLeaks, the Proposed SHIELD Act, and the First Amendment." *Journal of National Security Law and Policy* 5, no. 105 (2011): 105–18.

Stout, David. "Ex-Tobacco Official Enjoys the Aftermath of the Deal." *New York Times*, June 21, 1997.

"Supreme Court Will Not Revive Valerie Plame Lawsuit." *Washington Examiner*, June 21, 2009.

Swartz, Aaron. "Guerilla Open Access Manifesto," July 2008. Archive.org at http://archive.org/stream/GuerillaOpenAccessManifesto/Goamjuly2008_djvu.txt.

Sweeney, Paul. "Accommodating Would-Be Whistleblowers." *Financial Executive* 21, no. 2 (March 2005): 26.

Sylvia, Claire M. *The False Claims Act: Fraud against the Government*. 3rd ed. Eagan, MN: Thomson West, 2016.

Tanenhaus, Sam. "Gus Hall, Unreconstructed American Communist of Seven Decades, Dies at 90." *New York Times*, October 17, 2000.

Tavakolian, Hamid. "The Perils of Whistleblowing." *Management Research News* 16 (1993): 1–5.

Taylor, Marisa. "Rejection of NSA Whistleblower's Claim Draws Criticism." *McClatchy: D.C. Bureau*, February 23, 2015.

———. "Whistleblower in *Zero Dark Thirty* Case Gets Money and an Award." *McClatchy: D.C. Bureau*, September 30, 2016.

Teachout, Zephyr. *Corruption in America*. Cambridge, MA: Harvard University Press, 2014.

Tedesco, Theresa. "How Edward Snowden Escaped." *National Post*, September 6, 2016.

"Text of Letter to Enron's Chairman After Departure of Chief Executive." *New York Times*, January 16, 2002.

"Text of Study on Ellsberg." *New York Times*, August 3, 1973.

"Text: Victim Impact Statement." *New York Times*, August 11, 2005.

"This Is Not about Edward Snowden." Editorial. *Bloomberg*, June 24, 2013.

Thomas, Anthony C. "Release of Department of Defense Information to the Media (Report No. DODIG-2013-092)." Department of Defense, Office of the Deputy Inspector General for Intelligence and Special Program Assessments, June 14, 2013. http://www.dodig.mil/pubs/documents/DODIG-2013–092.pdf.

Thomas, Louisa. "Standing Alone." Review of *Beautiful Souls*, by Eyal Press. *New York Times*, March 9, 2012.

Thrush, Glenn. "George W. Bush's '4th term.'" *Politico*, June 6, 2013.

Timberg, Craig. "NSA Slide Shows Surveillance of Undersea Cables." *Washington Post*, July 10, 2013.

Ting, Michael M. "Whistleblowing." *American Political Science Review* 102, no. 2 (May 2008): 249–67.

"Top Secret America." *Washington Post*, last updated September 2010. http://projects.washingtonpost.com/top-secret-america/.

Transparency and Accountability in Military and Security Contracting Act of 2007: Hearings on H.R. 1507 before the Senate Democratic Policy Committee. 110th Cong., September 21, 2007. Statement of Bunnatine "Bunny" Greenhouse, former principal assistant responsible for contracting, U.S. Army Corps of Engineers.

Trent, Logan Douglas. *The Credit Mobilier*. New York: Arno, 1981.

"The Troubled Waters of 'Deepwater.'" *60 Minutes*, May 17, 2007, updated August 14, 2007.

Trumbo, Mitzi. "Hollywood Blacklisted My Father Dalton Trumbo: Now I'm Proud They've Put Him on Screen." Interview by Elizabeth Day. *Guardian*, January 16, 2016.

Tucker, Neely. "A Web of Truth." *Washington Post*, October 19, 2005.

Tucker, Robert C., ed. *The Marx-Engels Reader*. 2nd ed. New York: Norton, 1978.

———. *The Soviet Political Mind: Stalinism and Post-Stalin Change*. New York: Norton, 1972.

Tugend, Alina. "Opting to Blow the Whistle or Choosing to Walk Away." *New York Times*, September 20, 2013.

Turnage, Jack. Final paper for The Politics of Virtual Realities. Middlebury College, December 7, 2016.

Turner, Shawn. "DNI Clapper Declassifies and Releases Telephone Metadata Collection Documents." Office of the Director of National Intelligence, July 31, 2013.

Tweed, William "Boss." Interview. *New York Herald*, October 26, 1877, quoted in Kenneth Ackerman, *Boss Tweed: The Corrupt Pol Who Conceived the Soul of Modern New York*, Kindle ed. (Viral History Press, 2011).

"Tweed's Election: The Frauds Committed in His District, Full Evidence of Tweed's Rascality." *New York Times*, January 10, 1872.

United States of Secrets. Frontline, season 32, episode 12. Produced by Michael Kirk, Jim Gilmore, and Mike Wiser. PBS, May 13, 2014.

U.S. Air Force, "C-5 Galaxy." U.S. Air Force Archives, June 5, 2009. https://archive.fo/20120720095428/http://www.af.mil/information/factsheets/factsheet.asp?fsID=84.

U.S. Congressional Budget Office. "Table E-4: Discretionary Outlays since 1968." In *The Budget and Economic Outlook: 2018 to 2028*, April 9, 2018.

U.S. Council of the Inspectors General on Integrity and Efficiency. "Joint Statement on National Whistleblower Appreciation Day." Office of Special Counsel, August 2, 2016. https://osc.gov/News/pr16-21.pdf.

U.S. Department of Defense, Inspector General. "Whistleblower Reprisal Investigation: Thomas A. Drake." Report on Case No. 20121205-001567, March 19, 2014. Available in Marisa Taylor, "Rejection of NSA Whistleblower's Retaliation Claim Draws Criticism," *McClatchy: D.C. Bureau*, February 23, 2015. https://s3.amazonaws.com/s3.documentcloud.org/documents/1674432/dod-thomas-drake-final-response.pdf.

U.S. Department of Homeland Security, Office of the Inspector General. "110'/123' Maritime Patrol Boat Modernization Project." Department of Homeland Security, 2007. http://www1.cs.columbia.edu/~unger/articles/homelandSecRptFeb07.pdf.

U.S. Department of Justice, Civil Division. "Fraud Statistics." Department of Justice, November 23, 2010. http://www.taf.org/FCA-stats-2010.pdf.

U.S. Department of Justice, Office of Public Affairs. "Justice Department Celebrates 25th Anniversary of False Claims Act Amendments of 1986." Press release no. 12–142, January 31, 2012.

———. "Justice Department Recovers Nearly $5 Billion in False Claims Act Cases in Fiscal Year 2012." Press release, December 4, 2012.

———. "U.S. Investigation Services Agrees to Forego at Least $30 Million to Settle False Claims Act Allegations." Press release no. 15–1030, August 19, 2015.

U.S. Department of Justice and Office of the Director of National Intelligence. "Joint Statement on the Declassification of the Resumption of Collection under Section 215 of the USA Patriot Act." Press release, June 30, 2015.

U.S. Department of the Treasury. "Blueprint for a Modernized Financial Regulatory Structure." Department of the Treasury, March 2008. http://www.treasury.gov/press-center/press-releases/Documents/Blueprint.pdf.

———. "1600–1799." Department of the Treasury, last modified November 13, 2010. http://www.treasury.gov/about/history/Pages/1600–1799.aspx.

U.S. Deputy Inspector General for Intelligence. "Requirements for the TRAILBLAZER And THINTHREAD Systems." Report 05-INTEL-03. Department of Defense, Office of the Inspector General, December 15, 2004.

U.S. ex rel. DeKort v. Integrated Coast Guard Systems, 475 Fed. Appx. 521 (5th Cir. 2012).

U.S. ex rel. DeKort v. Integrated Coast Guard Systems, 2010 WL 4363379 (N.D. Tex. 2010).

U.S. ex rel. Marcus v. Hess. 317 U.S. 537 (1943).

U.S. Federal Bureau of Investigation. "SOLO: Part 01 of 125." Federal Bureau of Investigation Records Vault, March 5, 1958. http://vault.fbi.gov/solo/solo-part-01-of/view.

U.S. Foreign Intelligence Surveillance Court. "About the Foreign Intelligence Surveillance Court." Accessed December 18, 2018. https://www.fisc.uscourts.gov/about-foreign-intelligence-surveillance-court.

U.S. House of Representatives Committee on Un-American Activities. *100 Things You Should Know about Communism*. Washington, DC: House Un-American Activities Committee, 1949.

U.S. House of Representatives Permanent Select Committee on Intelligence. "Executive Summary of Review of the Unauthorized Disclosures of Former National Security Agency Contractor Edward Snowden," September 15, 2016. https://publicintelligence.net/us-hpsci-snowden/.

U.S. Merit Systems Protection Board. "About MSPB."

———. *Blowing the Whistle: Barriers to Federal Employees Making Disclosures*. Washington, DC: Government Printing Office, 2011.

———. *Blowing the Whistle in the Federal Government: A Comparative Analysis of 1980 and 1983 Survey Findings*. Washington, DC: Government Printing Office, 1984.

———. "Questions and Answers about Whistleblower Appeals." Accessed December 18, 2018. http://mspb.gov/appeals/whistleblower.htm.

———. *Whistleblowing and the Federal Employee: Blowing the Whistle on Fraud, Waste, and Mismanagement—Who Does it and What Happens?* Washington, DC: Government Printing Office, 1981.

———. *Whistleblowing in the Federal Government: An Update*. Washington, DC: Government Printing Office, 1993.

U.S. National Archives. "Pentagon Papers." National Archives. Accessed December 18, 2018. https://www.archives.gov/research/pentagon-papers.

U.S. National Security Agency, Office of the Inspector General. "ST-09-0002 Working Draft," March 24, 2009. https://www.aclu.org/sites/default/files/field_document/NSA%20IG%20Report.pdf.

U.S. Occupational Safety and Health Administration. "Whistleblower Investigation Data: FY2007–FY2017." Accessed December 18, 2018. https://www.whistleblowers.gov/sites/default/files/3DCharts-FY2007-FY2017.pdf.

U.S. Office of the Director of National Intelligence. "Assessing Russian Activities and Intentions in Recent US Elections." Intelligence Community Assessment 2017–01D, January 6, 2017. https://www.dni.gov/files/documents/ICA_2017_01.pdf.

———. "IC Legal Reference Book," last updated December 2016. https://www.dni.gov/index.php/who-we-are/organizations/ogc/ogc-related-menus/ogc-related-content/ic-legal-reference-book.

———. "Members of the IC." Accessed December 18, 2018. https://www.dni.gov/index.php/what-we-do/members-of-the-ic. "U.S. Intelligence Community Budget." Accessed December 18, 2018. https://www.dni.gov/index.php/what-we-do/ic-budget.

"US Reds Go Underground to Foil FBI, Hoover Says." *New York Times*, June 9, 1950.

U.S. Securities and Exchange Commission. "About the SEC." Accessed May 7, 2014. http://www.sec.gov/about.shtml.

———. "Whistleblower Program: 2017 Annual Report to Congress," 2017. https://www.sec.gov/files/sec-2017-annual-report-whistleblower-program.pdf.

U.S. Securities and Exchange Commission, Office of the Inspector General. "Assessment of the SEC's Bounty Program." Report No. 474, March 29, 2010. http://www.sec.gov/oig/reportspubs/474.pdf.

U.S. Senate Democratic Policy Committee Hearing. *Abuses in Private Security and Reconstruction Contracting in Iraq: Ensuring Accountability, Protecting Whistleblowers*, September 21, 2007. Bunnatine Greenhouse testimony. http://dpc.senate.gov/hearings/hearing40/greenhouse.pdf.

U.S. Senate Historical Office. *Election, Expulsion, and Censure Cases: 1793 to 1990*. Washington, DC: U.S. Senate Historical Office, 1995.

U.S. v. Griswold. 24 F. 361. United States District Court for the District of Oregon, 1885.

Van Buren, Peter. "Obama's War on Whistleblowers." *Mother Jones*, June 12, 2012.

Van Natta, Don, Jr., and Alex Berenson. "Enron's Collapse, the Overview: Enron's Chairman Received Warning about Accounting." *New York Times*, January 15, 2002.

Van Riper, Tom. "America's Richest Counties, 2014." *Forbes*, April 1, 2014.

Vaughn, Robert. "America's First Comprehensive Statute Protecting Corporate Whistleblowers." *Administrative Law Review* 57, no. 1 (Winter 2005): 1–105.

"Verizon Forced to Hand over Telephone Data—Full Court Ruling." *Guardian*, June 5, 2013.

Verlöy, André. "Documents Reveal Concern regarding Halliburton Contracts." Center for Public Integrity, November 3, 2004, updated May 19, 2014.

Verschoor, Curtis C. "Increased Motivation for Whistleblowing." *Strategic Finance*, November 18, 2010, 16–18, 61.

Volcker, Paul A. Speech given at a luncheon of the Economic Club of New York, NY, April 8, 2008.

"Voyage of the Slave Ship *Sally*: On the African Coast." Brown University Scholarly Technology Group. Accessed December 18, 2018. http://cds. library.brown.edu/projects/sally/narr_coast.html.

"Voyage of the Slave Ship *Sally*: The Middle Passage." Brown University Scholarly Technology Group. Accessed December 18, 2018. http://cds. library.brown.edu/projects/sally/narr_middle.html.

Vulliamy, Ed. "Focus: The Enron Scandal; The Woman Who Took on a Giant—Sherron Watkins's Memo Blew the Lid on Enron and Led to Sackings and a Suicide." *Observer*, January 27, 2002.

Wallace, William M. *Traitorous Hero: The Life and Fortunes of Benedict Arnold*. New York: Books for Libraries, 1954.

Walzer, Michael. *Just and Unjust Wars: A Moral Argument with Historical Illustrations*. 5th ed. New York: Basic Books, 2015.

Warren, Elizabeth. *A Fighting Chance*. New York: Metropolitan Books, 2014.

Washington, George. Letter to Gouverneur Morris, October 13, 1798. National Archives: Founders Online. http://founders.archives.gov/documents/Washington/05-04-02-0125. (Original source: *The Papers of George Washington*. Vol. 4, *8 September 1789–15 January 1790*. Edited by Dorothy Twohig. Presidential Series. Charlottesville: University Press of Virginia, 1993.)

"The Watergate Story: Deep Throat Revealed, Part IV." *Washington Post*. Accessed December 18, 2018. https://www.washingtonpost.com/wp-srv/politics/special/watergate/part4.html.

Watkins, Eli. "Trump Jr. Suggests Conspiracy of People Who Don't Want to Let 'America Be America.'" *CNN*, December 20, 2017.

Watkins, Sherron. "The Corporate Conscience: Interview; Sherron Watkins, Enron Whistleblower." Interview by Lesley Curwen. *Guardian*, June 21, 2003.

Waxman, Olivia. "America's First Anti-slavery Statute Was Passed in 1652. Here's Why It Was Ignored." *Time*, May 18, 2017.

Wayne, Leslie. "Troubled Times Bring Mini-Madoffs to Light." *New York Times*, January 27, 2009.

Webster, William. "I Led the F.B.I. Mueller Is Just Doing His Job." *New York Times*, July 17, 2018.

Weidner, David. "Harry Markopolos, SEC Chairman?" *Wall Street Journal*, March 11, 2010.

Weinberg, Neil. "The Dark Side of Whistleblowing." *Forbes*, March 14, 2005.

Weiner, Rachel. "A Suit over Abu Ghraib Getting to 'What Actually Happened.'" *Washington Post*, September 22, 2017.

Weiner, Tim. "Hoover Planned Mass Jailing in 1950." *New York Times*, December 23, 2007.

———. "Lockheed and the Future of Warfare." *New York Times*, November 28, 2004.

Weisberg, Jacob. "Cold War without End." *New York Times Magazine*, November 28, 1999.

Wells, Tom. *Wild Man: The Life and Times of Daniel Ellsberg*. New York: Palgrave, 2001.

Werner, M. R. *Tammany Hall*. Garden City, NY: Doubleday, 1928.

Whalen, Jeanne, and David Crawford. "How WikiLeaks Keeps Its Funding Secret." *Wall Street Journal*, August 23, 2010.

"A Whistle-blower Rocks an Industry." *Businessweek*, June 23, 2002.

White, Richard. "Information, Markets, and Corruption: Transcontinental Railroads in the Gilded Age." *Journal of American History* 90, no. 1 (June 2003): 19–43.

Whitehouse, Tammy. "More Clues on SEC Whistleblower Office." *Compliance Week*, February 2012.

"Why Is That a Secret?" Editorial. *New York Times*, August 24, 2011.

Wiebe, Kirk. Interview by author, February 6, 2014.

Wikibooks. "Ernest Fitzgerald and the Lockheed C-5A," last modified September 14, 2013. http://en.wikibooks.org/wiki/Professionalism/Ernest_Fitzgerald_and_the_Lockheed_C-5A.

Wikileaks. "Wikileaks: About." Accessed May 6, 2014. http://wikileaks.org/.

Wilhelm, Alex. "Microsoft Challenged a National Security Letter That Included a Gag Order—And Won." *TechCrunch.com*, May 22, 2014.

"William Marcy Tweed." *New York Tribune*, April 13, 1878. Quoted in Kenneth Ackerman, *Boss Tweed: The Corrupt Pol Who Conceived the Soul of Modern New York*, Kindle ed. (Viral History Press, 2011).

Williams, John H. *A Great and Shining Road: The Epic Story of the Transcontinental Railroad*. New York: Times Books, 1988.

Wilson, Duff. "Side Effects May Include Lawsuits." *New York Times*, October 2, 2010.

Wilson, Joseph C. *The Politics of Truth: Inside the Lies That Led to War and Betrayed My Wife's CIA Identity; A Diplomat's Memoir*. New York: Carroll & Graf, 2004.

Wilson, Woodrow. *The New Freedom: A Call for the Emancipation of the Generous Energies of a People*. New York: Doubleday, Page, 1918.

———. *Woodrow Wilson: The Essential Political Writings*. Edited by Ronald J. Pestritto. Lanham, MD: Lexington Books, 2005.

Wimsatt, Alison Ross. "The Struggles of Being Ernest." *Industrial Management Magazine*, January/February 1999, 12–19.

Witte, Griff. "On YouTube, Charges of Security Flaws." *Washington Post*, August 29, 2006.

Wittes, Benjamin. "Why Trump's War on the Deep State Is Failing—So Far." *Lawfare Institute*, January 1, 2018.

Wolff, Michael. "Donald Trump Didn't Want to Be President." *New York Magazine*, January 8, 2018.

———. *Fire and Fury: Inside the Trump White House*. New York: Henry Holt, 2018.

Wood, Gordon S. *The Americanization of Benjamin Franklin*. New York: Penguin Books, 2005.

———. *The Idea of America: Reflections on the Birth of the United States*. New York: Penguin Books, 2011.

———. *The Radicalism of the American Revolution*. New York: Knopf, 1992.

Woodward, Bob. *The Secret Man: The Story of Watergate's Deep Throat*. New York: Simon & Schuster, 2006.

Worth, Mark. "Most of Europe Has No Whistleblower Protection." *Deutsche Welle*, November 7, 2013.

———. "Whistleblowing in Europe: Legal Protections for Whistleblowers in the EU." *Transparency International*, October 2013. http://issuu.com/transparencyinternational/docs/2013_whistleblowingineurope_en.

Wu, Tim. "What Ever Happened to Google Books?" *New Yorker*, September 11, 2015.

———. "Why Monopolies Make Spying Easier." *New Yorker*, June 18, 2013.

Yardley, Jim. "Enron's Collapse, the Employee: Author of Letter to Enron Chief Is Called Tough." *New York Times*, January 16, 2002.

———. "With Warning on Enron, a Celebrity Is Born." *New York Times*, May 10, 2002.

Yates, Sally. "Who Are We as a Country? Time to Decide." *USA Today*, December 19, 2017.

Yoest, Patrick, and Michael R. Crittenden. "Fraud Investigator Blasts SEC over Madoff Lapses." *Wall Street Journal*, February 5, 2009.

Zetter, Kim. "Federal Judge Finds National Security Letters Unconstitutional, Bans Them." *Wired*, March 15, 2013.

Zetter, Kim, and Kevin Poulsen. "Unpublished Iraq War Logs Trigger Internal Wikileaks Revolt." *Wired*, September 27, 2010.

———. "U.S. Intelligence Analyst Arrested in Wikileaks Video Probe." *Wired*, June 6, 2010.

Zinn, Howard. "Eugene V. Debs and the Idea of Socialism." *Progressive*, January 1999.

Zittrain, Jonathan, and Molly Sauter. "Everything You Need to Know about Wikileaks." *MIT Technology Review*, December 9, 2010.

Acknowledgments

EVERY BOOK IS A journey, but this one was a veritable odyssey. The seeds were planted with unanswered questions from my previous book, *One Nation under Contract: The Privatization of American Power and the Future of Foreign Policy*. When government becomes shrouded in secrecy due to business proprietary or national security interests, citizens cannot see what their government is doing. Noting the way in which secrecy only further empowers the powerful, I wanted to think about how we might keep elites honest in this privatized world. Whistleblowers can serve that important function.

So I set out to explore the role whistleblowing and whistleblowers had played in American democracy. I had completed a full draft manuscript when the Snowden controversy broke, forcing me back to square one. Had I known the time and energy it would require to wrestle this topic to the ground in the Internet age, I would probably never have begun. With five full manuscript iterations and hundreds of pages of carefully sourced prose that had to be cut now behind me, I am grateful for the temporary insanity that permitted me to embark. As a result, the debts I have incurred along the way are larger than usual but thereby only all the more meaningful to recount.

First, there are my fantastic student research assistants at Middlebury College and the generous financial support I received from an Ace-Sloan Grant, the Undergraduate Collaborative Research

Fund, and the Rohatyn Center for Global Affairs that permitted me to employ them. I organized them into research teams for blitzkrieg campaigns, and they more than rose to the challenge. Heartfelt thanks therefore go to Caitlin Arnold, Charlie Arnowitz, Adam Beaser, Erin Benotti, Weijia Chu, Peter Coccoma, Francesca Conde, Andrew Fuller, Teddy Gold, Madelaine Hack, Helen Hur, Aly Jaquith, Max Kagan, Rachel Kogan, Wil Mackey, Alec Mac-Millen, Caroline Nutt, Mitchell Parrish, Sam Peisch, Tom Pesce, Brian Rowett, Hanna Salisbury, Collier Searle, Caroline Snell, Jake Springer, Connor Stoll, and Hyeon-Seok "Tom" Yu. Their creativity and curiosity were the rocket fuel for this project.

Any story of potential whistleblowing involves two competing narratives, often with very little in common. This becomes especially so in politically polarized times. I am grateful to the many individuals who generously shared their insights with me, both on and off the record, so that I might come closer to understanding each case in its full complexity. I am indebted to Kiron Skinner of Carnegie Mellon University for connecting me with the NSA, whose Public Affairs Office did its best to assist me in getting answers to my many questions. I'd also like to thank Mark Boal and Hugo Lindgren for asking good questions that helped me to clarify my book's key characters and overarching narrative.

I owe a good deal to CERGE-EI in Prague, New America in Washington, DC, the Santa Fe Institute, and the Hannah Arendt Center at Bard College for providing remarkable homes for thought and writing that also inspire action in the world. For critical financial support, I am grateful to Middlebury College's sabbatical leave program and to the Russell Leng '60 Professorship in International Politics and Economics.

Because this book turned out to be an extended exercise in redemption through suffering, the list of friends and colleagues who have helped me in thinking matters through by reading drafts, making time for extended conversation, or pointing me in the right direction is very long indeed. I am grateful for the collective brainpower and generosity of Emefa Agawa, Danielle Allen, Laura Bate, Adam Beaser, Roger Berkowitz, Joshua Berlowitz, Erik Bleich, Leon Botstein, David Bromwich, Arthur Brooks, Bill Burger, Keegan Callanan, Paul Carrese, Francesca Conde, Matt Dickinson, Rachel

Donadio, Stephen Donadio, Murray Dry, Tom Friedman, Robby George, Howard Gillman, Danny Goldhagen, Sarah Williams Goldhagen, Shalom Goldman, Susan Greenberg, Robyn Greene, Barbara Grosz, Anna Grzymala-Busse, Madelaine Hack, Helen Hur, Bert Johnson, Max Kagan, Hannah Kraus, Jakub Kraus, Michael Kraus, Cathy Lee, Wil Mackey, Alec MacMillen, Harvey Mansfield, Walter Russell Mead, Andrew Moravcsik, Andy Nagy-Benson, Will Nash, Darius Nassiry, Jay Parini, Paul Pierson, Robert Post, Jonathan Rauch, Gideon Rose, James Ross, Brian Rowett, David Sanger, Peter W. Singer, Anne-Marie Slaughter, Caroline Snell, Debora Spar, Geof Stone, Andrew Sullivan, Paula Throckmorton, Justin Vogt, Ian Wallace, Michael Walzer, Cornel West, Hyeon-Seok "Tom" Yu, Fareed Zakaria, and four anonymous reviewers. Roger Berkowitz, Danny Goldhagen, Andrew Moravcsik, Anne-Marie Slaughter, Debora Spar, and Fareed Zakaria deserve special mention for being there when it mattered, providing trenchant feedback on short notice, and enduring the occasional extended rant without prejudice. I am lucky to have such friends.

Yale University Press continues to be an inspiration in a fake-news world. It is a rare gift to have a publishing team that cares about books in the same way writers do. I couldn't imagine a better editor than the legendary Bill Frucht, who shares my love of mathematics and music, and always insists, sometimes maddeningly so, that I can do better. I hope that this final product finally pleases him. My agent and friend Will Lippincott continues to be a pleasure to work with and a fierce advocate. Best of all, he makes me laugh. I've been privileged to know Jeff Schier, now production editor, who flawlessly copyedited my previous book with Yale, and I was delighted to work with another enormously talented copyeditor for this one, Robin DuBlanc. Karen Olson made the whole process hum from start to finish.

Our beautiful children, Hannah Kraus and Jakub Kraus, are now adult book lovers and, best of all, incisive and reliable critics of any draft I send their way. Last but not least, my husband, Michael Kraus, has made all the difference from beginning to end. Our conversations have shaped this book in countless ways. A refugee from communist Prague who is an American by choice, he shares my faith in American ideals. This book is for him.

Index

Abramoff, Jack, 192
Abu Ghraib prison, 95–98
Ackerman, Bruce, 204
Ackerman, Kenneth, 191
Adams, Charles Francis, 49
Adams, John, 23, 25, 29; Alien and Sedition Acts signed by, 31; Hopkins investigated by, 26–27
Adams, Samuel, 21
Afghanistan, 91, 92, 96, 172, 178
Alexander, Keith, 132, 135, 138, 141–43, 157–61, 164, 165–66, 195
Alexis, Aaron, 160
Alfred (ship), 25, 28
Alien and Sedition Acts (1798), 31–32, 54
Allen, Danielle, 19–20
Allison, Graham, 74
Allison, William B., 49
al-Qaeda, 110, 140, 178, 195
All the President's Men (Woodward and Bernstein), 75
Amazon Web Services, 179
Ames, Oakes, 48–49, 50
Andrew Doria (ship), 25, 26
anonymity, 10
anonymizers, 158, 185
Anonymous (hacker group), 180

Anti-Federalists, 31, 32
anti-psychotic drugs, 220n34
AOL, 161
Apple Inc., 161, 180, 204
Arendt, Hannah, 4, 10, 73
Arkin, William, 89, 195
Assad, Bashar al-, 183
Assange, Julian, 151, 175; Ecuadorian asylum granted to, 156, 181; misleading video posted by, 172, 174; recklessness and grandiosity of, 176–78, 186; Russian links of, 180–84, 187; sexual assault charges against, 173, 181, 186; Snowden and, 144, 148, 156, 157
Australia, 163
Authorities Integration Group, 140–41

Babcock, Joshua, 25
Ballard, Joe, 99
Bamford, James, 128
Banks, Nathaniel P., 35
Bannon, Steve, 183
Bayard, James A., Jr., 49
Benkler, Yochai, 204
Bernstein, Carl, 75, 76
Biddle, Nicholas, 25, 26
Bigelow, Kathryn, 119